Advanced Artificial Intelligence Models and Its Applications

Advanced Artificial Intelligence Models and Its Applications

Editor

Tao Zhou

Basel • Beijing • Wuhan • Barcelona • Belgrade • Novi Sad • Cluj • Manchester

Editor
Tao Zhou
Nanjing University of Science and Technology
Nanjing
China

Editorial Office
MDPI
St. Alban-Anlage 66
4052 Basel, Switzerland

This is a reprint of articles from the Special Issue published online in the open access journal *Mathematics* (ISSN 2227-7390) (available at: https://www.mdpi.com/journal/mathematics/special_issues/advanced_artificial_intelligence_models_applications).

For citation purposes, cite each article independently as indicated on the article page online and as indicated below:

Lastname, A.A.; Lastname, B.B. Article Title. *Journal Name* **Year**, *Volume Number*, Page Range.

ISBN 978-3-0365-9132-2 (Hbk)
ISBN 978-3-0365-9133-9 (PDF)
doi.org/10.3390/books978-3-0365-9133-9

© 2023 by the authors. Articles in this book are Open Access and distributed under the Creative Commons Attribution (CC BY) license. The book as a whole is distributed by MDPI under the terms and conditions of the Creative Commons Attribution-NonCommercial-NoDerivs (CC BY-NC-ND) license.

Contents

About the Editor vii

Preface ix

Yanchun Zhao, Jiapeng Zhang, Rui Duan, fusheng Li and Huanlong Zhang
Lightweight Target-Aware Attention Learning Network-Based Target Tracking Method
Reprinted from: *Mathematics* 2022, 10, 2299, doi:10.3390/math10132299 1

Qasim M. Zainel, Saad M. Darwish and Murad B. Khorsheed
Employing Quantum Fruit Fly Optimization Algorithm for Solving Three-Dimensional Chaotic Equations
Reprinted from: *Mathematics* 2022, 10, 4147, doi:10.3390/math10214147 19

Na Liu, Haiming Mou, Jun Tang, Lihong Wan, Qingdu Li and Ye Yuan
Fully Connected Hashing Neural Networks for Indexing Large-Scale Remote Sensing Images
Reprinted from: *Mathematics* 2022, 10, 4716, doi:10.3390/math10244716 41

Zabir Mohammad, Muhammad Mohsin Kabir, Muhammad Mostafa Monowar, Md Abdul Hamid and Muhammad Firoz Mridha
Self-Writer: Clusterable Embedding Based Self-Supervised Writer Recognition from Unlabeled Data
Reprinted from: *Mathematics* 2022, 10, 4796, doi:10.3390/math10244796 57

Mohammed Abdullah Ammer, Zeyad A. T. Ahmed, Saleh Nagi Alsubari, Theyazn H. H. Aldhyani and Shahab Ahmad Almaaytah
Application of Artificial Intelligence for Better Investment in Human Capital
Reprinted from: *Mathematics* 2023, 11, 612, doi:10.3390/math11030612 77

Shuyu Li and Yunsick Sung
MRBERT: Pre-Training of Melody and Rhythm for Automatic Music Generation
Reprinted from: *Mathematics* 2023, 11, 798, doi:10.3390/math11040798 95

Shih-Che Lo and Ying-Lin Chuang
Vehicle Routing Optimization with Cross-Docking Based on an Artificial Immune System in Logistics Management
Reprinted from: *Mathematics* 2023, 11, 811, doi:10.3390/math11040811 109

Adegoke A. Muideen, Carman Ka Man Lee, Jeffery Chan, Brandon Pang and Hafiz Alaka
Broad Embedded Logistic Regression Classifier for Prediction of Air Pressure Systems Failure
Reprinted from: *Mathematics* 2023, 11, 1014, doi:10.3390/math11041014 129

Ye Yuan, Jiaqi Wang, Xin Xu, Ruoshi Li, Yongtong Zhu, Lihong Wan, et al.
Alleviating Long-Tailed Image Classification via Dynamical Classwise Splitting
Reprinted from: *Mathematics* 2023, 11, 2996, doi:10.3390/math11132996 147

Maha Alghawazi, Daniyal Alghazzawi and Suaad Alarifi
Deep Learning Architecture for Detecting SQL Injection Attacks Based on RNN Autoencoder Model
Reprinted from: *Mathematics* 2023, 11, 3286, doi:10.3390/math11153286 159

About the Editor

Tao Zhou

Tao Zhou is currently a Professor at the School of Computer Science and Engineering, Nanjing University of Science and Technology. He received his Ph.D. degree in Pattern Recognition and Intelligent Systems from Shanghai Jiao Tong University, China, in 2016. From 2016 to 2018, he was a Postdoctoral Fellow at the BRIC and IDEA lab, University of North Carolina, Chapel Hill (UNC-CH), USA. From 2018 to 2020, he was a Research Scientist in the Inception Institute of Artificial Intelligence (IIAI), Abu Dhabi, United Arab Emirates. He has published more than 80 technical papers in prominent journals and at conferences such as IEEE TPAMI, IEEE TIP, IEEE TMI, IEEE TCYB, IEEE TCSVT, IEEE TBME, CVPR, ICCV, IJCAI, MICCAI, etc. His research interests include computer vision, machine learning, medical image analysis, and AI in healthcare.

Preface

Artificial Intelligence (AI) has increasingly interweaved itself into our daily lives, revolutionizing industries and altering our interaction with technology. Within the vast AI landscape, advanced artificial intelligence models have emerged as formidable tools that push the boundaries of what once was conventionally considered achievable. Over time, AI has seen remarkable progress, driven by improvements in machine learning algorithms, deep neural networks, natural language processing, computer vision, and more. These advancements have set the stage for the creation of sophisticated AI models that display superior performance in intricate tasks, surpassing conventional methods.

This book presents ten articles accepted for publication in the Special Issue titled "Advanced Artificial Intelligence Models and Their Applications" of the MDPI Mathematics journal. The compilation of research papers explores the most recent developments in AI models and highlights their applications across diverse domains. The research topics encompass SQL injection attack detection, image classification, object tracking, vehicle routing and cross-docking, music generation, human capital investment, writer recognition, remote sensing image indexing, and optimization algorithms. These collective works underscore the varied applications of advanced AI models, demonstrating their potential to tackle complicated problems spanning different fields. The application of deep learning, self-supervised learning, optimization algorithms, and other AI methodologies has been instrumental in enhancing performance, efficiency, and decision making across various sectors.

The compilation is anticipated to be intriguing and valuable for those engaged in artificial intelligence, pattern recognition, machine learning, and computer vision, and those with an apt mathematical background who are keen to familiarize themselves with recent strides in artificial intelligence. As the Guest Editor of the Special Issue, I extend my gratitude to the authors for their quality contributions, the reviewers for their insightful comments that improved the submitted work, and the administrative staff of MDPI publications for their support in bringing this project to fruition. A special note of appreciation goes to Ms. Estelle Wang, the Managing Editor of the Special Issue, for her excellent cooperation and invaluable assistance.

Tao Zhou
Editor

Article

Lightweight Target-Aware Attention Learning Network-Based Target Tracking Method

Yanchun Zhao [1,†], Jiapeng Zhang [2], Rui Duan [2], Fusheng Li [1,*,†] and Huanlong Zhang [2]

1 School of Automation Engineering, University of Electronic Science and Technology of China, Chengdu 611731, China; yczhao@uestc.edu.cn
2 School of Electrical and Information Engineering, Zhengzhou University of Light Industry, Zhengzhou 450002, China; 331901050046@zzuli.edu.cn (J.Z.); 331901060053@zzuli.edu.cn (R.D.); hlzhang@zzuli.edu.cn (H.Z.)
* Correspondence: lifusheng@uestc.edu.cn
† These authors contributed equally to this work.

Abstract: Siamese network trackers based on pre-trained depth features have achieved good performance in recent years. However, the pre-trained depth features are trained in advance on large-scale datasets, which contain feature information of a large number of objects. There may be a pair of interference and redundant information for a single tracking target. To learn a more accurate target feature information, this paper proposes a lightweight target-aware attention learning network to learn the most effective channel features of the target online. The lightweight network uses a designed attention learning loss function to learn a series of channel features with weights online with no complex parameters. Compared with the pre-trained features, the channel features with weights can represent the target more accurately. Finally, the lightweight target-aware attention learning network is unified into a Siamese tracking network framework to implement target tracking effectively. Experiments on several datasets demonstrate that the tracker proposed in this paper has good performance.

Keywords: target features; siamese trackers; lightweight network; target tracking

MSC: 68T45

1. Introduction

Visual target tracking is a branch in the field of computer vision, and thanks to the development of deep learning techniques, especially the application of neural networks [1], target tracking has entered a new phase. In the target tracking task, the target being tracked is arbitrary, and the traditional trackers designed based on manual features [2] perform generally in target modeling. Thanks to the powerful generalization ability of depth features, which can model all kinds of targets well, depth feature-based trackers [3–5] have achieved excellent results in recent years.

Although the existing depth feature-based trackers perform well, we find that the pre-trained depth features still have some interference when modeling arbitrary targets. This is because, firstly, the targets being tracked are arbitrary, and if the dataset used to train the depth feature model does not contain such targets, that is, the depth feature model has not learned information about such targets, then when extracting the target features, it can only rely on the existing information for speculation, which often brings a lot of uncertainties and leads to more disturbances in the model. Secondly, even if the deep feature model has learned such targets, and when the general tracker uses the last layer or layers to extract the target features, it will lead to more disturbing factors in the feature model because of the huge amount of data. Finally, the existing pre-trained deep feature models are created mainly for the target recognition task, where its main task is to identify all similar targets that appear in each frame. The target tracking task, on the other hand, is different and is to identify the same target in subsequent frames, so the tracker based on pre-trained features may be wrong in the face of interference from similar targets in the same frame.

Some trackers use the designed lightweight network as the memory module and use the target appearance information in each frame to update network parameters, to achieve good appearance memory performance. In this paper, a lightweight target-aware attention learning network is designed to learn the most effective channel features of the target online, using the target information in the first frame template to learn a series of channel features with weights, and by recombining these channel features. A compact and effective deep feature is obtained, which can better distinguish the object from the background compared to the pre-trained features. At the same time, a new attention learning loss function is developed to optimize the training of the proposed network using the Adam optimization method. Different from other methods, the lightweight network designed in this paper does not require complex parameters and is easy to implement. It only needs to learn the most salient features through the reliable information of the first frame of the target and does not need to use too much memory temporarily, which is beneficial for the efficient use of hardware resources. Finally, the lightweight target-aware attention learning network is unified into the Siamese tracking network framework to effectively achieve target tracking. Figure 1 shows that our tracker yields better tracking performance when compared with other trackers.

Figure 1. Comparison of our tracker with other trackers for Bolt (**top**), Basketball (**bottom**).

The main contributions of this article are described in summary as follows:

(1) A lightweight target-aware attention learning network is designed to learn the most effective channel features of the target online. The new network mines the expressiveness of different channels to the target by the first frame template.

(2) A new attention learning loss function is developed to optimize the training of the proposed network using the Adam optimization method. The loss function effectively improves the modeling capability and tracking accuracy of the network by introducing the gradient information during training.

(3) The lightweight target-aware attention learning network is unified into the Siamese tracking network framework to effectively achieve target tracking. Moreover, the proposed method performs better against other trackers.

2. Related Work

There are a large number of researchers who have made many contributions in the field of visual tracking, and many excellent trackers have been proposed. In this section, we discuss some trackers that are similar to our work.

2.1. Lightweight Network-Based Tracker

Real-time target tracking is a very relevant research element. However, when the tracking speed increases, the tracking accuracy is bound to be affected. Therefore, many researchers have researched how to increase the tracking speed without affecting the tracking accuracy. Zhao et al. [6] use a pruned convolutional neural network to construct the tracker, which is trained by a mutual learning method to further improve the localization accuracy. Cheng et al. [7] propose a real-time semantic segmentation method based on extended convolution smoothing and lightweight up-sampling on the basis of a lightweight network, which can achieve high segmentation accuracy while maintaining high-speed real-time performance. Zhao et al. [8] design a lightweight memory network, which only needs reliable target frame information to fine-tune network parameters online, so as to enhance the memory ability of the target appearance. At the same time, it can maintain good discriminant performance without a complicated update strategy. Unlike them, this paper designs a lightweight network for online learning of the most salient features of the target and achieves redundant feature channel trimming by back-propagating the weights to determine the importance of the feature channels.

2.2. Siamese Network-Based Tracker

In recent years, the combination of Siamese networks and target tracking has led target tracking to enter a new stage. Bertinetto et al. [9] propose a new structure of fully convolutional Siamese networks. In the initial offline phase, deep convolutional networks are regarded as a more general similarity learning problem, and then the simple online estimation of the problem during tracking can achieve very competitive performance, and the frame rate at runtime far exceeds the requirements of real-time performance. Li et al. [10] developed a model consisting of a Siamese network and a region proposal network, which discards the traditional multi-scale testing and online tracking, divides the network into template branches and detection branches, and uses a large amount of data for offline training to achieve a good tracking result. Gao et al. [11] propose a Siamese Attentional Key-point Network for target tracking, by designing a new Siamese lightweight hourglass network and a novel cross-attentional module to obtain more accurate target features, and propose a key-points detection approach to accurately locate target location and scale regression.

3. Proposed Method

3.1. Basic Siamese Network for Visual Tracking

Siamese networks are originally applied to template matching problems and are later introduced into object tracking. It is composed of two networks with the same structure and the same weight. These two networks are used to extract the depth feature of the target and the depth feature of the search area, and finally the cross-correlation calculation is used to find the highest response value in the search area. The position of this point is the final target position. Moreover, the whole process can be expressed by the following formula:

$$f(z, x) = \varphi(z) * \varphi(x) + b \cdot 1 \qquad (1)$$

where z represents the initial frame position, x represents the position of the search region, $b \cdot 1$ denotes the deviation value, and $*$ represents the convolution operation.

As shown in Figure 2, the proposed tracker contains a pre-trained feature extraction network, a lightweight target-aware attention learning network, and a Siamese network matching module. The VGG feature extraction network is a very deep convolutional network for image classification and achieves the state-of-the-art performance on the ImageNet challenge dataset. It is trained offline in this paper, and the proposed lightweight target-aware attention learning network is trained online by using the given first frame target information, and then the cross-correlation operation of the Siamese network is used to locate target. The attention learning loss function used to train the lightweight target-aware attention learning network is redesigned on the basis of the MSE loss function, and the Adam optimization method is used for training, and the feature channel is determined according to the gradient value information of back propagation. The importance weight is weighted to the original depth feature to represent the target, and finally the template matching method of the Siamese network is used to locate the target. The calculation process is shown in Formula (2):

$$f_{new}(z,x) = (\varphi(z) \odot \alpha) * \varphi(x) + b \cdot 1 \tag{2}$$

where z denotes the template image, x denotes the image of the search region, $b \cdot 1$ denotes the deviation value of each, α is the channel attention weight vector of the feature channel, $\odot$ denotes the Hadamard product, $*$ denotes the convolution operation, and $f_{new}(z,x)$ denotes the response score.

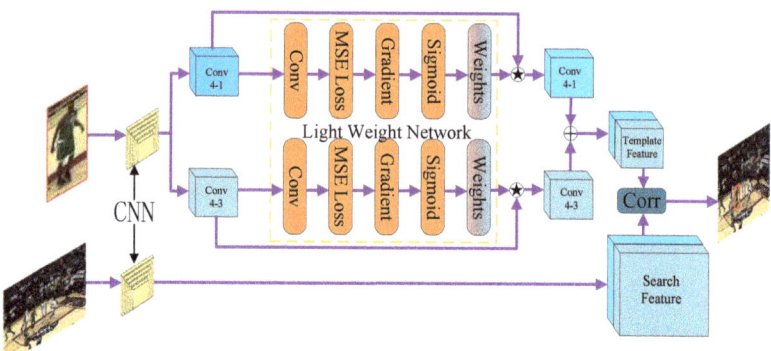

Figure 2. Overview of our network architecture for visual tracking.

3.2. Attentional Learning Loss Function

Most of the trackers based on correlation filtering use recurrent samples to train regression models, while Chen et al. [12] propose to use single-layer convolution to solve the linear regression problem and use the gradient-descent training method to solve the regression problem in target tracking, which this paper is inspired by. In the linear regression model of the work [12], the objective is to learn a linear function using the training samples $X \in R^{m \times n}$ and the corresponding regression objective $Y \in R^m$. Each element x_i in each row of the model X represents a training sample with feature dimensionality and the corresponding regression target x_i is the first element of the model Y. Then, the objective is to learn the coefficients w of a regression function by minimizing the objective function $f(x) = w^T \cdot x$ during the offline training process.

$$\arg\min_{w} \|X * w - Y\|^2 + \lambda\|w\|^2 \tag{3}$$

In Equation (3), $\|\cdot\|$ is the Euclidean parametrization, and λ is the regularization parameter to prevent overfitting.

The gradient values generated during the training of neural networks can be a good indication of the channel saliency feature information for different target classes [13], and this paper attempts to introduce this idea into a Siamese network-based tracker used for training to generate a set of weights that can represent the contribution of different feature channels to modeling, to enhance the target modeling capability of pre-trained depth features. To this end, this paper redefines its input based on Equation (3), which can be expressed by minimizing the following function:

$$\arg\min_{w} \sum_{i} \left((Z_i \cdot w'_i) * X_i - Y_i\right)^2 + \lambda' \sum_{i} w'^2_i \tag{4}$$

where · is the dot product operation, ∗ denotes the convolution operation, Z is the template depth feature, X is the search area depth feature; they are obtained from the same frame, and Z is located at the center of the X, λ' is regularization parameter, w' is the regression weight vector obtained by the network training, the dimension is the same as Z and X.

The comparison results of the target response maps are shown in Figure 3. Figure 3a shows the weighted features of the feature channels after learning using the attention learning loss function, and Figure 3b shows the target-specific diagnosis extracted directly using the original features.

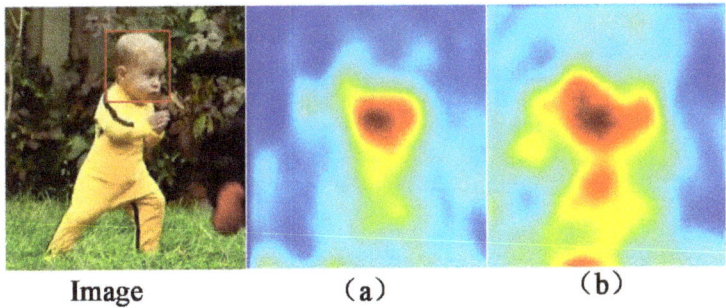

Figure 3. Comparison of the before and after learning characteristics of attentional learning loss.

Finally, the regression weights w' are mapped by the sigmoid function to obtain the channel weights corresponding to the sample images.

$$\alpha_i = 1 \Big/ \left(1 + e^{-w'_i}\right) \qquad (5)$$

where α_i denotes the i-th value in α, and $\alpha \in [0,1]$, w'_i denotes the i-th value in w'.

In summary, the loss function generates the gradient information by training the target information in the first frame. The gradient information is used to generate the weights of the different channels of the feature to the target information expression. The feature channel is determined according to the gradient value information of back propagation under the attentional learning loss function. The importance weight is weighted to the original depth feature to represent the target. Finally, the template matching method of the Siamese network is used to locate the target. However, the loss function is used under the assumption that the error between the model output and the groundtruth value obeys a Gaussian distribution. When this condition is not satisfied, the loss function is limited in its usefulness.

3.3. Lightweight Target-Aware Attention Learning Network

In a pre-trained deep model-based classification network, each feature channel contains a specific target feature pattern, and all feature channels together construct a feature space containing a priori information about different objects. The pre-trained network identifies object classes mainly through a subset of these feature channels, so the importance of each channel should not be calculated equally when used to track the target representation.

As shown in Figure 4, the lightweight target-aware attention learning network proposed in this paper is built on a single-layer convolutional network, which is used in the same way as a general neural network, and its kernel is set to match the size of the target template. However, to obtain better object appearance features, the lightweight target-aware attention learning network proposed in this paper only uses the given first frame object information for training and does not require complex offline training, while using the more advanced Adam Optimization method to obtain network parameters.

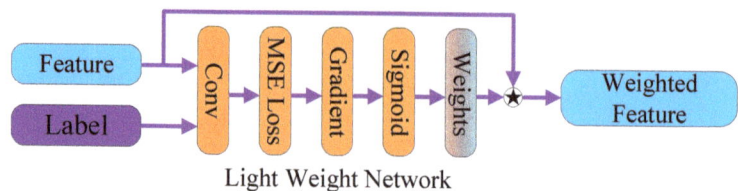

Figure 4. Lightweight target-aware attention learning network.

(1) Parameter learning process.

A search area of size X is intercepted around the given first frame target as an initial training sample, w_i' is a set of initial target feature channel weights with an initial value of 1. In the subsequent learning process, the gradient value information is calculated to update its value online according to the difference between the response values and labels of different channels. The larger the gradient value is, the smaller the contribution of the feature channel to the target model. Equation (4) is used to guide the online learning process, and the Adam optimization method is used to optimize the network by empirically setting the learning rate to, the momentum to 0.9, the weight decay to 1000, and the maximum number of iterations to 100. Compared with the traditional gradient descent (SGD) optimization method, the Adam optimization method is an improvement and extension of it, with high computational efficiency and small memory occupation. Moreover, the learning rate of the SGD optimization method is fixed, while the Adam optimization method can update the learning rate of the third training process adaptively based on the average of the first two training weights, which can improve the performance of the network on sparse gradient problems.

(2) Obvious characteristic of the lightweight target-aware attention learning network.

The network designed in this paper is implemented on a single-layer convolutional network, which learns the optimal representation of the target appearance by adjusting a certain number of feature channel weights through simple single-layer convolutional operations, using the proposed attention learning loss function to learn online, thus generating an optimal set of channel modeling parameters. This approach is computationally simple, does not require complex model computation strategies, does not take up too many valuable memory resources, and is easy to implement. Moreover, the number of parameters in the network is small, which facilitates fast computation and achieves real-time fast online tracking.

4. Experiment and Analysis

Our tracker is implemented on a PC with an i7-9700 3.0 GHz and a single NVIDIA GeForce RTX 2060 GPU with Pytorch. The algorithm proposed in this chapter uses the VGG-16 [14] neural network as the feature extraction network for the target and the search region, and the outputs of the Conv4-1 and Conv4-3 layers are used for target appearance modeling. The number of channel dimensions of the outputs is 512. Then the feature passes through the lightweight network and its feature channels are given different weights, and the number of channels is reduced to 380. Moreover, the kernel of the lightweight target-aware attention learning network is set to match the size of the target template. For the designed lightweight target-aware attention learning network, online training is performed using the attention learning loss function only in the first frame of each video sequence, setting the maximum number of iterations to 100, the momentum setting to 0.9, and the convergence loss threshold to 0.01. To handle scale variations, we also search for the object over three scales (0.957, 1, 1.047), and update the scales by scale weights (0.99, 1, 1.005). To evaluate the performance of the proposed algorithm, this section is tested on the OTB-50 [15] and OTB-100 [16] dataset, TC-128 [17] dataset, UAV123 [18] dataset set, VOT2016 [19] dataset and LaSOT dataset [20].

4.1. Ablation Studies

To better explain the validity of the proposed method, the ablation experiment of this work is analyzed on the OTB-100 dataset using one-pass evaluation. Our algorithm contains the base Siamese-based tracker and the proposed lightweight target-aware attention network. Figure 5 shows the precision and success rate of baseline without the proposed attention network and our method.

From Figure 5, we can see that when the proposed attention network is added, the accuracy and success rate of the tracking algorithm are improved. The network removes redundant and partial background information from the features to achieve superior tracking performance by online mining of different channels of the target depth features for their ability to represent the target information. The experimental results in Figure 5 show that the proposed attention network contributes to the performance of the tracking algorithm.

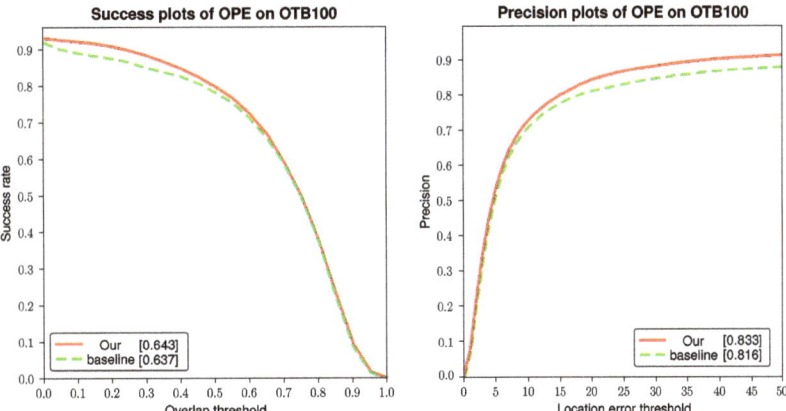

Figure 5. The ablation studies on the OTB-100 dataset.

4.2. OTB Dataset Experiments

In this paper, experiments are conducted on the popular OTB-50 and OTB-100 datasets in the field of target tracking, which consist of 50 and 100 fully annotated videos, respectively. In this paper, the accuracy maps in one-pass evaluation (OPE) are used to evaluate different trackers and are compared with 10 advanced trackers SiamFC, attention-based trackers MemTrack [21] and MemDTC [22], correlation filter-based trackers KCF [23], Staple [24], DSST [25] and SRDCF [26], deep learning and correlation filter-based tracker CF2 [27], CREST [28], and CSR-DCF [29] were compared for the results. As shown in Figures 6 and 7, the performance of the proposed tracker (Ours1) in this chapter is at the advanced level in both benchmark tests. Specifically, the proposed algorithm obtained success rate scores of 0.655 and 0.643 on OTB-50 and OTB-100, respectively, and the proposed algorithm gained 4.6% and 6.0% improvement over the Siamese network-based tracking method SiamFC, which confirms the advantages of the lightweight target-aware attention learning network and attention learning loss function proposed in this paper. CF2 algorithm uses the depth features of three layers in the VGG-16 network for target modeling to improve the discriminative power of the model, and obtains success rate scores of 0.603 and 0.562 for OTB-50 and OTB-100, respectively, and the performance of the proposed algorithm in this paper is 5.2% and 8.1% higher than that of the CF2 algorithm without using more depth features. The CREST algorithm achieves a higher success rate than the CF2 algorithm on the OTB-50 dataset and performs better than the algorithm proposed in this paper in terms of both success rate and accuracy; the reason for this is that the CREST algorithm introduces a residual network to extract the depth features of the target, and the residual network structure can be used to build a deeper network to improve the accuracy of the features and alleviate the gradient disappearance problem caused by the deep network.

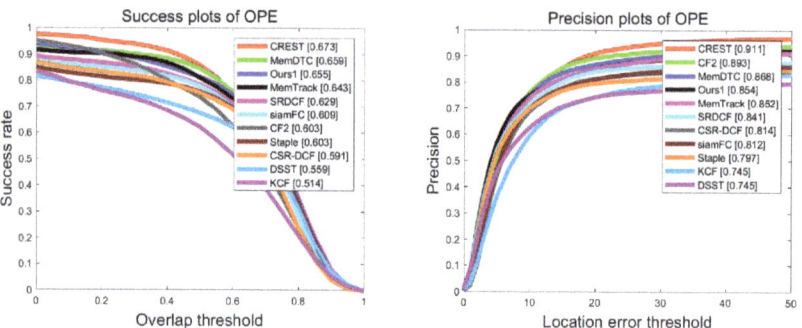

Figure 6. Success and precision rates on the OTB50 dataset.

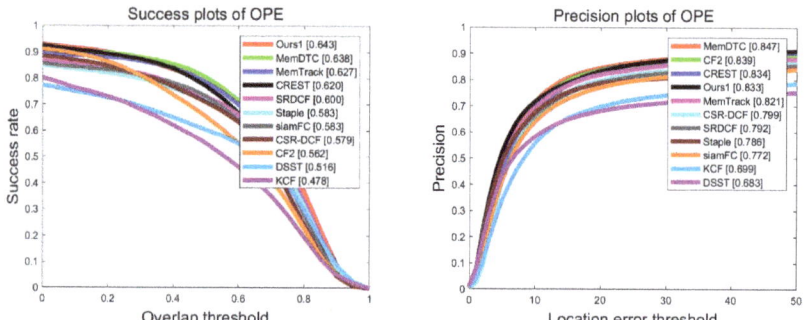

Figure 7. Success and precision rates on the OTB100 dataset.

For object-tracking algorithms, the real-time performance should also be used as one of the criteria for evaluating tracker performance. In Table 1, we compared the operational performance of some of the advanced trackers in terms of Precision score (%), Success rate (%), and Speed (FPS) on the OTB-100 dataset. Table 1 shows the results of our tracker compared with 7 advanced trackers including BaSiamIoU [30], ATOM [31], CFML [32], CREST [28], CSR-DCF [29], SRDCF [26], and SiamFC [9]. From Table 1, we can note that ATOM draws on the IoU-Net idea and proposes IoU modulation and IoU predictor to solve the scale challenge in the tracking process, achieving better tracking performance in terms of Precision score and Success rate. However, the speed performance of ATOM is not as satisfactory as our tracker. Meanwhile, although SiamFC is capable of reaching 102.3 FPS in speed, it is not able to adapt to changes in target appearance during tracking, resulting in lower tracking accuracy. Our tracker achieves 83.3% in Precision score and 64.3% in Success rate in 59 FPS. Overall, our tracker strikes a balance between Precision score, Success rate, and Speed. Therefore, for some scenes with higher requirements on tracking speed, SiamFC algorithm is a better choice, while for some scenarios where tracking accuracy is more preferred, ATOM algorithm should be chosen. Our method is more suitable for applications that require a certain degree of tracking accuracy and tracking speed.

Table 1. The real-time performance of the advanced trackers on the OTB-100 dataset. In the table, red, green and blue indicate the top three scores respectively.

Tracker	Precision Score (%)	Success Rate (%)	Speed (FPS)
Ours	83.3	64.3	59
BaSiamIoU	83.9	70.8	50
ATOM	87.9	66.7	30
CFML	85.3	64.9	32
SiamFC	77.2	58.3	102.3
CREST	83.4	62.0	1.8
CSR-DCF	79.9	57.9	8.5
SRDCF	79.2	60.0	4.2

(1) Challenge analysis of the OTB dataset

This part shows the success rate plots on the OTB-50 dataset for multiple challenge scenarios, as it contains 50 videos with relatively high tracking complexity in the OTB-100 dataset, which include: scale variation (SV), low resolution (LR), occlusion (OC), distortion (DF), motion blur (MB), fast motion (FM), in-plane rotation (IR), out-of-plane rotation (IR), out-of-field (OV), background clutter (BC), and illumination variation (IV).

More details of the performance of the proposed algorithm are shown in Figure 8. Overall, the proposed algorithm performs well in all 11 challenges. For the attributes of motion blur, distortion, and low resolution, the proposed algorithm outperforms the tracker SiamFC, which is also based on Siamese networks. The SiamRPN algorithm combines Siamese networks and region proposal network and has good tracking precision and speed, but the algorithm proposed in this paper has better performance under the background clutter challenge, indicating that the algorithm in this paper can extract the key features of the target. For exceeding the visual field, the proposed algorithm performs much better than the other nine compared trackers, which is attributed to the proposed lightweight target-aware attention learning network model and the attention learning loss function. In addition, the proposed algorithm performs better than most neural network-based trackers under the background clutter challenge, which indicates that the proposed lightweight target-aware attention learning network and attention learning loss function can effectively modify the pre-trained depth features to remove redundant information while enhancing the feature channels that are more important to the target representation, and thus it can improve the feature representation of the target. Overall, the proposed algorithm in this paper achieves good performance under several challenging attributes of the OTB-50 dataset.

(2) Qualitative experimental analysis of the OTB dataset

To qualitatively evaluate the proposed method, Figure 8 shows some tracking results of the proposed algorithm and other tracker on eleven challenging video sequences. SiamRPN is a deep learning-based algorithm, CF2 is a correlation filtering-based algorithm, where the SiamRPN algorithm also introduces region suggestion networks into the tracking, and SiamFC is a Siamese network-based algorithm, similar to the proposed algorithm in this paper. the proposed algorithm is similar.

In these six video sequences, there are many different challenges, including deformation (Bird1, MotorRolling, Skiing), occlusion (Soccer, Tiger), out-of-field (Bird1, Soccer), and background clutter (Football1, MotorRolling). SiamFC and the proposed algorithm can re-find the target after its occlusion disappears, while other trackers are unable to locate the target again due to untrustworthy samples introduced during model updates. CF2 and CREST drift rapidly in scenes where the target is out of view, and SiamFC and CF2 are unable to adapt to the challenge of scale changes in Bird1 and MotorRolling sequences. As the tracking task progresses, CREST, CF2, and SiamFC all lose targets one-by-one as the tracking drifts. In contrast, the algorithm proposed in this paper can adapt well to these challenges due to the introduction of a lightweight target-aware attention learning network and an attention learning loss function to learn the channel weight information of the target. As in these scenarios in Figure 9, the performance of the proposed algorithm is significantly better than other trackers.

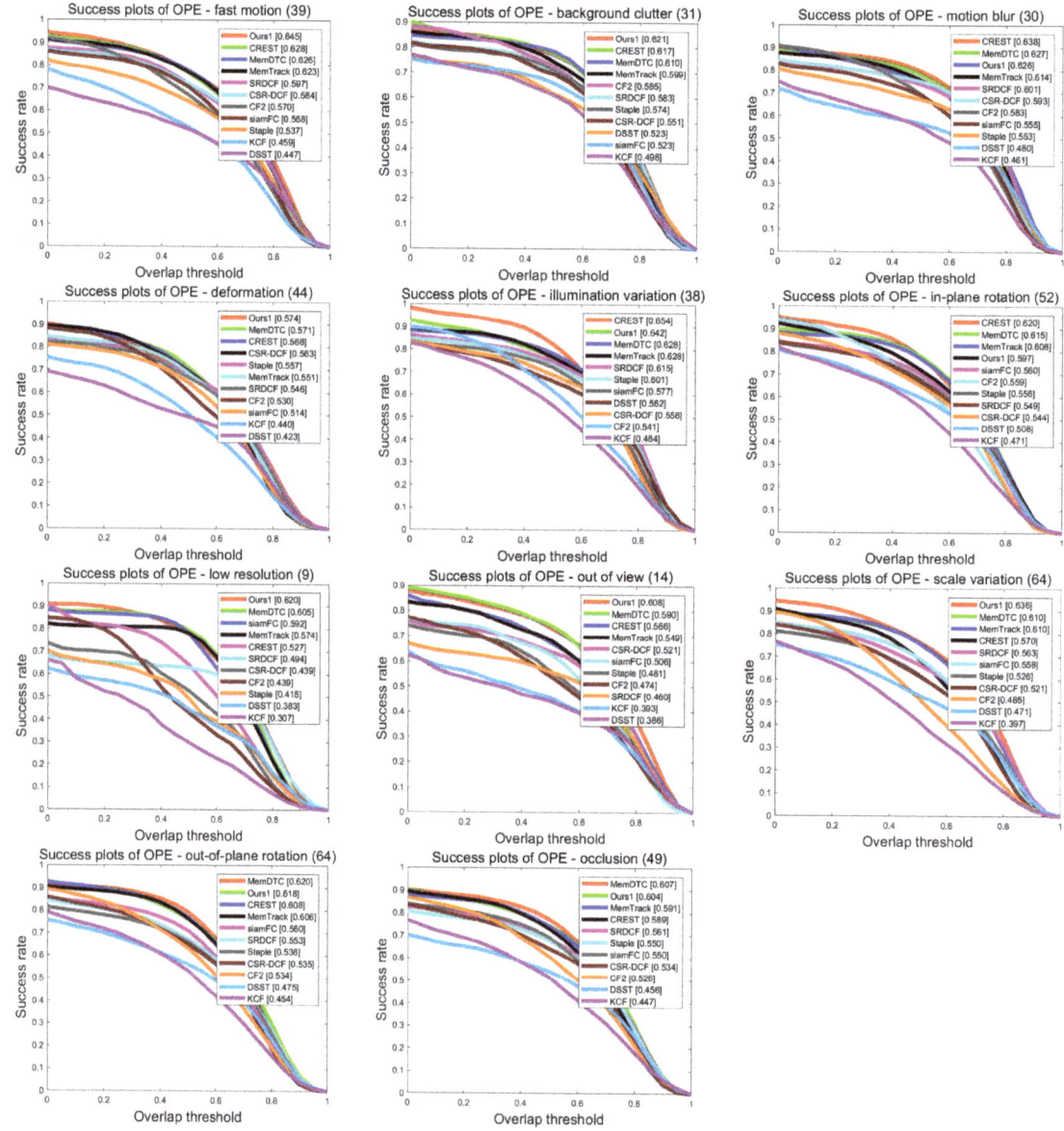

Figure 8. Comparison of 11 attribute challenge results.

Figure 9. Visualization of tracking results for focused challenge scenarios.

4.3. TC-128 Dataset Experiments

In this paper, the proposed method is evaluated on the Temple-Color (TC-128) dataset containing 128 videos. The evaluation method follows the guidelines in the OTB dataset and uses the accuracy plots in the one-time evaluation method (OPE) to compare the different trackers.

(1) Quantitative evaluation on TC-128 dataset: The proposed algorithm is compared quantitatively with 10 other trackers, including ECO [33], CREST [28], HCFTstar [34], CF2 [27], CACF [35], KCF [23], DSST [25], LOT [36], and CSK [37].

As shown in Figure 10, the proposed algorithm is in the top two positions among all trackers in terms of accuracy and success rate. Compared with the CF2 algorithm based on deep learning, the proposed algorithm achieves a higher success rate of 5.0% on TC-128, probably because CF2 uses unprocessed pre-trained deep features, while the proposed algorithm learns the most effective target channel weights through the designed lightweight target-aware attention learning network, so that the features better represent the appearance of the target. Moreover, the success rate of the proposed algorithm on TC-128 is 1.2% higher than that of CREST which learns linear regression on a single-layer convolutional network. It can also be seen that the CREST algorithm, which uses only one layer of depth features for target modeling, outperforms the CF2 algorithm, which uses multiple layers of depth features, which illustrates the great advantage of linear regression modeling on the network. The tracking robustness of the proposed algorithm is greater than that of the tracker CACF, which introduces contextual information. It can also be seen from the figure that trackers that use manual features to model targets such as KCF have significantly lower performance than other trackers that use depth features. The ECO algorithm combines color features and depth features to represent the target, and is sensitive to the color features of the target, so the performance on the TC-128 dataset designed for color features is better than the algorithm proposed in this paper. (2) Challenge analysis of TC-128 dataset: In this section, the success rate of the tracker associated with the work in this paper is tested on the TC-128 dataset for 11 challenging videos, including scale variation (SV), low-resolution (LR), occlusion (OC), distortion (DF), motion blur

(MB), fast motion (FM), in-plane rotation (IR), out-of-plane rotation (IR), out-of-field (OV), background clutter (BC), illumination variation (IV).

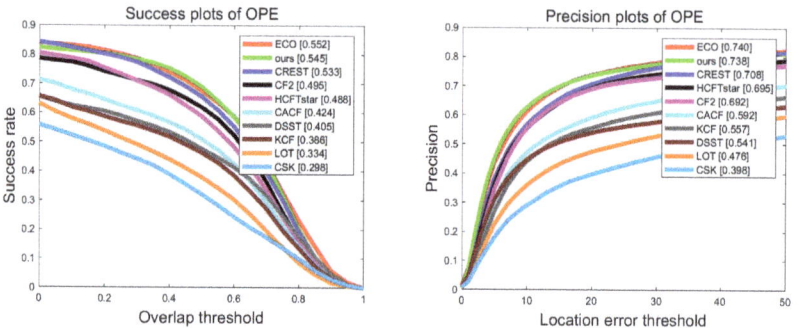

Figure 10. Success and precision rates on the TC-128 dataset.

Figure 11 shows the results of the proposed algorithm and other state-of-the-art trackers under 11 attribute challenges, and it is clear that the proposed algorithm outperforms the other trackers in overall performance. Thanks to the channel weight learning effect of the lightweight target-aware attention learning network, the proposed algorithm outperforms other trackers in the case of background clutter, motion blur, and deformation. ECO outperforms the proposed algorithm in deformation challenge scenarios due to the use of multi-feature fusion, but the proposed algorithm outperforms other trackers in several challenge scenarios with background clutter, motion blur, and out-of-field. In these scenarios, the targets often experience severe appearance changes or complex background disturbances, so the compared tracker experience tracking failures, while these compared tracker use sample update models that may contain noise, which prevents the tracker from obtaining an accurate model of the target appearance and leads to tracking failures. In contrast to these trackers, the lightweight target-aware attention learning network is introduced in this work to improve the modeling capability of depth features, allowing the tracker to adapt to target tracking tasks in complex scenes.

4.4. UAV123 Dataset Experiment

To further illustrate the performance of the proposed algorithm, the performance of the proposed algorithm is evaluated on the UAV (UAV123) dataset in this paper. Compared with typical visual object tracking datasets including OTB and TC-128, the UAV123 dataset provides low-altitude aerial video for target tracking. UAV123 is also one of the largest target tracking datasets, which contains 123 video sequences with over 110,000 images and an average sequence length of 915 frames. The UAV123 dataset has become increasingly popular due to real-life applications that are becoming increasingly popular, such as navigation, wildlife monitoring, crowd surveillance, etc. An algorithm that strikes a good balance between accuracy and real-time speed would be more practical for tracking these targets.

As shown in Figure 12, the proposed algorithm is tested on the UAV123 dataset in this paper to compare with 10 other trackers, including SRDCF [26], CREST [28], CF2 [27], SiamRPN [10], DSST [25], Struck [38], ECO [33], TADT [39], KCF [23], and CSK [37]. Thanks to the lightweight target-aware attention learning network introduced in the Siamese network framework, the proposed algorithm is higher than the TADT algorithm in terms of accuracy and success rate. Moreover, the success rate of the proposed algorithm on UAV123 is 5.8% higher than that of CREST which learns linear regression on a single convolutional layer. The performance of the CREST algorithm using only one layer of depth features outperforms that of CF2 and SRDCF using multiple layers of depth features. Trackers using manual features, such as DSST and KCF, have significantly lower performance than other trackers using depth features.

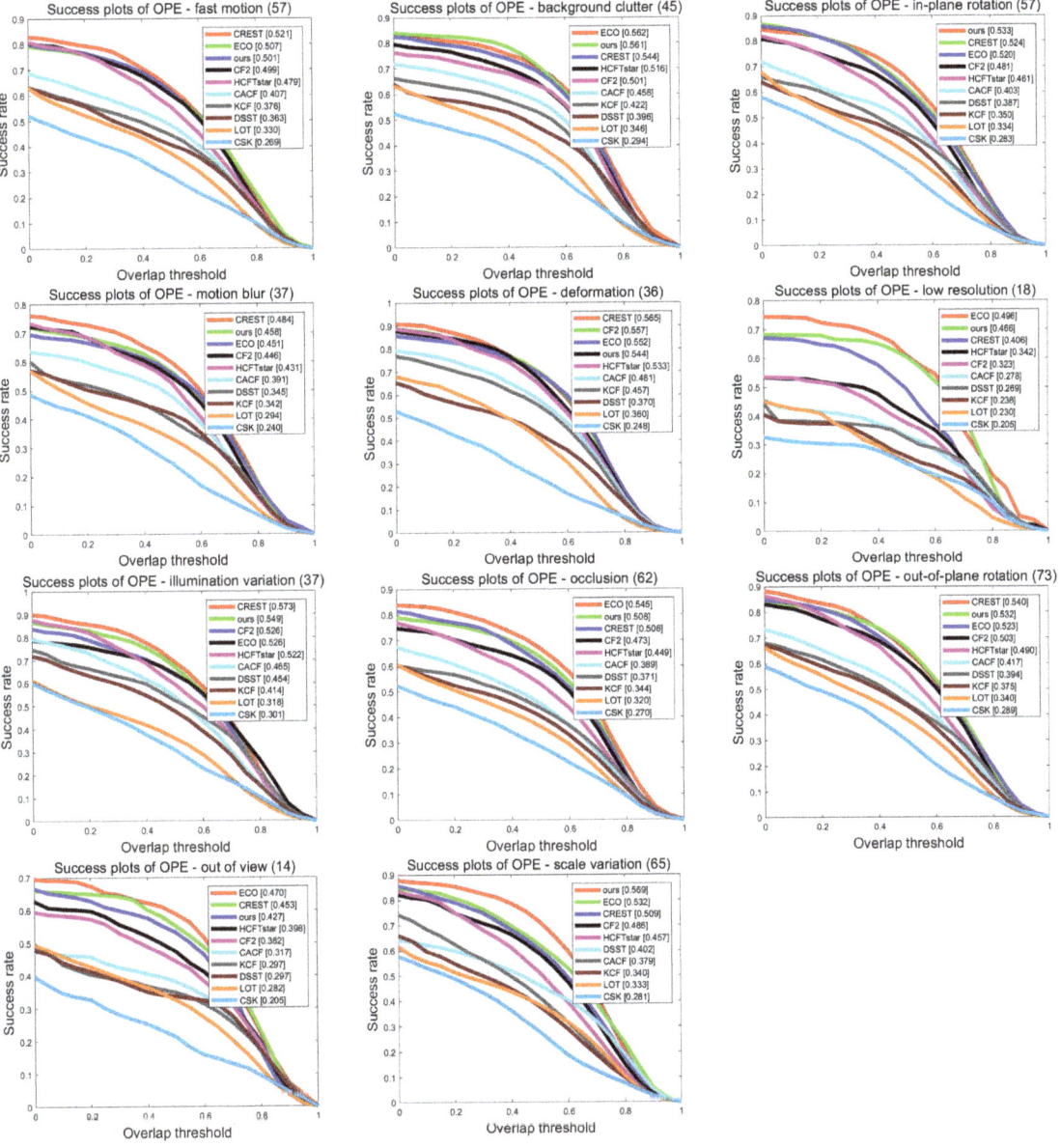

Figure 11. Comparison of 11 attribute challenge results.

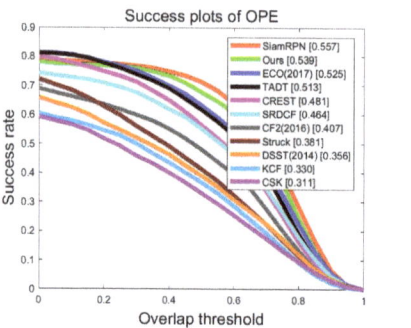 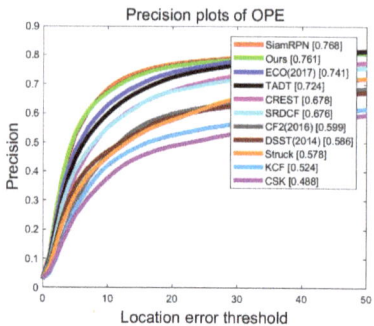

Figure 12. Success and precision rates on the UAV-123 dataset.

4.5. VOT2016 Dataset Experiment

The VOT dataset is a very popular dataset in the field of target tracking, and it uses two metrics, accuracy and robustness, to evaluate the performance of the trackers, as well as the average overlap metric (EAO) to rank the tracker. In this paper, the proposed algorithm is compared with other trackers on the VOT2016 dataset for experiments, and the compared trackers include SiamRPN++ [40], SiamRPN [10], TADT [39], DeepSRDCF [41], MDNet [42], SRDCF [26], HCF [27], DAT [43], and KCF [23]. The results of these tracker are obtained from the official results, and Figure 11 show the results of all tracker' ranking results.

As can be seen from Figure 13, thanks to the proposed lightweight target-aware attention learning network and the weight learning approach of the attention learning loss function, the proposed algorithm ranks third among all the compared trackers and performs better than the TADT algorithm that uses the regression loss function and the scale loss function for feature layer filtering. The performance of the proposed algorithm is weaker than that of SiamRPN and SiamRPN++ tracker, which also shows that SiamRPN introduces a region suggestion network to provide an accurate suggested target area and a classification regression mechanism to determine the target location and obtain a more accurate target scale through regression calculation. SiamRPN++ algorithm, on the other hand, introduces a deeper neural network to extract target features based on the SiamRPN algorithm, so it performs far ahead of the other tracker, which also shows that deep neural networks are more powerful in feature representation.

Table 2 shows some more detailed information comparing all the tracker, including the average overlap (EAO), overlap (Overlap), and failure (Failures), and the top three metrics on individual results are marked in red, green, and blue, respectively. As can be seen from the table, the proposed algorithm performs well overall in all three metrics, which reflects the ability of the proposed attention learning loss function and lightweight goal-aware attention learning network to learn reliable target features. The last column of the table shows the failure rate of the algorithm tracking, and it can be seen that the proposed algorithm ranks fourth place, which is not very far from the second-place SiamRPN and the third-place TADT, and there is still room for improvement.

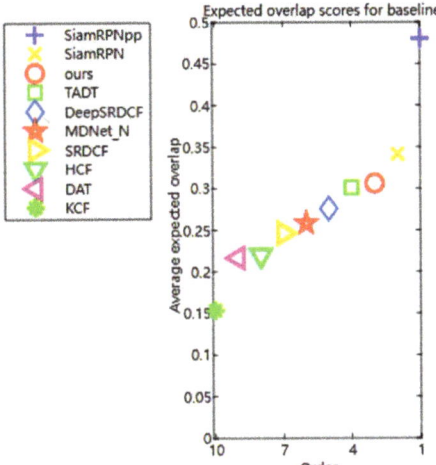

Figure 13. EAO score ranking of the compared trackers VOT2016 dataset.

Table 2. Overall performance on VOT2016 dataset, the top three trackers are marked with red, green and blue, respectively.

Tracker	EAO	Overlap	Failures
Ours	0.306	0.546	20.180
SiamRPN++	0.479	06356	11.586
SiamRPN	0.341	0.580	20.138
TADT	0.300	0.546	19.973
DeepSRDCF	0.275	0.522	20.346
MDNet	0.257	0.538	21.081
SRDCF	0.245	0.525	28.316
HCF	0.219	0.436	23.856
DAT	0.216	0.458	28.353
KCF	0.153	0.469	52.031

4.6. LaSOT Dataset Experiment

To further demonstrate the effectiveness of our method, the performance of the proposed algorithm is evaluated on the LaSOT dataset in this work. Compared with the above tracking dataset, LaSot dataset has a larger salce and more complex challenges for the tracker during the tracking process. LaSOT considers the connection between visual appearance and natural language, not only labeling the bounding box but also adding rich natural language descriptions. It contains 1400 video sequences with an average sequence length of 2500 frames and the test dataset contains 280 video sequences, with 4 videos per category.

As shown in Figure 14, our method achieved the third place in precision and success rate. Compared with the tracking algorithms based on the correlation filter, our method also obtains a good performance. However, the performance of our method is not competitive enough with the state-of-art tracking methods on the LaSOT dataset. The reason for this phenomenon is that our algorithm is not able to solve the challenge of target disappearance reproduction during long-term tracking.

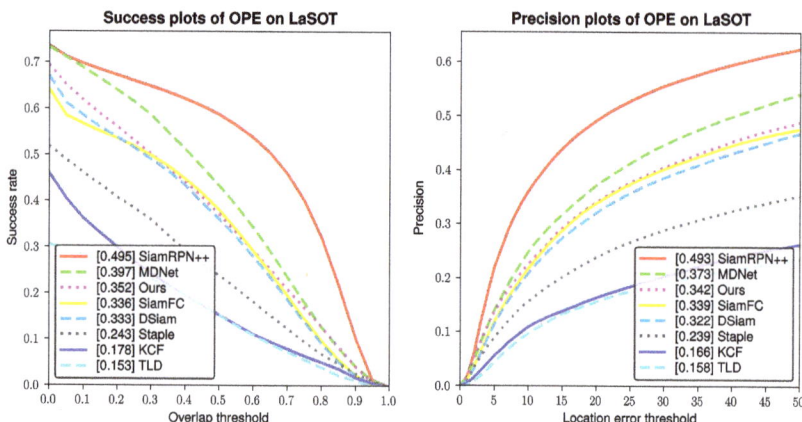

Figure 14. Success and precision plots of OPE on LaSOT dataset.

4.7. Discussions

The Siamese network tracker based on pre-trained depth features has achieved good performance in recent years. The pretrained depth features are trained in advance on large-scale datasets, and therefore contain feature information of a large number of objects. However, for a tracking video, the object being tracked is always the same, so the pretrained features contain some redundant features. To remove redundant and interfering information from pre-trained features and learn more accurate target information, this work presents a novel tracking method with the proposed lightweight target-aware attention learning network. This lightweight target-aware attention learning network uses reliable information that the ground truth of the target is given in the first frame of each video to train the weights of the network online and obtains gradient value information by backpropagation to determine the effect of different feature channels in the target feature layer on the target, and remodel the channel of the template feature by weighting this contribution. Then the compact and effective deep feature is obtained, which can better distinguish the object from the background. The network is the single-convolutional layer network which is relatively easy to implement and compared to complex convolutional neural networks, there are fewer parameters in the network. It is worth improving that although our method can refine the target features, it does not have the ability to deal with target failure, so its performance is constrained by the target disappearance reproduction challenge in long-term tracking.

5. Conclusions

In this paper, a novel Siamese network-based target tracking method is proposed to address the problem that different feature channels often have different importance for the target representation, which enhances the feature tracking target by designing a lightweight target-aware attention learning network and using a redesigned attention learning loss learning function to learn the most effective feature channel weights for the target using the Adam optimization method representation. This lightweight target-aware attention learning network uses reliable information from the first frame of each video sequence to train the weights of the network online, and obtains gradient value information by back propagation to determine the contribution of different feature channels in the target feature layer to model the target, and re-models the target by weighting this contribution to the channels of the template features. The network is relatively easy to implement and the small number of parameters facilitates fast computation. Finally, the proposed algorithm is evaluated on OTB, TC-128, UAV123, VOT2016, and LaSOT datasets, and both quantitative and qualitative analyses show that the method achieves satisfactory performance, demonstrating the effectiveness of the proposed lightweight target-aware attention learning network and attention learning loss function in a Siamese network framework-based tracker.

Author Contributions: Conceptualization: Y.Z., J.Z., R.D. and F.L.; methodology: Y.Z., J.Z., R.D. and F.L.; software: J.Z., R.D., H.Z.; validation: J.Z., R.D., H.Z.; analysis: Y.Z., R.D. and F.L.; investigation: H.Z.; resources: Y.Z., F.L.; writing—original draft preparation: J.Z., R.D.; writing—review and editing: Y.Z., J.Z., R.D.; visualization: R.D., H.Z.; supervision: H.Z. All authors have read and agreed to the published version of the manuscript.

Funding: This work was supported by the National Natural Science Foundation of China (61873246, 62072416, 6167241, 61702462), Program for Science & Technology Innovation Talents in Universities of Henan Province (21HASTIT028), Natural Science Foundation of Henan (202300410495), Zhongyuan Science and Technology Innovation Leadership Program (214200510026).

Institutional Review Board Statement: Not applicable.

Informed Consent Statement: Not applicable.

Data Availability Statement: Not applicable.

Conflicts of Interest: No conflict of interest exits in the submission of this manuscript, and this manuscript is approved by all authors for publication.

References

1. Farabet, C.; Couprie, C.; Laurent, N.; Yann, L. Learning Hierarchical Features for Scene Labeling. *IEEE Trans. Pattern Anal. Mach. Intell.* **2013**, *35*, 1915–1929. [CrossRef] [PubMed]
2. Bousetouane, F.; Dib, L.; Snoussi, H. Improved mean shift integrating texture and color features for robust real time object tracking. *Vis. Comput.* **2012**, *29*, 155–170. [CrossRef]
3. Zhang, H.; Chen, J.; Nie, G.; Hu, S. Uncertain motion tracking based on convolutional net with semantics estimation and region proposals. *Pattern Recognit.* **2020**, *102*, 107232. [CrossRef]
4. Guo, W.; Gao, J.; Tian, Y.; Yu, F.; Feng, Z. SAFS: Object Tracking Algorithm Based on Self-Adaptive Feature Selection. *Sensors* **2021**, *21*, 4030. [CrossRef] [PubMed]
5. Cao, Z.; Fu, C.; Ye, J.; Li, B.; Li, Y. HiFT: Hierarchical Feature Transformer for Aerial Tracking. In Proceedings of the IEEE International Conference on Computer Vision, Montreal, QC, Canada, 11–17 October 2021.
6. Zhao, H.; Yang, G.; Wang, D.; Lu, H. Lightweight Deep Neural Network for Real-Time Visual Tracking with Mutual Learning. In Proceedings of the 2019 IEEE International Conference on Image Processing (ICIP), Taipei, Taiwan, 22–25 September 2019.
7. Cheng, X.; Zhao, L.; Hu, Q. Real-Time Semantic Segmentation Based on Dilated Convolution Smoothing and Lightweight Up-Sampling. *Laser Optoelectron. Prog.* **2020**, *57*, 021017. [CrossRef]
8. Zhang, H.; Chen, J.; Nie, G.; Lin, Y.; Yang, G.; Zhang, W. Light regression memory and multi-perspective object special proposals for abrupt motion tracking. *Knowl.-Based Syst.* **2021**, *226*, 107127. [CrossRef]
9. Bertinetto, L.; Valmadre, J.; Henriques, J.F.; Vedaldi, A.; Torr, P.H.S. Fully-convolutional Siamese networks for object tracking. In Proceedings of the European Conference on Computer Vision, Amsterdam, The Netherlands, 11–14 October 2016.
10. Li, B.; Yan, J.; Wu, W.; Zhu, Z.; Hu, X. High performance visual tracking with Siamese region proposal network. In Proceedings of the IEEE Conference on Computer Vision and Pattern Recognition, Salt Lake City, UT, USA, 18–23 June 2018.
11. Gao, P.; Yuan, R.; Wang, F.; Xiao, L.; Hamido, F.; Zhang, Y. Siamese Attentional Keypoint Network for High Performance Visual Tracking. *Knowl.-Based Syst.* **2019**, *193*. [CrossRef]
12. Chen, K.; Tao, W. Learning linear regression via single-convolutional layer for visual object tracking. *IEEE Trans. Multimed.* **2018**, *21*, 86–97. [CrossRef]
13. Ramprasaath, R.S.; Michael, C.; Abhishek, D.; Ramakrishna, V.; Devi, P.; Dhruv, B. Grad-cam: Visual explanations from deep networks via gradient-based localization. Proceedings of the IEEE International Conference on Computer Vision, Venice, Italy, 22–29 October 2017; pp. 618–626.
14. Simonyan, K.; Zisserman, A. Very deep convolutional networks for large-scale image recognition. *arXiv* **2014**, arXiv:1409.1556.
15. Wu, Y.; Lim, J.; Yang, M.-H. Online object tracking: A benchmark. In Proceedings of the IEEE Conference on Computer Vision and Pattern Recognition, Portland, OR, USA, 23–28 June 2013; pp. 2411–2418.
16. Wu, Y.; Lim, J.; Yang, M.H. Object Tracking Benchmark. *IEEE Trans. Pattern Anal. Mach. Intell.* **2015**, *37*, 1834–1848. [CrossRef]
17. Liang, P.; Blasch, E.; Ling, H. Encoding color information for visual tracking: Tracker and benchmark. *IEEE Trans. Image Process.* **2015**, *24*, 5630–5644. [CrossRef] [PubMed]
18. Mueller, M.; Smith, N.; Ghanem, B. A benchmark and simulator for uav tracking. In Proceedings of the European Conference on Computer Vision, Amsterdam, The Netherlands, 11–14 October 2016; pp. 445–461.
19. Hadfield, S.; Bowden, R.; Lebeda, K. The visual object tracking VOT2016 challenge results. In Proceedings of the European Conference on Computer Vision, Amsterdam, The Netherlands, 11–14 October 2016; pp. 777–823.

20. Fan, H.; Bai, H.; Lin, L.; Yang, F.; Chu, P.; Deng, G.; Yu, S.; Huang, M.; Liu, J.; Xu, Y.; et al. Lasot: A high-quality large-scale single object tracking benchmark. *Int. J. Comput. Vis.* **2021**, *129*, 439–461. [CrossRef]
21. Yang, T.; Chan, A.B. Learning dynamic memory networks for object tracking. In Proceedings of the European Conference on Computer Vision, Munich, Germany, 8–14 September 2018.
22. Yang, T.; Chan, A.B. Visual tracking via dynamic memory networks. *IEEE Trans. Pattern Anal. Mach. Intell.* **2021**, *43*, 360–374. [CrossRef] [PubMed]
23. Henriques, J.F.; Caseiro, R.; Martins, P.; Batista, J. High-speed tracking with kernelized correlation filters. *IEEE Trans. Pattern Anal. Mach. Intell.* **2014**, *37*, 583–596. [CrossRef]
24. Bertinetto, L.; Valmadre, J.; Golodetz, S.; Miksik, O.; Torr, P.H.S. Staple: Complementary learners for real-time tracking. In Proceedings of the IEEE Conference on Computer Vision and Pattern Recognition, Las Vegas, NV, USA, 27–30 June 2016.
25. Danelljan, M.; Häger, G.; Khan, F.S.; Felsberg, F. Discriminative scale space tracking. *IEEE Trans. Pattern Anal. Mach. Intell.* **2016**, *39*, 1561–1575. [CrossRef]
26. Li, F.; Tian, C.; Zuo, W.; Zhang, L.; Yang, M.H. Learning spatial-temporal regularized correlation filters for visual tracking. In Proceedings of the IEEE Conference on Computer Vision and Pattern Recognition, Salt Lake City, UT, USA, 18–23 June 2018; pp. 4904–4913.
27. Ma, C.; Huang, J.B.; Yang, X.; Yang, M.H. Hierarchical convolutional features for visual tracking. In Proceedings of the IEEE International Conference on Computer Vision, Santiago, Chile, 7–13 December 2015; pp. 3074–3082.
28. Song, Y.; Ma, C.; Gong, L.; Zhang, L.; Lau, R.W.H.; Yang, M.H. Crest: Convolutional residual learning for visual tracking. In Proceedings of the IEEE Conference on Computer Vision and Pattern Recognition, Honolulu, HI, USA, 21–26 July 2017.
29. Lukezic, A.; Vojir, T.; Zajc, L.C.; Matas, J.; Kristan, M. Discriminative correlation filter with channel and spatial reliability. In Proceedings of the 2017 IEEE Conference on Computer Vision and Pattern Recognition, Honolulu, HI, USA, 21–26 July 2017; pp. 4847–4856. [CrossRef]
30. Tan, K.; Xu, T.B.; Wei, Z. Online visual tracking via background-aware Siamese networks. *Int. J. Mach. Learn. Cybern.* **2022**, 1–18. [CrossRef]
31. Danelljan, M.; Bhat, G.; Khan, F.S.; Felsberg, M. Atom: Accurate tracking by overlap maximization. In Proceedings of the IEEE/CVF Conference on Computer Vision and Pattern Recognition, Long Beach, CA, USA, 15–20 June 2019; pp. 4660–4669.
32. Yuan, D.; Kang, W.; He, Z. Robust visual tracking with correlation filters and metric learning. *Knowl.-Based Syst.* **2020**, *195*, 105697. [CrossRef]
33. Danelljan, M.; Bhat, G.; Khan, F.S.; Felsberg, M. Eco: Efficient convolution operators for tracking. In Proceedings of the IEEE Conference on Computer Vision and Pattern Recognition, Honolulu, HI, USA, 21–26 July 2017; pp. 6638–6646.
34. Ma, C.; Huang, J.B.; Yang, X.; Yang, M.H. Robust Visual Tracking via Hierarchical Convolutional Features. *IEEE Trans. Pattern Anal. Mach. Intell.* **2018**, *41*, 2709–2723. [CrossRef]
35. Mueller, M.; Smith, N.; Ghanem, B. Context-Aware Correlation Filter Tracking. In Proceedings of the IEEE Conference on Computer Vision and Pattern Recognition, Honolulu, HI, USA, 21–26 July 2017.
36. Oron, S.; Bar-Hillel, A.; Levi, D.; Avidan, S. Locally orderless tracking. *Int. J. Comput. Vis.* **2015**, *111*, 213–228. [CrossRef]
37. Henriques, J.F.; Rui, C.; Martins, P.; Batista, J. Exploiting the Circulant Structure of Tracking-by-Detection with Kernels. In Proceedings of the 12th European conference on Computer Vision—Volume Part IV, Florence, Italy, 7–13 October 2012; Springer: Berlin/Heidelberg, Germany, 2012.
38. Hare, S.; Golodetz, S.; Saffari, A.; Vineet, V.; Cheng, M.; Hicks, S.L.; Torr, P.H.S. Struck: Structured output tracking with kernels. *IEEE Trans. Pattern Anal. Mach. Intell.* **2016**, *38*, 2096–2109. [CrossRef]
39. Li, X.; Ma, C.; Wu, B.; He, Z.; Yang, M.H. Target-aware deep tracking. In Proceedings of the IEEE CVF Conference on Computer Vision and Pattern Recognition, Long Beach, CA, USA, 15–20 June 2019; pp. 1369–1378.
40. Li, B.; Wu, W.; Wang, Q.; Zhang, F.; Xing, J.; Yang, J. SiamRPN++: Evolution of Siamese Visual Tracking with Very Deep Networks. In Proceedings of the 2019 IEEE/CVF Conference on Computer Vision and Pattern Recognition (CVPR), Long Beach, CA, USA, 15–20 June 2019.
41. Danelljan, M.; Hager, G.; Khan, F.S.; Felsberg, M. Convolutional Features for Correlation Filter Based Visual Tracking. In Proceedings of the 2015 IEEE International Conference on Computer Vision Workshop (ICCVW), Santiago, Chile, 7–13 December 2015.
42. Nam, H.; Han, B. Learning Multi-Domain Convolutional Neural Networks for Visual Tracking. In Proceedings of the 2016 IEEE Conference on Computer Vision and Pattern Recognition (CVPR), Las Vegas, NV, USA, 27–30 June 2016.
43. Pu, S.; Song, Y.; Ma, C.; Zhang, H.; Yang, M.H. Deep attentive tracking via reciprocative learning. *Adv. Neural Inf. Process. Syst.* **2018**, *31*.

Article

Employing Quantum Fruit Fly Optimization Algorithm for Solving Three-Dimensional Chaotic Equations

Qasim M. Zainel [1], Saad M. Darwish [2,*] and Murad B. Khorsheed [3]

1. College of Physical Education and Sports Sciences, University of Kirkuk, Kirkuk 36001, Iraq
2. Department of Information Technology, Institute of Graduate Studies and Research, Alexandria University, Alexandria 21526, Egypt
3. College of Administration & Economics, University of Kirkuk, Kirkuk 36001, Iraq
* Correspondence: saad.darwish@alexu.edu.eg; Tel.: +2-01222632369

Abstract: In a chaotic system, deterministic, nonlinear, irregular, and initial-condition-sensitive features are desired. Due to its chaotic nature, it is difficult to quantify a chaotic system's parameters. Parameter estimation is a major issue because it depends on the stability analysis of a chaotic system, and communication systems that are based on chaos make it difficult to give accurate estimates or a fast rate of convergence. Several nature-inspired metaheuristic algorithms have been used to estimate chaotic system parameters; however, many are unable to balance exploration and exploitation. The fruit fly optimization algorithm (FOA) is not only efficient in solving difficult optimization problems, but also simpler and easier to construct than other currently available population-based algorithms. In this study, the quantum fruit fly optimization algorithm (QFOA) was suggested to find the optimum values for chaotic parameters that would help algorithms converge faster and avoid the local optimum. The recommended technique used quantum theory probability and uncertainty to overcome the classic FA's premature convergence and local optimum trapping. QFOA modifies the basic Newtonian-based search technique of FA by including a quantum behavior-based searching mechanism used to pinpoint the position of the fruit fly swarm. The suggested model has been assessed using a well-known Lorenz system with a specified set of parameter values and benchmarked signals. The results showed a considerable improvement in the accuracy of parameter estimates and better estimation power than state-of-the art parameter estimation approaches.

Keywords: chaotic system; fruit fly optimization algorithm; quantum-inspired computation; parameter estimation

MSC: 68T20

1. Introduction

Chaos theory studies nonlinear dynamic systems. Chaos is the interaction between regularity and probability-based unpredictability [1]. Weather and climate, biological and ecological processes, the economy, social structures, and other natural phenomena all exhibit chaotic regimes. The primary feature of chaos is its ability to generate a wide range of complex patterns. For use as cryptographic secret keys, relevant mathematical models may produce a vast amount of data. Confusion and diffusion are two key features of cryptography, and chaos theory has the unique quality of having a direct connection to both features. Furthermore, the deterministic but unexpected dynamics of chaotic systems may be a powerful tool in the development of a superior cryptosystem [2,3].

The fundamental benefit of chaos is that unauthorized users see chaotic signals as noise [2]. Chaotic-based encryption techniques are utilized for military, mobile, and private data [3]. These applications demand real-time, rapid, secure, and reliable monitoring. Most chaos-based secure communication systems use chaos synchronization [4]. Chaos synchronization is vital for achieving security after information has been transferred [5].

Therefore, many cryptographic algorithms have adopted popular chaotic models that depict chaos by employing mathematical models, such as a logistic map.

Chaos-based secure communication has issues. Due to the limitations of chaos theory and techniques for creating chaos, attackers may sometimes determine the chaotic system employed in encryption through state reconstruction. Second, transmission and sampling delays make chaotic synchronization difficult. Due to the limits of digital computer accuracy, computer chaotic maps are always periodic. Therefore, chaos-based public-key cryptography has collisions [6]. Finally, picking the input parameters limits chaos theory. The techniques used to determine these characteristics rely on the data dynamics and the desired analysis, which is often complicated and inaccurate. Due to a chaotic system's complicated nature, many practical characteristics are unknown and difficult to quantify [7]. Parameter estimation is a major issue.

Two parameter estimation methods exist. One is the synchronization method [3,8], which proposes updating parameter estimation based on chaotic system stability. Its methodologies and sensitivities rely on the considered system; hence, updating may be challenging due to the complexity of the chaotic system. Another method is through metaheuristic algorithms. Metaheuristic algorithms are intelligent optimization algorithms [9,10]. It translates parameter estimation into a multidimensional optimization problem using sample data from the original system. It is easier to implement than synchronization. Metaheuristic algorithms are popular for estimating chaotic system parameters [11,12]. Metaheuristic techniques require starting system settings. In many circumstances, the original values cannot be retrieved, making reconstruction and management of the chaotic system difficult. Most of these approaches are also used to estimate chaotic system parameters. Few apply to complex chaotic systems [13].

The fruit fly optimization algorithm (FOA) is simple and easy to comprehend compared with other sophisticated algorithms. FOA only requires adjusting the population size and maximum generation number. Traditional intelligent algorithms need at least three parameters. The influence of numerous factors on algorithm performance is hard to examine; hence, they are generally determined via several tests. An incorrect parameter will impair algorithm performance and complexity [14]. However, there is still a lot of potential for development of FOA variations to obtain greater performance, particularly for complicated practical issues related to convergence speed or avoiding being trapped into the local optimum.

When it comes to population-based optimization methods, variability in the population and unpredictability in the search process are two factors that often play a pivotal role. By using quantum mechanics instead of Newtonian dynamics, the quantum-behaved particle swarm optimization (QPSO) increases the particles' capacity to escape the local optimum. Classical quantum mechanics is the theoretical underpinnings of quantum theory, which aims to appropriate some of the mysteriousness of quantum behavior processes. Integrating quantum theory into the original FA, the quantum firefly algorithm (QFA) is able to combat the loss of variety [15]. Quantum mechanics may be used to explain how fruit flies navigate the environment in search of food; their actions are characterized by a wave function of uncertainty. A quantum-behaved approach can avoid premature convergence and help escape from the local optimum.

1.1. Problem Statement and Motivation

Chaotic systems are very sensitive to initial parameter choices. Long-term system behavior prediction is difficult. Synchronization and chaos control in nonlinear systems depend on exact parameter values in chaotic systems; if one of these values is uncertain, the system will not perform as intended. Some parameters are unknown or difficult to quantify due to the complexity of chaotic systems (such as secure communication). If we wish to control or synchronize chaotic systems, we must estimate unknown system parameters. Too many factors may cause the parameter estimation algorithm for 3D chaotic systems to become more complex, which in turn increases the amount of effort required to calculate the results. This is why most algorithms struggle to find the global optimum. As a result of its effectiveness, FA has been used to tackle a wide range of optimization issues, leading to significant progress in a short period of time. The motivation is to take insights from quantum theory to improve upon the FA for estimating the parameters of a 3D chaotic system.

1.2. Contribution and Methodology

The work presented in this paper is an extension of the work introduced in Ref. [16], where quantum mechanics was used in the fruit fly optimization algorithm to make it easier for particles to get out of the local optimum, so that the chaotic system parameters could be estimated. In this paper, the QFOA was adopted to solve the parameter estimation problem of the Lorenz chaotic system to achieve the synchronization with the aim of transmitting data correctly. Fitness function based on the mean square error was utilized to find the minimum error between the original and estimated ones in different directions. To achieve high performance in terms of time and accuracy, the suggested model selected only some samples from the received signal to check the synchronization early. QFOA variables were tuned to estimate the unknown chaotic system parameters. Then, these estimated parameters were used later, inside the well-known fourth-order Runge–Kutta algorithm, to build the estimated original signal (a chaotic signal with a known structure) to yield synchronization.

The rest of this paper is organized as follows: Section 2 provides a background and literature review of some studies related to estimating the parameters of the chaotic system; Section 3 presents the proposed methodology based on the analysis of the previous techniques; Section 4 reports a complete evaluation of the proposed methodology, along with the results and the discussion; and the final section contains the conclusion based on the previous sections and future directions for research.

2. Background and Related Work

This section offers some important background related to the proposed model and includes a literature review on parameters estimation of the chaotic system as one of the most important techniques to achieve chaotic synchronization concerns on wireless communication networks.

2.1. Preliminaries

2.1.1. Chaos Theory

Chaos theory is an alternative description and explanation of the behavior of nonlinear dynamical systems [17]. In mathematical language, a dynamical system is classified as a chaotic system [18–21] if it has the following properties:

- Sensitive to initial conditions—each point in a system is arbitrarily near other points with drastically different behavior. Qualitatively, two paths with a starting separation δX_0 diverge.

$$|\delta X(t)| \approx e^{\lambda t} |\delta X_0| \tag{1}$$

λ is the Lyapunov exponent. One positive Lyapunov exponent indicates chaotic behavior, whereas more than one indicates hyperchaotic behavior.

- Topological mixing—implies system evolution, so that every area or open set of its phase space will overlap. This assumption has profound implications for one-dimensional systems.
- Periodic orbit density—each space point is arbitrarily near periodic orbits and is regular. Not meeting this requirement may prevent topological mixing systems from becoming chaotic. In chaos theory, the butterfly effect is the sensitivity of a system to starting conditions. Small changes in a dynamical system's starting state may have huge long-term effects. Time makes such systems unpredictable.

2.1.2. Lyapunov Exponents

The Lyapunov exponents help investigate chaotic or hyperchaotic dynamical systems. Lyapunov exponents categorize dynamical systems so that we can see their behavior. A dynamical system is chaotic if it has one positive Lyapunov exponent, and hyperchaotic if it has more [22–24]. Consider two locations in space, X_0 and $X_0 + \Delta X_0$, which form orbits using an equation or set of equations. Sensitive dependency may only occur in particular parts of a system; hence, this separation depends on the beginning value, $\Delta x(X_0, t)$. For chaotic points, $\Delta x(X_0, t)$ acts unpredictably. The mean exponential rate of divergence of two near orbits is defined as [25].

$$\lambda = \lim_{\substack{t \to \infty \\ |\Delta X_0| \to 0}} \frac{1}{t} \ln \left| \frac{\Delta x(X_0, t)}{\Delta X_0} \right| \qquad (2)$$

The Lyapunov exponent, λ, is used to differentiate orbits. If $\lambda < 0$, the orbit attracts a stable fixed point or periodic orbit. The more negative the exponent, the better the stability. If $\lambda = 0$, the system is steady state. A conservative system has this exponent and are Lyapunov stable. In this case, orbits would stay apart. For $\lambda > 0$, the orbit is chaotic. Nearby points diverge to any arbitrary separation.

To define sphere trajectories, we require linearized systems or variational equations. $\vec{x} = \vec{F}(\vec{x})$, where $\vec{x} = (x_1, x_2, \ldots, x_n)$ and $\vec{F} = (f_1, f_2, \ldots, f_n)$. Any ordinary numerical differential equation solution may create $\emptyset(\vec{x_0})$. Formally, partial derivatives explain how these perturbations respond. Consider the Lorenz system [26–28]:

$$\begin{cases} \dot{x} = \theta_1(y - x) \\ \dot{y} = \theta_2 x - y - xz \\ \dot{z} = -\theta_3 z + xy \end{cases} \qquad (3)$$

$\theta_1, \theta_2,$ and θ_3 are Lorenz parameters. To set up the linearized system for the above equations, the right-hand Jacobian is needed.

$$J = \begin{bmatrix} \frac{\partial f_1}{\partial x} & \frac{\partial f_1}{\partial y} & \frac{\partial f_1}{\partial z} \\ \frac{\partial f_2}{\partial x} & \frac{\partial f_2}{\partial y} & \frac{\partial f_2}{\partial z} \\ \frac{\partial f_3}{\partial x} & \frac{\partial f_3}{\partial y} & \frac{\partial f_3}{\partial z} \end{bmatrix} \qquad (4)$$

$$J = \begin{bmatrix} -\theta_1 & \theta_1 & 0 \\ \theta_2 - Z & -1 & -x \\ y & x & -\theta_3 \end{bmatrix} \qquad (5)$$

$$J = \begin{bmatrix} \delta_{x1} & \delta_{y1} & \delta_{z1} \\ \delta_{x2} & \delta_{y2} & \delta_{z2} \\ \delta_{x3} & \delta_{y3} & \delta_{z3} \end{bmatrix} \qquad (6)$$

The ith equation's x variation component is δ_{xi}. Column sums are the x, y, and z coordinates of the evolving variant. The rows represent the vector coordinates of the original x, y, and z variations. Linear equations:

$$\begin{bmatrix} \dot{\delta}_{x1} & \dot{\delta}_{y1} & \dot{\delta}_{z1} \\ \dot{\delta}_{x2} & \dot{\delta}_{y2} & \dot{\delta}_{z2} \\ \dot{\delta}_{x3} & \dot{\delta}_{y3} & \dot{\delta}_{z3} \end{bmatrix} = \begin{bmatrix} \frac{\partial f_1}{\partial x} & \frac{\partial f_1}{\partial y} & \frac{\partial f_1}{\partial z} \\ \frac{\partial f_2}{\partial x} & \frac{\partial f_2}{\partial y} & \frac{\partial f_2}{\partial z} \\ \frac{\partial f_3}{\partial x} & \frac{\partial f_3}{\partial y} & \frac{\partial f_3}{\partial z} \end{bmatrix} \begin{bmatrix} \delta_{x1} & \delta_{y1} & \delta_{z1} \\ \delta_{x2} & \delta_{y2} & \delta_{z2} \\ \delta_{x3} & \delta_{y3} & \delta_{z3} \end{bmatrix} \qquad (7)$$

$$\begin{bmatrix} \dot{\delta}_{x1} & \dot{\delta}_{y1} & \dot{\delta}_{z1} \\ \dot{\delta}_{x2} & \dot{\delta}_{y2} & \dot{\delta}_{z2} \\ \dot{\delta}_{x3} & \dot{\delta}_{y3} & \dot{\delta}_{z3} \end{bmatrix} = \begin{bmatrix} -\theta_1 & \theta_1 & 0 \\ \theta_2 - Z & -1 & -x \\ y & x & -\theta_3 \end{bmatrix} \begin{bmatrix} \delta_{x1} & \delta_{y1} & \delta_{z1} \\ \delta_{x2} & \delta_{y2} & \delta_{z2} \\ \delta_{x3} & \delta_{y3} & \delta_{z3} \end{bmatrix} \quad (8)$$

2.1.3. Chaos Synchronization

Chaos synchronization occurs when two (or more) chaotic systems (identical or non-identical) adapt a characteristic of their motion to the same behavior, owed to force or coupling. This includes trajectories and phase locking. Complete, projective, and antiphase synchronization have been explored [29]. These three synchronization types are usually of interest for master-slave configurations, i.e., two connected systems. However, for a more general case of networks, the less regular synchronization regimes such as multi-clustering and synchronization of groups of nodes are of relevance. See [30,31] for more details.

Complete synchronization means having equivalent state variables over time. Generalized synchronization for master-slave systems implies a functional relation between connected chaotic oscillators, $x_2(t) = F[x_1(t)]$.:

1. Complete Synchronization

    Considering the following master and slave systems:

    $$\dot{x} = \theta(x), \quad (9)$$

    $$\dot{y} = \psi(y) + u(x, y), \quad (10)$$

    State vectors $x, y \in \mathbb{R}$ is the vector controller for $f, g: \mathbb{R}^n \to \mathbb{R}^n$. The system error dynamics are:

    $$e(t) = y(x) - x(t), \quad (11)$$

    The systems are said to be in complete synchronization if:

    $$\lim_{t \to \infty} \|e(t)\| = 0 \quad (12)$$

2. Anti-Phase Synchronization

    In this type, given the same master-slave systems, the error dynamics for the systems are defined as:

    $$e(t) = y(x) + x(t) \quad (13)$$

    The systems are said to be in anti-synchronization if Equation (12) is satisfied.

3. Projective Synchronization

    In this type, given the same master-slave systems, the error dynamics for the systems are defined as:

    $$e(t) = y(x) - \alpha x(t) \quad (14)$$

where $\alpha \neq 0$ is the constant, called a scaling factor. The systems are said to be in projective synchronization if Equation (12) is satisfied. By setting appropriate values for α, synchronized systems may be scaled to desired levels and proportionally grow. Complete synchronization and anti-synchronization are specific examples of projective synchronization where $\alpha = 1$ and $\alpha = -1$. Greater mathematical complexity and chaos characterize the Lorenz map because of its higher dimension. As one-dimensional chaotic maps need fewer computing processes, they are better suited for applications that need to run with minimal latency. More basic chaotic maps, however, have serious security flaws. This shortcoming arises because of the restricted chaotic range, reduced chaotic complexity, and accelerated rate of degradation of dynamic behavior [32,33].

Several approaches for chaotic synchronization have been presented. Active nonlinear control and adaptive mode control have been widely employed for synchronization in recent literature [29]. Based on the Lyapunov stability theory, active nonlinear control has gained popularity in recent years. Adaptive control assumes that there is a controller with a fixed structure and complexity for each potential plant parameter value, which can achieve the required performance with suitable controller parameter values. All these strategies are not applicable if the parameters of the chaotic system are unknown. Chaos control and synchronization focus on estimating the unknown parameters of chaotic dynamical systems. Parameter identification may be transformed into a multi-dimensional optimization problem using an objective function [34–36].

2.1.4. Chaotic Maps

Chaotic maps are differential equations that describe chaotic discrete dynamics [18]. Chaos can only be detected in deterministic, continuous systems with a three-dimensional phase space or more. Low-dimensional chaotic systems are resource-efficient. The logistic map is a typical low-dimensional system [37]. Chaos is degenerative in these systems. It is hard to give the output sequence a long period. High-dimensional chaotic systems are more nonlinear. However, they have the drawbacks of excessive resource consumption and low-speed performance. Therefore, a large-period, high-dimensional, digital chaotic system with high speed and minimal resources is needed. Chen, Rossler, and Henon are 3D chaotic systems utilized in wireless communication [38].

1. Chen Chaotic System

Chen identified a classical chaotic attractor in a basic 3D system [38]:

$$\begin{cases} \dot{x} = a(y-x) \\ \dot{y} = (c-a)x - xz - cy \\ \dot{z} = xy + bz \end{cases} \quad (15)$$

x, y, and z are state variables, whereas a, b, and c are parameters. Chen chaotic-based encryption relies on secret keys. An invader cannot guess the wireless key. As Chen chaotic systems are sensitive to beginning circumstances and system characteristics, two near-initial conditions lead to diverse paths, as shown in Figure 1a.

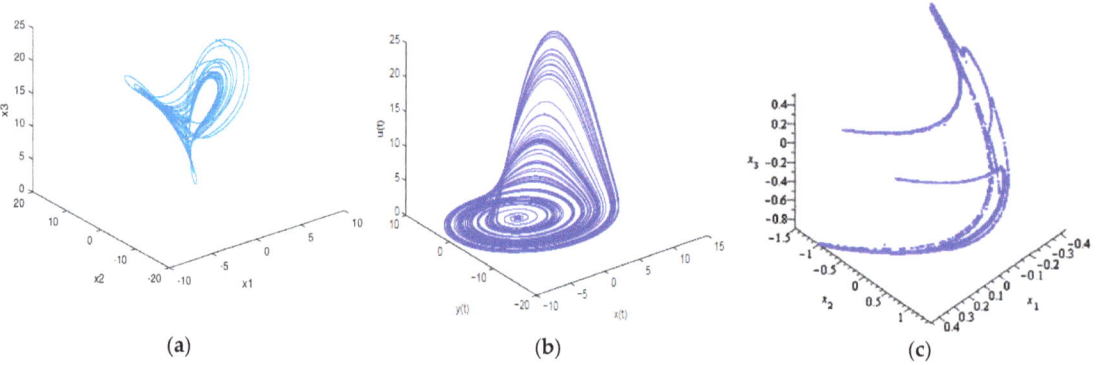

(a)　　　　　　　　　　(b)　　　　　　　　　　(c)

Figure 1. 3D view of (**a**) Chen chaotic, (**b**) Rossler chaotic, and (**c**) Henon chaotic map.

2. Rossler Chaotic System

Rossler is a basic chaotic dynamical system with one non-linear term with standard system equations [39]:

$$\begin{cases} \dot{x} = a(y-x) \\ \dot{y} = x + ay \\ \dot{z} = b + xz - cz \end{cases} \quad (16)$$

x, y, and z are state variables; a and b are fixed; and c is the control parameter. Rossler attractor parameters are $a = 0.2$, $b = 0.2$, and $c = 5.7$. Figure 1b shows the Rossler chaotic attractor. This system is the minimum for continuous chaos for at least three reasons: (1) Its phase space has minimal dimensions, (2) Nonlinearity is minimal because there is a single quadratic term, and (3) It generates a chaotic attractor with a single lobe, unlike the Lorenz attractor, which has two.

3. Henon Chaotic System

The Henon chaotic map is a chaotic discrete-time dynamical system. The map simplifies the Lorenz model's Poincare portion. The plane will either approach the Henon odd attractor or diverge to infinity.

$$\begin{cases} \dot{x} = a - (y^2 + bz) \\ \dot{y} = x \\ \dot{z} = y \end{cases}, \quad (17)$$

The Henon chaotic map parameters are $a = 1.4$ and $b = 0.3$. The conventional Henon map is chaotic (Figure 1c).

2.1.5. Quantum Fruit Fly Optimization Algorithm

Optimizing means picking the best element (based on some criteria) from a group of options or finding the least or maximum output for an experiment [34]. Heuristic methods are intelligent search strategies that speed up the process of obtaining a satisfying or near-optimal solution in bio-inspired procedures. A heuristic approach is simpler than an analytical one. However, precision is lost. Metaheuristics are iterative processes that help identify near-optimal solutions. Metaheuristics combine heuristic approaches to improve their performance [10,40]. Recent metaheuristic algorithms include the FOA [41]. FOA is inspired by fruit fly foraging. FOA has fewer adjusting parameters, less computational quantity, and offers great global search and convergence abilities. FOA is two-phased. The first step is smelling. In this phase, flies travel toward food by smelling it. Second phase begins when they are closer to the food supply: the vision stage. The fruit flies utilize their eyesight to come closer to the food. This phase repeats until the fruit fly eats the food. The steps of FOA include [42,43]:

(1) The random initial position of a fruit fly. Init X_axis; Init Y_axis.
(2) A fruit fly's sense of smell searches randomly for food.

$$\begin{cases} X_i = X_{axis} + Random\ Value\ R_1 \\ Y_i = Y_{axis} + Random\ Value\ R_2 \end{cases} \quad (18)$$

(3) As the food's location is unknown, the distance ($Dist$) to the origin is inferred before calculating the decision value of smell concentration (S).

$$\begin{cases} Dist_i = \sqrt{X_i^2 + Y_i^2} \\ S_i = \frac{1}{Dist_i} \end{cases} \quad (19)$$

(4) The smell concentration decision value (S) is inserted in the Fitness function to calculate the fruit fly's $Smell_i$.

$$Smell_i = Function(S_i) \quad (20)$$

(5) Determine the fruit fly swarm's strongest smell (seek for the maximum value)

$$[bestSmell\ \ bestIndex] = \max(Smell) \quad (21)$$

(6) Using the best smell concentration and x, y coordinates, the fruit fly swarm flies to the position.

$$\begin{cases} Smellbest = bestSmell \\ X\_axis = X(bestindex) \\ Y\_axis = Y(bestindex) \end{cases} \quad (22)$$

(7) If the smell concentration is better than the previous iteration of smell concentration, execute Step 6.

Quantum theory assigns the fruit fly swarm to move in quantum space. The delta potential well model increases the uncertainty that fruit flies recognize and migrate to food. All quantum objects have wave-like features and may be in several locations at once; hence, they are characterized in quantum theory by the wave function (x, t), rather than by their position x and velocity v. A location's likelihood of hosting the item in quantum space is determined by the strength of the wave function at that location, as shown below in module form [15].

$$|\psi(x,t)|^2 dxdydz = Qdxdydz \tag{23}$$

$Qdxdydz$ is the object's probability of appearing at (x, y, z) at time t. Thus, $|\psi(x,t)|^2$ is the probability density function meeting the equation:

$$\int_{-\infty}^{+\infty} |\psi|^2 dxdydz = \int_{-\infty}^{+\infty} Qdxdydz = 1 \tag{24}$$

Schrödinger's equation describes object motion in quantum physics.

$$i\hbar \frac{\partial}{\partial t} \psi(X,t) = \hat{H}\psi(X,t) \tag{25}$$

$$\hat{H} = -\frac{\hbar}{2m}\nabla^2 + V(t) \tag{26}$$

$\hbar$ is the Planck Constant, $\hat{H}$ is the Hamiltonian operator, m is the object mass, and $V(t)$ denotes the potential field of the object. Fruit flies search for food in the delta potential well, where they move in quantum space. Quantum behavior replaces fruit fly foraging and random search in quantum space. Both fruit fly smell and vision become more uncertain, increasing population diversity. One-dimensional space was used for simplicity. If food source location is x, its potential energy in the one-dimensional delta potential well is:

$$V(x) = -\gamma \delta(x - \rho_{axis}) = -\gamma \delta(y) \tag{27}$$

where the location of the fruit fly swarm, ρ_{axis}, is in the center of the delta potential well. According to Schrödinger's equation, the following normalized wave function can be obtained:

$$\psi(y) = \frac{1}{\sqrt{L}} e^{-|y|/L} \tag{28}$$

L is the delta potential well length. Thus, the probability density function is:

$$Q(y) = |\psi(y)|^2 = \frac{1}{L} e^{-|y|/L} \tag{29}$$

This equals

$$y = \pm \frac{L}{2} \ln \frac{1}{u} \tag{30}$$

u is a random number (0, 1). Thus, we can determine the fruit fly's food source location:

$$x = \rho_{axis} \pm \frac{L}{2} \ln \frac{1}{u} \tag{31}$$

The model assumes that a 1D delta potential well is on each dimension at the swarm center attractor point, and osphresis-based search has quantum properties. The fruit fly's quantum-behaved foraging is shown by the wave function, not randomly. The employed QFOA model included swarm location initialization, osphresis-based search, and vision-based search. The employed QFOA model used quantum-behaved searching instead of random osphresis-based searching. In the osphresis-based search process, M_{osp}, new food source locations (X_{axis}, Y_{axis}) were generated in the delta potential well. FOA's quantum-behaved searching mechanism is:

$$\begin{cases} X_i = X_{axis} \pm \frac{L_{x,i}}{2} \ln \frac{1}{r_x} \\ Y_i = Y_{axis} \pm \frac{L_{y,i}}{2} \ln \frac{1}{r_y} \end{cases} \quad (32)$$

where $i = 1, 2, \ldots, M_{osp}$, r_x and r_y are random [0, 1] values. $L_{x,i}$ and $L_{y,i}$ are delta potential well characteristic lengths of the corresponding dimension, determined by the fruit fly's last search location, based on their olfactory senses.

$$\begin{cases} L_{x,i} = 2b|X_{axis} - X_i| \\ L_{y,i} = 2b|Y_{axis} - Y_i| \end{cases} \quad (33)$$

i is the iteration number and b controls the quantum searching range.

$$b = b_1 \, logsig\left(10 \cdot \left(0.5 - \frac{g}{G_{max}}\right)\right) + b_2 \quad (34)$$

b_1 and b_2 restrict the value range to $b \in [b_2, b_1 + b_2]$.

2.2. Related Work

Several works on estimating chaotic system parameters have been recently published [13,44,45]. Real-world estimation is difficult for parameters of a complex 3D chaotic system. Most gradient-based methods are sensitive to initial conditions, trapping them in local minima. Estimating 3D chaotic parameters using soft computing techniques at a suitable cost function, is one solution, such as global optimization algorithms. Several cases of chaotic system parameter estimation using optimization algorithms have been reported [44,46,47]. The following section summarizes these algorithms.

Li et al. [35] combined the artificial bee colony algorithm (ABC) and differential evolution (DE) to estimate chaotic system parameters. Gao et al. [48] proposed chaos firefly optimization (CFA) for identifying Lorenz chaotic system parameters. Using chaotic search to update the standard Firefly algorithm improved optimization accuracy and speed. Recent pioneering work has combined the cuckoo search (CS) algorithm and orthogonal learning to estimate Lorenz and Chen chaotic system parameters [49]. He et al. also used particle swarm optimization (PSO) to estimate Lorenz system parameters [50]. This technique does not sufficiently explore the solution space. Small populations produce poor results. Li et al. [51] introduced the chaotic ant swarm (CAS) algorithm to determine chaotic system parameters.

Gholipour et al. [52] estimated chaotic system parameters with the artificial bee colony algorithm. Wei and Yu [53] presented a hybrid cuckoo search (HCS) algorithm inspired by differential evolution. The presented HCS offers two novel mutation strategies to fully exploit the neighborhood. Three chaotic systems with and without time delays were simulated and compared to other optimization methods to test HCS. Experimental results showed HCS's superiority in chaotic system parameter estimation due to its high calculation accuracy, fast convergence speed, and strong robustness. In [54], the authors introduced a two-stage estimation technique that combined the guaranteed approach and swarm intelligence.

Zhuang et al. [55] presented a new hybrid Jaya–Powell method for estimating the parameters of a Lorenz chaotic system. The proposed Jaya–Powell algorithm combines the Jaya algorithm, which seeks the relatively global optimum, with the Powell algorithm, which seeks the relatively local optimum, to provide a more precise and efficient estimate. This algorithm's searching technique makes it easier to strike a middle ground between exploration and exploitation throughout the optimization process. The suggested Jaya–Powell algorithm does not need the careful adjustment of appropriate parameters as it does not rely on any algorithm-specific parameters. Compared with seven benchmark methods, the proposed hybrid Jaya–Powell algorithm provided more precise estimates and converged more quickly.

The work presented in [56] explored how to use several metaheuristic algorithms for the recognition of parameters in a fractional-order financial chaotic system. The algorithms that have been put into place are the ant colony optimizer, grey wolf optimizer, whale optimization algorithm, and artificial bee colony optimizer. As an objective function, mean square error was used to estimate the system's parameters. Zhang et al. [57] offered a novel method of parameter estimation that made use of numerical differentiation to streamline the preparation of observational data. Given the noisy observations on a subset of dependent variables, numerical differentiation may be used to approximately determine the values of the dependent variables and their derivatives. The parameter estimation issue may be simplified by substituting these approximations into the original system. The precision and efficiency of their technology are shown by numerical examples.

Encouraged by recent developments in data assimilation, Carlson et al. [58] built a dynamic learning technique to estimate missing parameters of a chaotic system using just a subset of available data. The authors convincingly proved, under plausible assumptions that this approach converged to the right parameters when the system under issue was the standard three-dimensional Lorenz system. They computationally showed the effectiveness of this technique on the Lorenz system by recovering any correct subset of the three non-dimensional parameters of the system, provided that an appropriate subset of the state was observable. Over the last two decades, studies on how to synchronize a Lorenz chaotic system have been more prominent. Model reference adaptive control (MRAC) synchronization scheme design has been the primary focus of the majority of the research. For this problem, C. Peng, and Y. Li [59] suggested two system identification strategies. The observer–Kalman filter identification method was the first method used. The second kind of discretization was the bilinear transform. The new approach significantly improved the accuracy of the discovered parameters, which were therefore already very near to actual values.

Rizk-Allah et al. [60] presented a unique approach to parameter estimation for the chaotic Lorenz system, using a modified form of particle swarm optimization (PSO). The suggested technique, a memory-based particle swarm optimization (MbPSO) algorithm, modeled the parameter estimation of the Lorenz system as a multidimensional issue. To change the population's orientation and improve search efficiency, MbPSO added two additional variables to the classic PSO. The results showed that the suggested algorithm performed much better than the original PSO, when particle memories were linked to those of other particles. The primary goal of the study [61] was to apply a deep learning technique to the problem of estimating the parameters of chaotic systems, such as the Lorenz system. In this research, the authors used the k-means technique to build out the workflow of a deep neural network (DNN)-based approach. The DNN approach works well for difficult, nonlinear problems. Using the proposed approach, 98% of correct training data and 73% of test data were predicted.

The parameter identification for the discrete memristive chaotic map was the primary topic of the research presented by Peng et al. [62], in which a novel intelligent optimization technique called the adaptive differential evolution algorithm was suggested. To handle the hyperchaotic and attractors that coexist in the investigated discrete memristive chaotic maps, the identification objective function had two unique components: time sequences and return maps. It was shown via numerical simulations that the suggested approach outperformed the other six existing algorithms and maintained the ability to correctly identify the original system's properties, even when subjected to noise interference.

Although chaotic system parameter estimation has been studied for decades, it can still be improved. According to the review, past studies focused on: (1) Estimating a single chaotic system parameter and (2) Not addressing the best optimization technique for exploration and exploitation in a unified framework. Most bio-inspired optimization techniques for chaotic system parameter estimation combine two or more algorithms to improve exploration and exploitation. To the best of our knowledge, little attention has been paid to developing a bio-inspired parameter estimation technique for a chaotic system with few training samples.

3. Materials and Methods

Let $\dot{X} = F(X, X_0, \theta_0)$ be a continuous nonlinear chaotic system, where $X = (x_1, x_2, \ldots, x_N)' \in \mathbb{R}^n$ is the chaotic system's state vector, $\dot{X}$ is X's derivative, the resulting solution is parameterized by the initial value X_0, and $\theta_0 = (\theta_{1,0}, \theta_{2,0}, \ldots, \theta_{d,0})'$ are the original parameters. If the system's structure is known, the estimated system may be expressed as $\dot{\widetilde{X}} = F(\widetilde{X}, X_0, \widetilde{\theta})$, where $\widetilde{X} = (\widetilde{x}_1, \widetilde{x}_2, \ldots, \widetilde{x}_N)' \in \mathbb{R}^n$ is the state vector and $\widetilde{\theta} = (\widetilde{\theta}_1, \widetilde{\theta}_2, \ldots, \widetilde{\theta}_d)'$ is a collection of estimated parameters. Based on X, the fitness function is [49,51]:

$$f\left(\widetilde{\theta}_i^n\right) = \sum_{i=0}^{W} \left[(x_1(t) - \widetilde{x}_{i,t}^n(t))^2 + \ldots + (X_N(t) - \widetilde{x}_{i,N}^n(t))^2\right], \quad (35)$$

where $t = 0, 1, \ldots \ldots W$ and i is the ith state vector. Estimating chaotic system parameters aim to reduce fitness function by minimizing $\widetilde{\theta}_i^n$. Dynamic instability makes chaotic systems difficult to estimate. Due to the problem's many variables and various local search optima, typical optimization in the local optima is difficult [63,64].

A chaos communication system comprises of transmitter, receiver, and channel (noise) performance. In the transmitter, the modulation methods utilized to combine the message signal and chaotic carrier are crucial for system security. As a signal must be sent to the receiver, there is a possibility that intruders may receive the signal. Even if intruders do not know the structure or parameters of a chaotic system, they may use signal processing or sophisticated algorithms to extract the message from the transmitter signal. In chaotic masking, the signal is directly added to the chaotic signal; thus, the fluctuation may be recognized by non-linear dynamic forecasting techniques or power spectrum analysis, if the message amplitude/frequency is high enough. Mixing the message should remove any pattern or information from the sent signal. The carrier chaotic signal will be distorted by channel noise before reaching the receiver. Message recovery requires chaotic synchronization at the receiver. Demodulation is an issue in chaotic communication systems. The recommended solution uses a few signal samples instead of large samples that need more calculation. The communication channel is assumed to be free noise, as the emphasis is on estimating the chaotic system's unknown parameters, not channel attacks.

As discussed later, in a quantum model of FOA, each fruit fly represents a particle that has a state depicted by a wave function, instead of position and velocity. The dynamic behavior of the fruit fly is different from that of the fruit fly in standard FOA algorithms; that is, the accurate values of x and v cannot be simultaneously calculated. Its searching performance is better than the original particle swarm optimization algorithm. The quantum particle swarm optimization algorithm is a global convergence guarantee algorithm. The capabilities of a QFOA algorithm to enhance convergence speed and low optimization accuracy were achieved through: (1) A mutation operator to increase the diversity of particles in a population (the delta potential well concept to speed up the convergence speed); (2) An operator based on evolutionary generations to update a contraction expansion coefficient (objective or fitness function for global optimization); (3) An elitist strategy to remain the strong particles.

3.1. At the Transmitter Side

The original signal was hidden using a known 3D Lorenz chaotic signal. Lorenz used $\theta_1 = 10$, $\theta_2 = 28$, and $\theta_3 = 8/3$. This system shows chaotic behavior [65]. Three phases applied chaotic masking. First, we used the fourth-order Runge–Kutta (RK4) to solve the 3D Lorenz chaotic system equation to create the chaotic signal. RK4 examines iterative steps in four places [66,67]. Runge–Kutta was run three times for each point in phase space with h = 0.01 [49–52].

$$\vec{k_2} = h\vec{f}\left(\vec{x}_c + \frac{1}{2}\vec{k_1}\right), \tag{36}$$

$$\vec{k_3} = h\vec{f}\left(\vec{x}_c + \frac{1}{2}\vec{k_2}\right), \tag{37}$$

$$\vec{k_4} = h\vec{f}\left(\vec{x}_c + \frac{1}{2}\vec{k_3}\right), \tag{38}$$

$$\vec{x}_c(t_0 + h) = \vec{x}_c(t_0) + (\vec{k_1} + 2\vec{k_2} + 2\vec{k_3} + \vec{k_4}), \tag{39}$$

$$\vec{k_1} = h\vec{f}(\vec{x}_c), \tag{40}$$

$$\vec{x}_c(t_0 + h) = \vec{x}_c(t_0) + (\vec{k_1} + 2\vec{k_2} + 2\vec{k_3} + \vec{k_4}), \tag{41}$$

$$\vec{k_1} = \begin{bmatrix} k_{1x} \\ k_{1y} \\ k_{1z} \end{bmatrix} = h\vec{f}(\vec{x}_c) = h\vec{f}\begin{bmatrix} x_c \\ y_c \\ z_c \end{bmatrix} = h\vec{f}\begin{bmatrix} x_{c0} \\ y_{c0} \\ z_{c0} \end{bmatrix} = h\begin{bmatrix} \theta_1(y_{c0} - x_{c0}) \\ \theta_2 x_{c0} - y_{c0} - x_{c0}z_{c0} \\ -\theta_3 z_{c0} + x_{c0}y_{c0} \end{bmatrix} \tag{42}$$

$$\vec{k_2} = \begin{bmatrix} k_{2x} \\ k_{2y} \\ k_{2z} \end{bmatrix} = h\vec{f}\left(\vec{x}_c + \frac{1}{2}\vec{k_1}\right) = h\vec{f}\left(\begin{bmatrix} x_c \\ y_c \\ z_c \end{bmatrix}_{t=0} + \frac{1}{2}\begin{bmatrix} x_{1x} \\ y_{1y} \\ z_{1z} \end{bmatrix}\right) \tag{43}$$

$$\vec{k_3} = \begin{bmatrix} k_{3x} \\ k_{3y} \\ k_{3z} \end{bmatrix} = h\vec{f}\left(\vec{x}_c + \frac{1}{2}\vec{k_2}\right) = h\vec{f}\left(\begin{bmatrix} x_c \\ y_c \\ z_c \end{bmatrix}_{t=0} + \frac{1}{2}\begin{bmatrix} x_{2x} \\ y_{2y} \\ z_{2z} \end{bmatrix}\right) \tag{44}$$

$$\vec{k_4} = \begin{bmatrix} k_{4x} \\ k_{4y} \\ k_{4z} \end{bmatrix} = h\vec{f}\left(\vec{x}_c + \frac{1}{2}\vec{k_3}\right) = h\vec{f}\left(\begin{bmatrix} x_c \\ y_c \\ z_c \end{bmatrix}_{t=0} + \frac{1}{2}\begin{bmatrix} x_{3x} \\ y_{3y} \\ z_{3z} \end{bmatrix}\right) \tag{45}$$

$$\vec{c}(t) = \begin{bmatrix} k_{4x} \\ k_{4y} \\ k_{4z} \end{bmatrix} = \begin{bmatrix} x_{c0} \\ y_{c0} \\ z_{c0} \end{bmatrix} + \frac{1}{6}(\vec{k_1} + 2\vec{k_2} + 2\vec{k_3} + \vec{k_4}) \tag{46}$$

The second stage involved sampling the original input to create a discrete signal or accumulating an analogue or continuous signal [47]. Sampling is described by the following arithmetic statement, where $\delta(t)$ represents the impulse train of period Ts [68]:

$$\text{Sampled Signal } x_s(t) = x(t) \cdot \delta(t) \tag{47}$$

$$\delta(t) = a_0 + \sum_{n=1}^{\infty}(a_n \cos(nw_s t) + b_n \sin(nw_s t)) \tag{48}$$

$$a_0 = \frac{1}{T_s}\int_{-\frac{T}{2}}^{\frac{T}{2}}\delta(t)dt = \frac{1}{T_s}\delta(0) = \frac{1}{T_s} \tag{49}$$

$$a_n = \frac{2}{T_s}\int_{-\frac{T}{2}}^{\frac{T}{2}}\delta(t)\cos(nw_s)dt = \frac{2}{T_s}\delta(0) = \frac{1}{T_s}\cos(nw_s 0) = \frac{2}{T_s} \tag{50}$$

$$b_n = \frac{2}{T_s}\int_{-\frac{T}{2}}^{\frac{T}{2}}\delta(t)\sin(nw_s)dt = \frac{2}{T_s}\delta(0) = \frac{1}{T_s}\sin(nw_s 0) = 0 \tag{51}$$

$$\delta(t) = \frac{1}{T_s}\sum_{n=1}^{\infty}\frac{2}{T_s}\delta(t)\cos(nw_s t) + 0) \tag{52}$$

$$x_s(t) = x(t)[\frac{1}{T_s} + \sum_{n=1}^{\infty}\left(\frac{2}{T_s}\cos(n_s t)\right) + 0)] = \frac{1}{T_s}[x(t) + 2\sum_{n=1}^{\infty}(\cos(nw_s t))x(t)] \tag{53}$$

$$x_s(t) = \frac{1}{T_s}[x(t) + 2\cos(nw_s t).x(t) + 2\cos(n2w_s t).x(t) + 2\cos(n3w_s t).x(t) + \ldots] \quad (54)$$

After sampling the original signal, downsampling reduced the signal's sampling rate by M. When a signal is downsampled, only every Mth sample is taken and all others are discarded. Downsampling balances a dataset by matching the majority class (3D original signal) with minority class samples (3D chaotic signal). In the third stage, the downsampled original signal $\vec{x}_d(t)$ was added, or masked, to the chaotic oscillator output at the transmitter before transmission. The transmitter is represented as follows:

$$\vec{c}(t) = K(\vec{x}_c(t)), \quad (55)$$

$\vec{c}(t)$ is the chaotic system's output after applying RK4. $\vec{x}_m$ is formed by adding $\vec{c}(t)$ to $\vec{x}_d(t)$

$$\vec{x}_m(t) = \vec{c}(t) + \vec{x}_d(t) \quad (56)$$

$$\vec{x}_m = \begin{bmatrix} x_m \\ y_m \\ z_m \end{bmatrix}, \quad \vec{x}_m = \begin{bmatrix} x_d \\ y_d \\ z_d \end{bmatrix} \quad (57)$$

Before transmitting the signal via the channel, upsampling and interpolation were used to rebuild it. The upsampling procedure increases the sampling rate by an integer factor M (interpolation factor) by adding M-1 evenly spaced zeroes between each pair of samples. Mathematically, upsampling is provided by the following equations, where $l = 0, \pm 1, \pm 2, \ldots$. The impulse train [n] represents the sampling function.

$$x_U[n] = \begin{cases} x_m\left[\frac{n}{M}\right]. & n = 0, \pm M, \pm 2M, \ldots \\ 0 & \text{otherwise} \end{cases} \quad (58)$$

$$x_U[n] = x_m[n]p[n] = \sum_{J=-\infty}^{+\infty} x_m[l]\delta[n - lM] \quad (59)$$

$$p[n] = \sum_{t=-8}^{+\infty} \delta[n - lM] \quad (60)$$

After upsampling, interpolation was used to create new data points within a specified range. If the sampling instants are near enough, the signal can be accurately recreated by low-pass filter interpolation. Low-pass filtering $x_U[n]$ reconstructs $x_m[n]$. The interpolated signal $x_T[n]$ is calculated as [69]:

$$x_T[N] = x_U[n] * h[n] \quad (61)$$

$h[n]$ denotes the impulse response of the low-pass filter:

$$h[n] = \frac{M\Omega_C}{2\pi}\text{sinc}\left(\frac{n\Omega_C}{\pi}\right) \quad (62)$$

Ω_C is the cutoff frequency of the discrete time filter. So, the equivalent interpolation formula can be written as:

$$x_T[n] = \sum_{J=-\infty}^{+\infty} x_m[lM]h_T[n - lM] \quad (63)$$

$$x_T[n - lM] = \frac{M\Omega_C}{2\pi}\text{sinc}\left[\frac{\Omega_C}{\pi}(n - lM)\right] \quad (64)$$

$h[n]$ is the impulse response of the interpolating filter. The interpolation using the *sinc* function is commonly referred to as band limited interpolation.

3.2. On the Receiver Side

On the receiver side, the received signal (masked original signal) was downsampled. To use chaotic communications, two identical chaotic oscillators were needed in the transmitter (or master) and receiver (or slave). Unknown receiver-side parameters $(\tilde{\theta}_1, \tilde{\theta}_2, \tilde{\theta}_3)$ needed to be approximated. The quantum fruit fly optimization algorithm (QFOA) estimates the 3D Lorenz chaotic system's unknown parameters. The fundamental QFOA includes a setup step and a cycle of smelling, evaluating, and flocking [15,43,70]. The QFOA control parameters were set, including the maximum number of generations and population size, and the fruit fly swarm's location was randomized. As the original FOA can only solve continuous optimization issues, it was adapted to tackle synchronization in chaos-based communication networks. Each fly picked randomly from the search space group, including $\tilde{\theta}_1$, $\tilde{\theta}_2$, and $\tilde{\theta}_3$. As stated in [71], the search space for unknown chaotic system parameters is [9 11], [20 30], and [2 3]. Given these initial answers, QFOA repeated the following steps [72]:

- These solutions were input to a predefined chaotic receiver system. The RK4 was used in the 3D Lorenz equations to create chaotic signals (one for each fruit fly).
- Each fly determined food concentration using the mean square error between the predicted chaotic signal and the downsampled received signal (smelling process).
- Each fly shared its position with others. The flies compared their solutions to choose the best one.
- Flies migrated to the solution with the lowest fitness value, which became the new best solution (vision process).

This stage outputs the 3D Lorenz chaotic system's ideal parameters. The second stage of synchronization used these characteristics as inputs. RK4 was used again to create the estimated 3D chaotic signal. The third stage received this estimated signal and the downsampled received signal. We then subtracted the two signals to get the sampled signal. The original signal was reconstructed using upsampling and interpolation. Perfect synchronization is key to reconstructing the original signal. Table 1 provides the link between QFOA parameters and the parameters estimation problem of the chaotic system.

Table 1. The link between QFOA parameters and the parameters estimation problem of the chaotic system.

QFOA Parameters	Chaotic Synchronization Problem
Number of iterations	The search process's best solution iteration count.
Number of swarms m	$m = 25$.
Initial location	The initial solution is randomly selected from each parameter's search space.
Smell concentration	Mean square error (Objective or fitness function).
Vision	Smell concentration-based parameter selection.

4. Results

This section analyses the model's efficiency. Experiments were performed to test the model's reliability in estimating chaotic system parameters. The suggested approach optimized synchronization with the Lorenz chaotic system and speech signal. The 20 to 30 dB weaker speech signal was combined with the chaotic mask signal to create a broadcast signal. Table 2 shows the experiment's algorithm settings. The recommended model was implemented in MATLAB R2017b (9.3.0.713579) 64-bit. The model was constructed using a laptop with an Intel (R), Core (TM) i5-8250U CPU@ 1.60 GHZ @ 1.80 GHz, 8 GB, and 64-bit operating system, with a x64 processor.

In the proposed chaotic parameters estimate model, various statistical parameters were employed to evaluate model performance. These evaluations included [45] the mean (average) of best fitness values and standard deviations. For a robust model, these means (mean of best fitness) needed to be as low as possible, where optimum fitness quantifies the difference between estimated and sent signals. Standard deviations (Std.) shows how measurements for a group are spread apart from the average (mean) or anticipated value. A low standard deviation suggests that most data points are near to the mean (more reliable). A large standard deviation suggests the data points are widely scattered (less reliable).

Table 2. The parameters of the optimization algorithms (Reference parameters collected from previous studies).

Algorithm	Parameters	Values
Fruit fly (FOA)	Number of swarms	25
	Maximum number of iterations	50
Cuckoo search (CS)	Number of swarms	25
	Probability rate	0.20
	Maximum number of iterations	50
Practical swarm (PSO)	Number of swarms	25
	Inertia weight	0.8
	Acceleration coefficient	1.5
	Maximum number of iterations	50
Genetic algorithm (GA)	Number of swarms	25
	Crossover rate	0.7
	Mutation rate	0.3
	Maximum number of iterations	50
Firefly algorithm (FA)	Number of swarm	25
	Initial brightness of each fly	1
	Absorption coefficient of light	1
	Step size (α)	1
	Maximum number of iterations	50

4.1. Experiment 1: Comparison with Existing Methods

The first batch of tests compared the proposed model to comparable techniques [44] that used the GA, PSO, and CS to find the 3D Lorenz chaotic system characteristics solely using chaotic signals. Default swarm parameters were utilized. Table 3 shows that the suggested model is superior to the prior techniques. QFOA's calculated parameters matched the original parameters' real values. According to [49], the 3D Lorenz chaotic system's initial parameters are $\theta_1 = 10$, $\theta_2 = 28$, and $\theta_3 = 8/3$, allowing complete synchronization between the master and slave chaotic systems. The estimated parameters matched the CS-based model, but the QFOA outperformed in terms of the optimal function's mean and standard deviation. Most data points were close to the mean with a low standard deviation (more reliable). QFOA was more effective and resilient than other chaotic system parameter estimation strategies. The model and system responses were synchronized. This gain was due to the proposed model's higher coverage and exploration of the searching space, which improved parameter estimate accuracy and led to the discovery of optimum chaotic parameter values compared with existing techniques.

Table 3. Comparison of statistical results for the Lorenz system, in case of only using chaotic signal.

Models	Means of the Best Fitness	Std. Dev. of the Best Fitness	θ_1	θ_2	θ_3
QFOA	9.53×10^{-9}	5.83×10^{-9}	10.00	28.00	2.6666
CS	1.71×10^{-4}	1.69×10^{-4}	10.00	28.00	2.6664
PSO	0.118	0.269	9.998	27.99	2.6665
GA	1.332	2.784	10.027	28.01	2.6691

4.2. Experiment 2: Effect of QFOA Iteration

The second set of experiments investigated the effect of the QFOA number of iterations on the proposed model to identify the correct parameters of the 3D Lorenz chaotic system using only chaotic signals and masking voice signals with the chaotic signals. QFOA was performed 30 times every iteration, with 50 iterations total and $W = 30$ for data sampling. Default swarms were utilized. After 20 iteration, the parameters θ_1, θ_2, and θ_3 converge to the actual values. QFOA reached stable values in 25 iterations. As the fitness function value declines rapidly to zero, indicating that QFOA may converge quickly to the global optimum. These few iterations did not require complex calculations. By adjusting the location of the QFOA swarms by modifying the number of iterations, the algorithm could reach an ideal balance between exploitation and exploration. At the same time, elitism in population iteration may have sped up the convergence and assured continual optimization. This highlights the remarkable efficiency of QFOA in accomplishing global optimization.

4.3. Experiment 3: Effect of Number of Swarms

The third set of experiments was implemented to find a suitable number of QFOA swarms that helped to reduce computational effort without sacrificing estimation precision. For the three-dimensional Lorenz system, the proposed model was run by setting the QFOA swarm numbers as 10, 30, and 100, respectively. In general, tiny populations provide poor outcomes. As the population grows, outcomes improve, but more fitness tests are needed. Beyond a certain point, outcomes are not significantly influenced. When there are too few swarms, the solution space is not sufficiently searched, resulting in unsatisfactory outcomes. Considering search quality and computational effort, a population size between 30 and 60 is suggested. A larger population size is suggested for estimating additional parameters. Size 25 performed well. Considering processing costs and estimating accuracy, a large population size is unnecessary.

4.4. Experiment 4: Influence of the Data Sampling W

The fourth series of experiments tested how data sampling affected model accuracy. To reduce the amount of parameter setting combinations, the model changed one parameter W at a time, while leaving other parameters (number of swarms, number of iterations, etc.) at default values. The impact of modifying these variables was also considered. General factors for selecting W were minimum fitness mean and highest estimate accuracy. All scenarios were run 30 times for comparison. Table 4 lists the estimation results and the means of the best fitness values for different data sampling W. As shown, the estimation accuracy declined as W increased. Moving from 30 samples to 100 decreased the mean of fitness values by 36%, whereas moving from 100 samples to 200 decreased the mean of fitness values by 45%. These three groups of input data may have provided a satisfactory estimate, but the 30 samples of data had the least variation. Different inputs impacted the first iteration, but for all instances, it took roughly 25 iterations for the algorithm to converge to zero, indicating these three conditions could all acquire quite accurate anticipated outcomes. As expected, chaotic parameter estimate accuracy falls as W rises. The crucial sensitivity of the nonlinear system to starting circumstances and parameters made the fitness function more difficult as W increased. To decrease estimate bias in target nonlinear systems, it is vital to sample enough data.

Table 4. Statistical results for the extended Lorenz chaotic system with varied data sampling.

Number of Samples	Means of the Best Fitness	θ_1	θ_2	θ_3
W = 30	9.45×10^{-9}	10.00	28.000	2.6667
W = 100	1.49×10^{-8}	10.00	27.998	2.6666
W = 200	2.18×10^{-8}	9.99	27.997	2.6666

4.5. Experiment 5: Comparison with another Quantum Metaheuristic Algorithm

The fifth series of tests compared the proposed model with a comparable strategy that used the quantum firefly (QFA) algorithm to determine the ideal chaotic parameters of the 3D Lorenz chaotic system exclusively using chaotic signal and masking speech sounds with chaotic signal. Both techniques were performed 30 times to compare fitness means and standard deviations. Default swarms were utilized. Table 5 shows that the estimated chaotic parameters while masking speech signals with chaotic signals are similar to the

QFA-based model. The mean fitness values and standard deviations of QFOA were 37 and 66% lower than in QFA.

Table 5. Statistical results for the Lorenz system.

	Model	Means of the Best Fitness	Std. Dev. of the Best Fitness	θ_1	θ_2	θ_3
Masking voice signal with chaotic signal	QFOA	1.04×10^{-8}	6.27×10^{-9}	10.00	28.00	2.6667
	QFA	1.61×10^{-8}	1.85×10^{-8}	10.00	27.99	2.6666
Chaotic only	QFOA	9.53×10^{-9}	5.79×10^{-9}	10.00	28.00	2.6667
	QFA	1.42×10^{-8}	1.18×10^{-8}	10.00	28.00	2.6667

In general, the quantum-inspired firefly algorithm (QFA) ensured the diversification of firefly-based generated solution sets, using the superstitions quantum states of the quantum computing concept. However, it suffered from premature convergence and stagnation; this was mainly dependent on the ability of the employed potential field to handle movement uncertainty. The suggested QFOA algorithm, inspired by the delta potential field, presented the most balanced computational performance in terms of exploitation (accuracy and precision) and exploration (convergence speed, and acceleration). The advantage of such models, on the one hand, is that they are "exactly solvable", e.g., the spectrum and eigenvectors are explicitly known; on the other hand, many interesting physical features are retained, despite the simplification involved in approximating short-range with zero-range. Thus, QFOA was more effective and resilient than QFA in estimating chaotic parameters.

4.6. Experiment 6: Estimation Accuracy with Different Chaotic Systems

The sixth group of experiments was conducted to determine the efficiency of the proposed model regarding the different chaotic systems, including the 3D Chen and 3D Rossler chaotic systems in cases of only using the chaotic signal. The algorithm was run 30 times and the default parameters of QFOA were used. Table 6 shows that the estimated parameters derived by QFOA were close to the original parameters for chaotic systems. As stated in [44], the original parameters of 3D Chen chaotic system were $\theta_1 = 35$, $\theta_2 = 3$, and $\theta_3 = 28$; whereas, as stated in [73], the original parameters of 3D Rossler chaotic system were $\theta_1 = 0.2$, $\theta_2 = 0.4$, and $\theta_3 = 5.7$, through which perfect synchronization could be obtained between the master and slave chaotic systems. In the search process, fruit flies modified their places based on individual and swarm experiences. This expanded the solution search space and prevented premature convergence. This also improved the algorithm's convergence speed. Generalized synchronization was possible with certain parameters [74].

Table 6. Estimation accuracy for different chaotic system using default QFOA parameters.

Chaotic Systems	θ_1	θ_2	θ_3
Lorenz	10.000	28.0000	2.6667
Chen	35.000	2.9999	27.999
Rossler	0.2000	0.3999	5.6999

Computer simulations of the three 3D chaotic systems and comparisons with other metaheuristic approaches proved the suggested method's efficiency. The impact of data sampling, iterations, and swarms on estimating accuracy was also studied. Theoretical study and computer simulation led to the following conclusions: (1) A shorter data sample length improves estimate accuracy because a longer sample length complicates the objective function. (2) The highest number of iterations improves estimating accuracy by moving the swarms. Thus, exploitation and exploration balance each other. (3) Many swarms will investigate enough space for study, improving estimate accuracy. These swarms are computationally intensive. To decrease estimate bias in chaotic systems, use the right data sampling, iterations, and swarms.

For our simulations, we used some of the most famous chaotic systems as examples. The number of parameters for these chaotic systems was not large, and the system was not complex. At present, the most studied chaotic neural network systems have many parameters, and the weight of these systems affects the complexity of the network. However, the suggested simpler model may be adapted to deal with chaotic neural network systems and other complicated chaotic systems. In our case, instead of searching for only three chaotic parameters, which represented the final solution picked from the search space based on a quantum-inspired particle's movement, more parameters could be correctly estimated by increasing the number of fruit flies. Therefore, there is a trade-off between computational cost and required best fitness evaluation function that must be balanced.

4.7. Industrial Application Case: Financial Chaotic System

Due to the nonlinear nature of the financial markets, chaos models using nonlinear dynamics have been a popular topic in recent years. Uncertainty in the market environment has a particularly negative impact on the financial system. Therefore, describing the financial chaos model with random elements is more practical. Due to deterministic instability, financial chaos, such as the extreme turbulence of the financial market and the financial crisis, occurs during the functioning of the financial system, which has significant detrimental effects on economic development and social stability. Controlling the financial system from a chaotic to a periodic state is as simple as modifying the controller settings. As a first step, we theoretically obtained a range of values for the controller parameters by analyzing the financial system's dynamic equations and controllers. Later, we investigated the effects of these parameters on the system.

5. Conclusions

Chaotic synchronization is key for chaotic signals in a communication system. On the receiver end, the chaotic system's parameters are unknown; thus, the task is to determine the ideal values to retrieve the message signal. Using the fruit fly optimization technique, this article improved chaotic synchronization in chaos-based wireless networks. In this study, parameter estimation for a three-dimensional Lorenz chaotic system was set up as a multi-dimensional optimization problem and solved using the quantum fruit fly optimization method. Quantum theory was employed by the FOA model and replaced the osphresis-based search of FOA with a quantum behavior-based searching mechanism. The quantum fruit fly optimization technique improved parameter estimation accuracy by carefully exploiting the search space and converging, which suggested that the algorithm could estimate optimum parameter values. Furthermore, it enhanced the exploration of optimal solutions by sharing information regarding parameter values. The difference between the proposed model and existing metaheuristic algorithms was the use of fruit fly optimization to produce better quality solutions and convergence speed, i.e., establishing an optimal trade-off between exploration and exploitation. This model may be extended to other chaotic systems.

The results and discussion of this study led to the following conclusions (important results): (1) Numerical simulations indicate the proposed approach can accurately predict chaotic system parameters. The suggested model is faster and more accurate than current techniques. This outcome is due to balancing exploitation and exploration in the search space. (2) Even with the original signal added to the chaotic signal, the current algorithm can still identify it well, especially for the Lorenz system. (3) As with final estimated results, 30 samples of data has the highest accuracy and least variation, proving that the amount of input data affects algorithm stability.

For future work, the proposed model should be applied to different chaotic systems, such as in high-dimensional, hyper chaotic systems, and time-delay chaotic systems. Implementation and testing in a real testbed are important in the field of wireless communication. Real deployment tests can bring up issues that did not come up in simulation. To work well in real implementations, changes to the proposed model may be required.

Author Contributions: Conceptualization, S.M.D.; methodology, S.M.D.; software, Q.M.Z. and M.B.K.; validation, S.M.D.; formal analysis, S.M.D. and M.B.K.; investigation, S.M.D., Q.M.Z. and M.B.K. resources, Q.M.Z. and M.B.K.; data curation, S.M.D.; writing—original draft preparation, S.M.D., Q.M.Z. and M.B.K.; writing—review and editing, S.M.D.; visualization, Q.M.Z. and M.B.K.; supervision, S.M.D.; project administration, Q.M.Z. and M.B.K.; funding acquisition, Q.M.Z. and M.B.K. All authors have read and agreed to the published version of the manuscript.

Funding: This research received no external funding.

Institutional Review Board Statement: The study did not require ethical approval.

Informed Consent Statement: Not applicable.

Data Availability Statement: The study did not report any data.

Conflicts of Interest: The authors declare no conflict of interest.

References

1. Shukla, P.; Khare, A.; Rizvi, M.; Stalin, S.; Kumar, S. Applied Cryptography Using Chaos Function for Fast Digital Logic-Based Systems in Ubiquitous Computing. *Entropy* **2015**, *17*, 1387–1410. [CrossRef]
2. Sadkhan, S.; Al-Sherbaz, A.; Mohammed, R. Chaos based Cryptography for Voice Encryption in Wireless Communication. In Proceedings of the First International Conference of Electrical, Communication, Computer, Power and Control Engineering, Mosul, Iraq, 17–18 December 2013; pp. 191–197.
3. Mondal, B.; Mandal, T. A Multilevel Security Scheme using Chaos based Encryption and Steganography for Secure Audio Communication. *Int. J. Res. Eng. Technol.* **2013**, *2*, 399–403.
4. Fadhel, S.; Shafry, M.; Farook, O. Chaos Image Encryption Methods: A Survey Study. *Bull. Electr. Eng. Inform.* **2017**, *6*, 99–104. [CrossRef]
5. Pecora, L.; Carroll, T. Synchronization of Chaotic Systems Chaos: An Interdisciplinary. *J. Nonlinear Sci.* **2015**, *25*, 097611. [CrossRef]
6. Zhang, H. Chaos Synchronization and Its Application to Secure Communication. Ph.D. Dissertation, Electrical and Computer Engineering, University of Waterloo, Waterloo, ON, USA, 2010.
7. Shewale, G.; Shinde, N.; Shirode, A.; Singh, S.; Solanki, J.; Tajane, M.; Tripathi, G. *Chaos Theory Technical Report-60*; Sardar Patel Institute of Technology: Mumbai, India, 2012; pp. 1–39.
8. Yau, H.; Pu, Y.; Li, S. An FPGA-Based PID Controller Design for Chaos Synchronization by Evolutionary Programming. *Discret. Dyn. Nat. Soc.* **2011**, *2011*, 516031. [CrossRef]
9. Rai, D.; Tyagi, K. Bio-Inspired Optimization Techniques—A Critical Comparative Study. *ACM SIGSOFT Softw. Eng. Notes* **2013**, *38*, 1–7. [CrossRef]
10. Wahab, M.; Meziani, S.; Atyabi, A. A Comprehensive Review of Swarm Optimization Algorithms. *PLoS ONE* **2015**, *10*, e0122827. [CrossRef]
11. Shan, D.; Cao, G.; Dong, H. LGMS-FOA: An Improved Fruit Fly Optimization Algorithm for Solving Optimization Problems. *Math. Probl. Eng.* **2013**, *2013*, 108768. [CrossRef]
12. Ding, S.; Zhang, X.; Yu, J. Twin Support Vector Machines based on Fruit Fly Optimization Algorithm. *Int. J. Mach. Learn. Cybern.* **2016**, *7*, 193–203. [CrossRef]
13. Li, S.; Xu, W.; Li, R.; Zhao, X. A General Method for Chaos Synchronization and Parameters Estimation between Different Systems. *J. Sound Vib.* **2007**, *302*, 777–788. [CrossRef]
14. Niu, J.; Zhong, W.; Liang, Y.; Luo, N.; Qian, F. Fruit Fly Optimization Algorithm based on Differential Evolution and Its Application on Gasification Process Operation Optimization. *Knowl. Based Syst.* **2015**, *88*, 253–263. [CrossRef]
15. Zhang, X.; Xia, S.; Li, X. Quantum Behavior-Based Enhanced Fruit Fly Optimization Algorithm with Application to UAV Path Planning. *Int. J. Comput. Intell. Syst.* **2020**, *13*, 1315–1331. [CrossRef]
16. Abdo, A.H. Optimized Chaotic Parameters Estimation Algorithm to Enhance the Synchronization of Wireless Communication Networks. Master Thesis, Alexandria University, Alexandria, Egypt, 2019.
17. Cattani, M.; Caldas, I.; Souza, S.; Iarosz, K. Deterministic Chaos Theory: Basic Concepts. *Rev. Bras. Ensino Física* **2017**, *39*, 1315. [CrossRef]
18. Fradkov, A.; Evans, R.; Andrievsky, B. Control of Chaos: Methods and Applications in Mechanics Philosophical Transactions of the Royal Society A: Mathematical. *Phys. Eng. Sci.* **2006**, *364*, 2279–2307.
19. Gauthier, Y. The Construction of Chaos Theory. *Found. Sci.* **2009**, *14*, 153–165. [CrossRef]

20. Ren, H.; Baptista, M.; Grebogi, C. Wireless Communication with Chaos. *Phys. Rev. Lett.* **2013**, *110*, 2–5. [CrossRef]
21. Kamil, I.; Fakolujo, O. Lorenz-Based Chaotic Secure Communication Schemes. *Ubiquitous Comput. Commun. J.* **2015**, *7*, 1248–1254.
22. Meador, C. Numerical Calculation of Lyapunov Exponents for Three Dimensional Systems of Ordinary Differential Equations. Master Thesis, Marshall Digital Scholar, Marshal University, Huntington, WV, USA, 2011.
23. Pukdeboon, C. A Review of Fundamentals of Lyapunov Theory. *J. Appl. Sci.* **2011**, *10*, 55–61.
24. Balibrea, F.; Caballero, M. *Examples of Lyapunov Exponents in Two Dimensional Systems Nonlinear Maps and their Applications*; Springer: New York, NY, USA, 2014; pp. 9–15.
25. Bespalov, A.; Polyakhov, N. Determination of the Largest Lyapunov Exponents Based on Time Series. *World Appl. Sci.* **2013**, *26*, 157–164.
26. Leonov, G.; Kuznetsov, N. On Differences and Similarities in the Analysis of Lorenz, Chen, and Lu Systems. *Appl. Math. Comput.* **2015**, *256*, 334–343. [CrossRef]
27. Thanoon, T.; L-Azzawi, S.A. Stability of Lorenz Differential System by Parameters Tikrit. *J. Pure Sci.* **2010**, *15*, 118–222.
28. Chenthittayil, S. Determination of Chaos in Different Dynamical Systems. Master Thesis, the Graduate School of Clemson University, Clemson, SC, USA, 2015.
29. Kose, E.; Akcayoglu, A. Examination of the Eigenvalues Lorenz Chaotic System. *Eur. Sci. J.* **2014**, *10*, 114–121.
30. Feketa, P.; Schaum, A.; Meurer, T. Synchronization and Multicluster Capabilities of Oscillatory Networks with Adaptive Coupling. *IEEE Trans. Autom. Control* **2020**, *66*, 3084–3096. [CrossRef]
31. Gambuzza, L.; Frasca, M.; Latora, V. Distributed Control of Synchronization of a Group of Network Nodes. *IEEE Trans. Autom. Control* **2018**, *64*, 365–372. [CrossRef]
32. Feketa, P.; Schaum, A.; Meurer, T.; Michaelis, D.; Ochs, K. Synchronization of Nonlinearly Coupled Networks of Chua Oscillators. *IFAC-PapersOnLine* **2019**, *52*, 628–633. [CrossRef]
33. Ochs, K.; Michaelis, D.; Solan, E.; Feketa, P.; Schaum, A.; Meurer, T. Synthesis, Design, and Synchronization Analysis of Coupled Linear Electrical Networks. *IEEE Trans. Circuits Syst. I Regul. Pap.* **2020**, *67*, 4521–4532. [CrossRef]
34. George, G.; Raimond, K. A Survey on Optimization Algorithms for Optimizing the Numerical Functions. *Int. J. Comput. Appl.* **2013**, *61*, 41–46. [CrossRef]
35. Li, X.; Yin, M. Parameter Estimation for Chaotic Systems by Hybrid Differential Evolution Algorithm and Artificial Bee Colony Algorithm. *Nonlinear Dyn.* **2014**, *77*, 61–71. [CrossRef]
36. Jadon, S.; Tiwari, R.; Sharma, H.; Bansal, J. Hybrid Artificial Bee Colony Algorithm with Differential Evolution. *Appl. Soft Comput.* **2017**, *58*, 11–24. [CrossRef]
37. Jessa, M. Designing Security for Number Sequences Generated by Means of the Sawtooth Chaotic Map. *IEEE Trans. Circuits Syst.* **2006**, *53*, 1140–1150. [CrossRef]
38. Hao, D.; Xin, J.; Meng, H.; Quan, S. A New Three-Dimensional Chaotic System and Its Modified Generalized Projective Synchronization. *Chin. Phys. B* **2011**, *20*, 040507.
39. Ding, Y.; Jiang, Y.; Wang, H. Delayed Feedback Control and Bifurcation Analysis of Rossler Chaotic System. *Nonlinear Dyn.* **2010**, *61*, 707–715. [CrossRef]
40. Abdmouleh, Z.; Gastli, A.; Brahim, L.; Haouari, M.; Al-Emadi, N. Review of Optimization Techniques Applied for the Integration of Distributed Generation from Renewable Energy Sources. *Renew. Energy* **2017**, *113*, 266–280. [CrossRef]
41. Jiang, H.; Zhao, D.; Zheng, R.; Ma, X. Construction of Pancreatic Cancer Classifier Based on SVM Optimized by Improved FOA. *BioMed Res. Int.* **2015**, *2015*, 781023. [CrossRef]
42. Pan, W. A New Fruit Fly Optimization Algorithm: Taking the Financial Distress Model as an Example. *Knowl. Based Syst.* **2012**, *26*, 69–74. [CrossRef]
43. Yin, L.; Li, X.; Gao, L.; Lu, C. A New Improved Fruit Fly Optimization Algorithm for Traveling Salesman Problem. In Proceedings of the Eighth International Conference on Advanced Computational Intelligence, Chiang Mai, Thailand, 14–16 February 2016; pp. 21–28.
44. Peng, Y.; Sun, K.; He, S.; Yang, X. Parameter Estimation of a Complex Chaotic System with Unknown Initial Values. *Eur. Phys. J. Plus* **2018**, *133*, 305. [CrossRef]
45. Lazzus, J.; Rivera, M.; Caraballo, C. Parameter Estimation of Lorenz Chaotic System using a Hybrid Swarm Intelligence Algorithm. *Phys. Lett. A* **2016**, *380*, 1164–1171. [CrossRef]
46. Sun, J.; Zhao, J.; Wu, X.; Fang, W.; Cai, Y.; Xu, W. Parameter Estimation for Chaotic Systems with a Drift Particle Swarm Optimization Method. *Phys. Lett. A* **2010**, *374*, 2816–2822. [CrossRef]
47. Qiang, L.; Wei, P.; Shan, Y.; Bin, L.; Feng, X.; Ning, J. Parameter Estimation for Chaotic Systems with and without Noise using Differential Evolution-based Method. *Chin. Phys. B* **2011**, *20*, 060502. [CrossRef]
48. Gao, W.; Zhang, Z.; Chong, Y. Chaotic System Parameter Identification based on Firefly Optimization. *Appl. Mech. Mater.* **2013**, *347–350*, 3821–3826. [CrossRef]
49. Xiang-Tao, L.; Ming-Hao, Y. Parameter Estimation for Chaotic Systems using the Cuckoo Search Algorithm with an Orthogonal Learning Method. *Chin. Phys. B* **2012**, *21*, 050507.
50. He, Q.; Wang, L.; Liu, B. Parameter Estimation for Chaotic Systems by Particle Swarm Optimization. *Chaos Solitons Fractals* **2007**, *34*, 654–661. [CrossRef]

51. Li, L.; Yang, Y.; Peng, H.; Wang, X. Parameters Identification of Chaotic Systems via Chaotic Ant Swarm. *Chaos Solitons Fractals* **2006**, *28*, 1204–1211. [CrossRef]
52. Gholipour, R.; Khosravi, A.; Mojallali, H. Parameter Estimation of Lorenz Chaotic Dynamic System using Bees Algorithm. *Int. J. Eng.* **2013**, *26*, 257–262. [CrossRef]
53. Wei, J.; Yu, Y. An Effective Hybrid Cuckoo Search Algorithm for Unknown Parameters and Time Delays Estimation of Chaotic Systems. *IEEE Access* **2018**, *6*, 6560–6571. [CrossRef]
54. Sheludko, A. Parameter Estimation for One-Dimensional Chaotic Systems by Guaranteed Algorithm and Particle Swarm Optimization. *IFAC-PapersOnLine* **2018**, *51*, 337–342. [CrossRef]
55. Zhuang, L.; Cao, L.; Wu, Y.; Zhong, Y.; Zhangzhong, L.; Zheng, W.; Wang, L. Parameter Estimation of Lorenz Chaotic System Based on A Hybrid Jaya-Powell Algorithm. *IEEE Access* **2020**, *8*, 20514–20522. [CrossRef]
56. Gupta, S.; Gautam, G.; Vats, D.; Varshney, P.; Srivastava, S. Estimation of Parameters in Fractional Order Financial Chaotic System with Nature Inspired Algorithms. *Procedia Comput. Sci.* **2020**, *173*, 18–27. [CrossRef]
57. Zhang, J.; Huang, S.; Cheng, J. Parameter Estimation for A Chaotic Dynamical System with Partial Observations. *J. Inverse Ill-Posed Probl.* **2021**, *29*, 515–524. [CrossRef]
58. Carlson, E.; Hudson, J.; Larios, A.; Martinez, V.; Ng, E.; Whitehead, J. Dynamically Learning the Parameters of a Chaotic System Using Partial Observations. *arXiv* **2021**, arXiv:2108.08354. [CrossRef]
59. Peng, C.; Li, Y. Parameters Identification of Nonlinear Lorenz Chaotic System for High-Precision Model Reference Synchronization. *Nonlinear Dyn.* **2022**, *108*, 1733–1754. [CrossRef]
60. Rizk-Allah, R.; Farag, M.; Barghout, M.; Hassanien, A. A Memory-Based Particle Swarm Optimization for Parameter Identification of Lorenz Chaotic System. In *Proceedings of International Conference on Computing and Communication Networks*; Springer: Singapore, 2022; pp. 571–587.
61. Ann, N.; Pebrianti, D.; Abas, M.; Bayuaji, L. Parameter Estimation of Lorenz Attractor: A Combined Deep Neural Network and K-Means Clustering Approach. In *Recent Trends in Mechatronics towards Industry*; Springer: Singapore, 2022; pp. 321–331.
62. Peng, Y.; He, S.; Sun, K. Parameter Identification for Discrete Memristive Chaotic Map using Adaptive Differential Evolution Algorithm. *Nonlinear Dyn.* **2022**, *107*, 1263–1275. [CrossRef]
63. Chang, W. Parameter Identification of Rossler's Chaotic System by an Evolutionary Algorithm. *Chaos Solitons Fractals* **2006**, *29*, 1047–1053. [CrossRef]
64. Chang, W. Parameter Identification of Chen and Lü Systems: A Differential Evolution Approach. *Chaos Solitons Fractals* **2007**, *32*, 1469–1476. [CrossRef]
65. Gonzales, O.; Han, G.; De, G.; Sánchez, E. Lorenz-Based Chaotic Cryptosystem: A Monolithic Implementation. *IEEE Trans. Circuits Syst. I Fundam. Theory Appl.* **2000**, *47*, 1243–1247. [CrossRef]
66. Roslan, U.; Salleh, Z.; Kilicman, A. Solving Zhou Chaotic System using Fourth-Order Runge-Kutta Method. *World Appl. Sci. J.* **2013**, *21*, 939–944.
67. Garoma, H.; Kabeto, M. Numerical Solution of Fourth Order Ordinary Differential Equations using Fifth Order Runge—Kutta Method. *Asian J. Sci. Technol.* **2017**, *8*, 4332–4339.
68. Meneny, S. *An Introduction to Digital Signal Processing: A Focus on Implementation*, 1st ed.; River Press: Fort Benton, MT, USA, 2008.
69. Mandal, M.; Asif, A. *Continuous and Discrete Time Signals and Systems*, 1st ed.; Cambridge University Press: Cambridge, UK, 2007.
70. Jiang, Z.; Yang, Q. A Discrete Fruit Fly Optimization Algorithm for the Traveling Salesman Problem. *PLoS ONE* **2016**, *11*, e0165804. [CrossRef]
71. Zhang, H.; Li, B.; Zhang, J.; Qin, Y.; Feng, X.; Liu, B. Parameter Estimation of Nonlinear Chaotic System by Improved TLBO Strategy. *Soft Comput.* **2016**, *20*, 4965–4980. [CrossRef]
72. Kundra, H.; Khan, W.; Malik, M.; Rane, K.; Neware, R.; Jain, V. Quantum-Inspired Firefly Algorithm Integrated with Cuckoo Search for Optimal Path Planning. *Int. J. Mod. Phys. C* **2022**, *33*, 2250018. [CrossRef]
73. Li, H.; Bai, P.; Xue, J.; Zhu, J.; Zhang, H. Parameter Estimation of Chaotic Systems using Fireworks Algorithm. *Adv. Swarm Comput. Intell.* **2015**, *9141*, 457–467.
74. Abarbanel, H.; Kennel, M.; Illing, L.; Tang, S.; Chen, H.; Liu, J. Synchronization and Communication using Semiconductor Lasers with Optoelectronic Feedback. *IEEE J. Quantum Electron.* **2001**, *37*, 1301–1311. [CrossRef]

Article

Fully Connected Hashing Neural Networks for Indexing Large-Scale Remote Sensing Images

Na Liu, Haiming Mou, Jun Tang, Lihong Wan, Qingdu Li and Ye Yuan *

Institute of Machine Intelligence, University of Shanghai for Science and Technology, Shanghai 200093, China
* Correspondence: yuanye_usst@usst.edu.cn

Abstract: With the emergence of big data, the efficiency of data querying and data storage has become a critical bottleneck in the remote sensing community. In this letter, we explore hash learning for the indexing of large-scale remote sensing images (RSIs) with a supervised pairwise neural network with the aim of improving RSI retrieval performance with a few binary bits. First, a fully connected hashing neural network (FCHNN) is proposed in order to map RSI features into binary (feature-to-binary) codes. Compared with pixel-to-binary frameworks, such as DPSH (deep pairwise-supervised hashing), FCHNN only contains three fully connected layers and incorporates another new constraint, so it can be significantly accelerated to obtain desirable performance. Second, five types of image features, including mid-level and deep features, were investigated in the learning of the FCHNN to achieve state-of-the-art performances. The mid-level features were based on Fisher encoding with affine-invariant local descriptors, and the deep features were extracted by pretrained or fine-tuned CNNs (e.g., CaffeNet and VGG-VD16). Experiments on five recently released large-scale RSI datasets (i.e., AID, NWPU45, PatternNet, RSI-CB128, and RSI-CB256) demonstrated the effectiveness of the proposed method in comparison with existing handcrafted or deep-based hashing methods.

Keywords: neural network; binary hash code; image retrieval; remote sensing

MSC: 68T09

1. Introduction

Nowadays, we are living in a period of big remote sensing data [1] because numerous Earth observation sensors provide a huge amount of remote sensing data for our lives; therefore, the development of fast and accurate content-based image retrieval (CBIR) methods is becoming increasingly important in the remote sensing community. In order to make better use of big data, machine learning methods are essential [2]. In 2007, Salakhutdinov and Hinton [3,4] proposed a hash learning method in the field of machine learning. Since then, the hashing method has been widely studied and applied in the fields of computer vision, information retrieval, pattern recognition, data mining, etc. [?]. Hash learning methods convert high-dimensional data into the form of binary codes through machine learning methods. At the same time, the transformed binary codes retain the neighboring relationships in the original high-dimensional space. In recent years, hash learning methods have rapidly developed into a research hotspot in the field of machine learning and big data.

Traditionally, the representation of remote sensing images (RSIs) is described by a real number vector with thousands of dimensions. Traditional remote sensing image retrieval methods usually describe images by using real vectors with thousands of dimensions. Each dimension can be stored in computer memory by floating-point data with four bytes, which may lead to the following issues: (1) The storage of a large-scale dataset requires many hard disks; (2) exhaustively searching for relevant images in a large-scale dataset is computationally expensive. When a 4096-dimensional feature of the fully connected

Citation: Liu, N.; Mou, H.; Tang, J.; Wan, L.; Li, Q.; Yuan, Y. Fully Connected Hashing Neural Networks for Indexing Large-Scale Remote Sensing Images. *Mathematics* **2022**, *10*, 4716. https://doi.org/10.3390/math10244716

Academic Editor: Danilo Costarelli

Received: 22 September 2022
Accepted: 6 December 2022
Published: 12 December 2022

Publisher's Note: MDPI stays neutral with regard to jurisdictional claims in published maps and institutional affiliations.

Copyright: © 2022 by the authors. Licensee MDPI, Basel, Switzerland. This article is an open access article distributed under the terms and conditions of the Creative Commons Attribution (CC BY) license (https://creativecommons.org/licenses/by/4.0/).

layer in a deep network is expressed and stored, it takes 4096 × 4 bytes of storage space. Since one byte is equal to eight bits, the storage space of a 4096-dimensional real vector is 4096 × 4 × 8 bits. In contrast, when hash learning is used to map deep features, supposing that the deep features are mapped to 64 bits through hashing coding, the storage space used is eight bytes. In this case, in comparison with the storage space of 4096 × 4 × 8 bits, the hash learning method can greatly reduce the hard disk storage space of data and greatly improve the computational efficiency of image retrieval. To address the above issue, hashing-based approximate nearest neighbor search, which is a highly time-efficient search with a low storage space, is becoming a popular retrieval technique due to the emergence of big data. Hash mapping [5] represents an image as binary codes that contain a small number of bits, such as 32 bits (4 bytes), thereby significantly helping in the reduction of the amount of memory required for storage.

2. Related Work

Hashing-based retrieval methods can generally be divided into two categories: data-independent and data-dependent methods. As a popular data-independent method, random projection without training data is usually employed to generate hash functions, such as locality-sensitive hashing (LSH). Due to the limitation of data-independent hashing approaches [6], many recent methods based on an unsupervised or supervised manner were proposed in order to design more efficient hash functions. In the remote sensing community, there are only a few works on hash-based RSI retrieval. Demir and Bruzzone investigated two types of learning-based nonlinear hashing methods, namely, kernel-based unsupervised hashing (KULSH) and the kernel-based supervised LSH method (KSLSH). KULSH extended LSH to nonlinearly separable data by modeling each hash function as a nonlinear kernel hyperplane constructed from unlabeled data. KSLSH defined hash functions in the kernel space such that the Hamming distances from within-class images were minimized and those from between-class images were maximized. Both KULSH and KSLSH were used on bag-of-visual-words (BOVW) representations with SIFT descriptors [7]. Li and Ren [8,9] proposed partial randomness hashing (PRH) for RSI retrieval in two stages: (1) Random projections were generated to map image features (e.g., a 512-dimensional GIST descriptor) to a lower Hamming space in a data-independent manner; (2) a transformation weight matrix was used to learn based on training images. In KULSH, KSLSH, and PRH, the image representations (BOVW or GIST) were based on handcrafted feature extraction.

Benefiting from the rapid development of deep learning, Li et al. [10,11] investigated a deep hashing neural network (DHNN) and conducted comparisons of the binary quantization loss between the L1 and L2 norms. As an improved version of DPSH (deep pairwise-supervised hashing) [12], the DHNN improved the design of the sigmoid function and could perform feature learning and hash function learning simultaneously. Rather than designing handcrafted features, the DHNN could automatically learn different levels of feature abstraction, thereby resulting in a better description ability. However, the learning of the DHNN was time-consuming because deep feature learning and hash learning were performed in an end-to-end framework.

2.1. Convolutional Neural Network Hashing (CNNH)

CNNH combines the extraction of depth features and the learning of hash functions into a joint learning model [13,14]. Unlike the traditional method based on handcrafted features, CNNH is a supervised hash learning method, and it can automatically learn the appropriate feature representation and hash function from the pairwise labels by using the feature learning method of the neural network. CNNH is also the first deep hashing method to use paired label information as an input.

The CNNH method consists of two processes:

(1) **Using the data samples to learn the hash function of the information.**

Given n images, $\mathbf{X} = \{x_1, x_2, \cdots, x_n\}$, and the similarity matrix S is defined as follows:

$$S_{ij} = \begin{cases} +1 & x_i, x_j \text{ are similiar} \\ -1 & x_i, x_j \text{ are disimiliar} \end{cases} \quad (1)$$

The hash function that needs to be learned is defined as:

$$H(X) = \{h_1(x), h_2(x), \cdots, h_c(x)\} \quad (2)$$

where $H(X)$ is an n by q binary matrix, and $h_k(x) \in \{-1, 1\}^q$ is the k-th hash function in the matrix (the length of the function is q) and is also the hash code of the image x_k.

Supervised hashing uses the similarity matrix S and the data sample $\mathbf{X}$ to calculate a series of hash functions, that is, to decompose the similarity matrix S into HH^T through gradient descent, where each row of H represents each the approximate hash codes corresponding to an image. The objective function of the above process is as follows:

$$\min_H \sum_{i=1}^n \sum_{j=1}^n \left(s_{ij} - \frac{1}{q} H_i H_j^T\right)^2 = \min_H \left\| S - \frac{1}{q} HH^T \right\|_F^2 \quad (3)$$

where $\|\cdot\|_F$ is the Frobenius norm and H is the hash coding matrix.

(2) **Learning the image feature representation and hash functions.**

A convolutional network is used to learn the hash codes, and the learning process uses the cross-entropy loss function. The network has three convolutional layers, three pooling layers, one fully connected layer, and an output layer. The parameters of each layer are as follows: The numbers of filters of the first, second, and third convolutional layers are 32, 64, and 128 (with the size of 5×5); a dropout operation with a ratio of 0.5 is used in the fully connected layer.

After training the network, the image pixels can be used as inputs in order to obtain the image representation and hash codes. However, CNNH is not an end-to-end network.

2.2. Network-in-Network Hashing (NINH)

Rather than the paired labels used by the CNNH method, the NINH network uses triplets of images to train the model, which makes it an end-to-end deep hash learning method, and the layer is deeper than that of CNNH [15]. NINH integrates the feature representation and the learning of hash functions in a framework that allows them to promote each other and further improve performance.

Given the sample space of $\mathbf{X}$, we define the mapping function as $F: X \to \{0,1\}^q$. The triplet information is $(\mathbf{X}, \mathbf{X}_+, \mathbf{X}_-)$ and satisfies the following: The similarity between $\mathbf{X}$ and $\mathbf{X}_+$ is greater than that between $\mathbf{X}$ and $\mathbf{X}_-$. After mapping, the similarity between $F(X)$ and $F(X_+)$ is greater than that between $F(X)$ and $F(X_-)$.

The NINH method consists of three parts:

(1) **The loss function.**

The triplet-ranking hinge loss function is composed of three images, wherein the first image and the second image are similar, and the first image and the third image are dissimilar. The function is defined as:

$$\begin{aligned} L_{\text{trilet}}(F(X), F(X_+), F(X_-)) = \\ \max(0, 1 - (\|F(X) - F(X_-)\|_H - \|F(X) - F(X_+)\|_H)) \end{aligned} \quad (4)$$

where $F(X), F(X_+), F(X_-) \in \{0,1\}^q$, $\|\cdot\|_H$ represents the Hamming distance.

(2) **The feature representation.**

The CNN model is used to extract an effective feature representation from the input image. The CNN model that we used is an improved NIN (network-in-network) [16] network. The improvement of the network is the introduction of the convolution kernel, and the size of a convolutional layer is 1×1. In addition, an average pooled layer is used instead of the fully connected layer.

(3) **The hash coding.**

The feature-to-hash code mapping is performed by using the divide-and-encode module to reduce the redundancy between hash codes. At the same time, the sigmoid function is used to restrict the range of the output to [0,1], thereby avoiding discrete constraints.

2.3. Deep Pairwise-Supervised Hashing (DPSH)

DPSH based on pairs of images is used to compensate for the large workload of triplets [12,17]. Although the CNNH and DPSH methods are both based on pairs of information, the processes of feature learning and hash function learning are performed in two phases in the CNNH method. The two processes are independent of each other, and the DPSH method is an end-to-end deep learning framework that can perform feature learning and hash coding learning at the same time. The DPSH method mainly includes:

(1) **Feature learning.**

A convolutional neural network with a seven-layer structure is used for feature learning.

(2) **Hash coding learning.**

A discrete method is used to solve the NP-hard discrete optimization problem. For a set of binary hash codes $B = \{b_i\}_{i=1}^n$, the likelihood function L of the paired samples is defined as follows:

$$p(l_{i,j} \mid B) = \begin{cases} \text{sigmoid}(\Psi_{i,j}) & l_{i,j} = 1 \\ 1 - \text{sigmoid}(\Psi_{i,j}) & l_{i,j} = 0 \end{cases} \quad (5)$$

where $\text{sigmoid}(\Psi_{i,j}) = \frac{1}{1+e^{-\psi_{i,j}}}$, $\psi_{i,j} = \frac{b_i^T b_j}{p}$, and the value of p is 2. By taking the negative log-likelihood function $L[\cdot]$ of the paired $l_{i,j}$, the following optimization problem can be obtained:

$$\min_{B} \zeta = -\log p(L \mid B) = -\sum_{l_{i,j} \in L} \log p(l_{i,j} \mid B) - \sum_{l_{i,j} \in L} \left(l_{i,j} \Psi_{i,j} - \log\left(1 + e^{-\Psi_{i,j}}\right) \right) \quad (6)$$

Although existing methods cover handcrafted and CNN-based features, hash-based RSI retrieval still needs to be developed because the related works are scarce. For example, CNNH is an early representative model that combines deep convolutional networks with hash coding. It firstly decomposes the similarity matrix of samples in order to obtain the binary code of each sample, and then uses convolutional neural networks to fit the binary code. The fitting process is equivalent to a multi-label prediction problem. Although it has achieved significant performance improvements in comparison with traditional hand-designed-feature-based methods, it is still not an end-to-end method, and the image representation that is learned cannot be used, in turn, to update the binary code. Therefore, it still cannot fully exploit the powerful capabilities of deep models. To better tap into the potential of deep models, in this study, we propose a fully connected hashing neural network (FCHNN) to map the BOVW, pretrained, or fine-tuned deep features into binary codes with the aim of improving the RSI retrieval performance and learning efficiency. The main contributions are as follows: (1) An extended BOVW representation based on the affine-invariant local description and Fisher encoding is introduced, and this representation is competitive with deep features after hashing. (2) The FCHNN with three layers is proposed for pairwise-supervised hashing learning. The framework of the proposed feature-to-binary method has more advantages than that of a pixel-to-binary method (e.g.,

DPSH) in terms of the retrieval performance and efficiency. (3) In comparison with DSPH, another constraint is incorporated into the objective function of the FCHNN to accelerate the speed with which the desired results are obtained.

3. Proposed Method

The FCHNN consists of two parts: (1) feature extraction and (2) hashing learning based on a feature-to-binary framework, as shown in Figure 1. The proposed framework is beneficial for studying different types of features (either handcrafted or deep-based features). Based on the feature extraction, the FCHNN implements the hash coding of five types of features. These five types of features are Fisher vectors based on the affine-invariant local description, activation vector features extracted from the full connection layer based on pretrained and fine-tuning strategies, and activation vectors extracted using the CaffeNet and VGG-VD16 models, respectively. In order to be consistent, the Fisher vector also uses 4096-dimensional features. In the learning of the FCHNN, the same pair information as that used in DPSH is used for supervised learning, and the optimized learning process of the fully connected network is completed through random gradient descent.

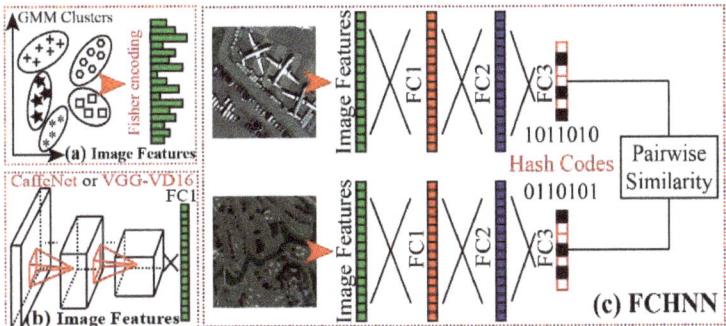

Figure 1. Framework of the proposed feature extraction and the FCHNN: (a,b) feature extraction stages; (c) the learning of the FCHNN.

A. Feature Extraction

To give a comprehensive analysis of RSI representation and to investigate the generality of the FCHNN for different features, five types of feature extraction were employed.

Mid-Level Features: Mid-level representation consists of the detection of affine-invariant points of interest, extraction of SIFT descriptors, and Fisher encoding with GMM clustering. The interest-point detector selects a multi-scale Hessian implemented with the VLFeat toolbox [18], and a 128-dimensional SIFT descriptor is extracted for each point of interest. The SIFT descriptors are then transformed into RootSIFT [19] and 64-dimensional PCA-SIFT [20]. In the stage of Fisher encoding, a 4096-dimensional ($2 \times 32 \times 64$) Fisher vector can be obtained based on the PCA-SIFT and 32 GMM (Gaussian mixture model) clusters.

Deep Features: Two types of pretrained convolutional neural networks (CNNs), namely, CaffeNet and VGG-VD16, were employed to extract deep features. Both CNNs were implemented with MatConvNet [21] and trained on the ImageNet dataset. Both CaffeNet and VGG-VD16 included three fully connected layers. Given an input image and a CNN model, we extracted a 4096-dimensional activation vector from the antepenultimate fully connected layer as the deep features.

With the use of the fine-tuning strategy proposed by [22], the fine-tuned CaffeNet and VGG-VD16 could also be obtained by retraining the corresponding pretrained CNN on a training dataset until convergence. Given an input image and a fine-tuned CNN, 4096-dimensional activation vectors could also be obtained, similarly to the feature extraction using the pretrained CNN.

B. FCHNN

Architecture: As shown in Figure 1, the FCHNN consisted of three fully connected layers, with the aim of mapping the image features into a set of binary codes (0 or 1). The first two fully connected layers (denoted by FC1 and FC2) of the FCHNN contained 4096 neurons. Both FC1 and FC2 were followed by a nonlinear operation called rectified linear units (ReLU). The last fully connected layer (denoted as FC3) was the binary output containing N neural nodes. N corresponded to the desired number of bits after hashing. The architecture of the FCHNN was similar to that of the last three fully connected layers of AlexNet, except for the number of output nodes. The FCHNN has the following characteristics: (1) It is a feature-to-binary rather than pixel-to-binary framework; (2) it is general for both handcrafted and deep features; (3) the use of fewer layers can significantly improve its learning speed.

Object Function: Given n training images, $Z = \{z_i\}_{i=1}^n$, where z_i is a vector (image features shown in Figure 1) of the ith image. A set of pairwise labels $L = \{l_{i,j}\}$ that satisfy $l_{i,j} \in \{0,1\}$ is constructed to provide the supervised information. $l_{i,j} = 1$ indicates that z_i and z_j are similar (within-class samples); otherwise ($l_{i,j} = 0$), z_i and z_j are dissimilar (between-class samples). The FCHNN aims to map z_i to binary codes $b_i \in \{-1,1\}^d$ with d bits, causing b_i and b_j to have a low Hamming distance if $l_{i,j} = 1$ or a high Hamming distance if $l_{i,j} = 0$.

Here, we adopt the same definition as that in Equation (5). Inspired by deep hashing neural networks (DHNNs), we parameterize Equation (5) as $p = sd$, where s is the similarity factor and d is the length of the hash codes. This operation can not only enhance the flexibility of the algorithm, but can also enable the algorithm to have optimal performance when facing hash codes of different lengths. To solve the optimization problem of Equation (6), its discrete form can be rewritten as follows:

$$\min_{B,A} \zeta = -\sum_{l_{i,j} \in L} \left(l_{i,j} \Lambda_{i,j} - \log\left(1 + e^{\Lambda_{i,j}}\right) \right)$$
$$\text{s.t. } a_i = b_i \quad \forall i = 1,2,\cdots,n \quad (7)$$
$$a_i \in \mathbb{R}^{c \times 1} \quad \forall i = 1,2,\cdots,n$$
$$b_i \in \{-1,1\}^c \quad \forall i = 1,2,\cdots,n$$

where $\Lambda_{i,j} = \frac{a_i^T a_j}{sd}$ and $A = \{a_i\}_{i=1}^n$.

By taking the negative log-likelihood of the pairwise labels $l_{i,j}$ in L, the following objective function can be formed:

$$\min_{B,A} \zeta = -\sum_{l_{i,j} \in L} \left(l_{i,j} \Lambda_{i,j} - \log\left(1 + e^{\Lambda_{i,j}}\right) \right) + \alpha \sum_{i=1}^n \|b_i - a_i\|_2^2 \quad (8)$$

where $A = \{a_i\}_{i=1}^n$; $a_i = W^T f(z_i; \theta) + v$, and θ denotes the FC1 and FC2 parameters of the FCHNN; $f(z_i; \theta)$ denotes the FC2 output, $W \in \mathbb{R}^{4096 \times d}$ denotes a weighted matrix containing the fully connected weights between FC2 and FC3, $v \in \mathbb{R}^{c \times 1}$ is a bias vector, and α is a hyper-parameter.

Equation (8) aims to make the FCHNN's output and the final binary code b_i as similar as possible. In addition, we introduce another constraint into the objective function, and Equation (8) can be rewritten as follows:

$$\min_{B,A} \zeta = -\sum_{l_{i,j} \in L} \left(l_{i,j} \Lambda_{i,j} - \log\left(1 + e^{\Lambda_{i,j}}\right) \right) + \alpha \sum_{i=1}^n \|b_i - a_i\|_2^2 + \beta \sum_{l_{i,j} \in L} \left(\Psi_{i,j} - l_{i,j} \right) b_i^T a_i \quad (9)$$

where $b_i^T a_i$ should be as large as possible, while $\Psi_{i,j} - l_{i,j}$ should be as small as possible. The third term, which can significantly accelerate the learning speed in order to obtain desirable results, considers the performance of the final hash codes. Thus, we can obtain:

$$\min_{\mathbf{B},\mathbf{W},v,\theta} \zeta = - \sum_{l_{i,j} \in \mathbf{L}} \left(l_{i,j} \Lambda_{i,j} - \log\left(1 + e^{\Lambda_{i,j}}\right)\right) + \text{alpha} \sum_{i=1}^{n} \left\| b_i - \mathbf{W}^T f(z_i;\theta) + v \right\|_2^2 + \beta \sum_{l_{i,j} \in \mathbf{L}} (\Psi_{i,j} - l_{i,j}) b_i^T \left(\mathbf{W}^T f(z_i;\theta) + v\right) \quad (10)$$

where $\mathbf{B}, \mathbf{W}, v$ and θ are the parameters that need to to be learned.

Learning: The learning of the FCHNN is summarized in Algorithm 1. In each iteration, a mini-batch of training images is collected from the entire training set in order to alternately update the parameters. In particular, b_i can be directly optimized by $b_i = sign(a_i) = sign(\mathbf{W}^T f(z_i;\theta) + v)$. For $\mathbf{W}, v$ and θ, we first compute the derivatives of the objective function for a_i:

$$\frac{\partial \zeta}{\partial a_i} = \sum_{j=1}^{n} (\Lambda_{i,j} - l_{i,j}) a_j + 2\alpha (a_i - b_i) + \beta \sum_{j=1}^{n} (\Psi_{i,j} - l_{i,j}) b_j \quad (11)$$

Then, $\mathbf{W}, v$ and θ can be updated through back-propagation, as in [23,24].

Algorithm 1: Learning for the FCHNN

Input: Training samples $\mathbf{Z} = \{\mathbf{z}_i\}_{i=1}^{n}$ and pairwise labels $\mathbf{L} = \{l_{i,j}\}$
Output: **B**, **W**, **v**, and θ
FCHNN initialization: All fully connected weights are randomly initialized by a Gaussian distribution with a mean of 0 and variance of 0.01.
Repeat: Sampling a minibatch of samples randomly from **Z**, each sample $\mathbf{Z}_i$ in the minibatch performs:
(1) Calculation of $f(\mathbf{Z}_i;\theta)$ by using forward propagation
(2) Computation of $\mathbf{a}_i = \mathbf{W}^T f(\mathbf{z}_i;\theta) + \mathbf{v}$
(3) Computation of the binary code of $\mathbf{Z}_i$ by using $\mathbf{b}_i = sign(\mathbf{a}_i)$
(4) Computation of derivatives for $\mathbf{Z}_i$
(5) Update of **W**, **v**, and θ via back-propagation
Until a fixed number of iterations is reachd

Output of the FCHNN: The model obtained after the network learning of the FCHNN can be applied to the mapping of image features other than those in the training set. For any given input image, first, we can extract the corresponding image features as the input of the FCHNN, extract the output of the FCHNN through forward propagation, and do the following:

$$b_i = \text{sign}\left(\mathbf{W}^T f(z_i;\theta) + v\right) \quad (12)$$

where b_i represents the final hash codes.

4. Experiments and Discussion

Extensive experiments were conducted on five recently released large-scale datasets, namely, AID [25], NWPU [26], PatternNet [27], RSI-CB128 [28], and RSI-CB256 [28], as shown in Figure 2. AID contains 30 RSI scene classes collected from multi-source-based Google Earth imagery, including 10,000 RGB images with 600 × 600 pixels. Each class consists of different numbers of images, ranging from 220 to 420; the spatial resolution of this dataset ranges from 0.5 to 8 m. NWPU contains 45 RSI scene classes collected from Google Earth, including 31,500 RGB images with 256 × 256 pixels. Each class contains 700 images, and the spatial resolution of this dataset ranges from 0.2 to 30 m in most cases. PatternNet contains 38 RSI classes collected from Google Earth imagery or the

Google Maps API, including 30,400 RGB images with 256 × 256 pixels. Each class contains 800 images, and the spatial resolution of this dataset ranges from 0.062 to 4.693. RSI-CB is composed of RSI-CB128 and RSI-CB256, which are two large-scale RSI datasets collected from Google Earth and Bing Maps. RSI-CB128 contains 45 RSI scene classes, including more than 36,000 RGB images with 128 × 128 pixels. RSI-CB256 contains 35 RSI scene classes, including more than 24,000 RGB images with 256 × 256 pixels. The resolution of RSI-CB (both RSI-CB128 and RSI-CB256) ranges from 0.22 to 3 m.

Figure 2. Datasets. From top to bottom: AID, NWPU, PatternNet, RSI-CB128, and RSI-CB256.

A. Experimental setup and evaluation strategy

Each dataset was randomly divided into five parts—four parts for training and one for testing. Given a dataset, the fine-tuning process of CaffeNet or VGG-VD16 was performed on the training set with a workstation with a 3.4 GHz Intel CPU and 32 GB of memory, and an NVIDIA Quadro K2200 GPU was used for acceleration. The fine-tuning parameters, such as the learning rate, batchSize, weightDecay, and momentum, were set to 0.001, 256, 0.0005, and 0.9, respectively.

For the FCHNN, we used a validation set to choose the hyper-parameters s, α, and β, and we found that good performance could be achieved by setting $s = 2, \alpha = 50$, and $\beta = 1$, which were then used for all dataset experiments with $d = 16, d = 32$, and $d = 64$, where $s = 2$ was the similarity factor. After the feature vectors were normalized, they needed to be dot-multiplied by 500. In the experiment, to better adapt the Fisher vector to the FCHNN, we found that scaling up the Fisher vector by a certain ratio could improve the accuracy of hash retrieval. Thus, 500 was the empirical value that we obtained after a series of comparative analyses. Of course, if we did not scale up the Fisher vector, we could also obtain a considerable retrieval effect.

To evaluate the retrieval performance, each image (represented by binary codes) in the testing dataset was used as a query to sequentially compute the Hamming distance between the query and training images in order to obtain the ranking results, which were then used to compute the average precision. The final mean average precision (mAP) [18,29,30] was the averaged result over all queries. Precision–recall curves were also used to plot the tradeoff between precision (Precision = TP/(TP + FP)) and recall (Recall = TP/(TP + FN)), where TP is a true positive, FP is a false positive, and FN is a false negative.

B. *Evaluation of the retrieval performance*

Given a training dataset with multiple classes, the optimization of the FCHNN was based on supervised learning with back-propagation (BP) by computing the derivatives of a defined objective function. The supervised information could be obtained with pairs of images (similar or dissimilar) from the training dataset; meanwhile, the objective function was based on pairwise images (labels).

Unlike DPSH and DHNNs, the FCHNN has a small-sized network architecture and learns the linear–nonlinear transformation with multiple layers for mid-level or deep features, rather than the original image. There are two differences between DPSH [31] and the proposed FCHNN in terms of optimization: (1) Firstly, the weighted sigmoid function is selected to allow the FCHNN to have better performance; (2) secondly, the FCHNN introduces another constraint term in order to improve the convergence of the network learning.

Table 1 and Figure 3 show comparisons of the hash retrieval performance (mAP) on five datasets, on which four methods were compared; these were PRH [8], KULSH [32], KSLSH [32], and DPSH [24,31]. PRH is a method of learning hash functions by using a locally random strategy. Firstly, images are mapped to Hamming space in a data-independent manner by using a random projection algorithm. Secondly, learning transforms the weight matrix from the training data of remote sensing images in a more efficient way. However, this method only extracts GIST features; it is a hash coding method based on handcrafted features. For a comprehensive comparative analysis, we further combined PRH with BOW and Fisher vector coding in order to extract mid-level features and use them for hash coding. KULSH [32–34] is based on the LSH method, and it is for achieving fast processing of kernel data with arbitrary kernel functions. KULSH [35] only exploits the BOVW method. Similarly, in order to ensure the comprehensiveness of our comparative research, we also combined the KULSH method with the GIST features and the Fisher vector coding method as the middle-layer expression, and then with hash coding. KSLSH [32,36] is a limited supervised method that uses similar and dissimilar pairwise information, achieves high-quality hash function learning based on sufficient training datasets, and, finally, maps data to Hamming space. The distance within similar data is the smallest, and the distance within dissimilar data is the largest in the Hamming space.

In general, the PRH, KULSH, and KSLSH methods are hash coding methods that use handcrafted features. Deep pairwise-supervised hashing (DPSH) is a deep hashing method that implements both feature learning and hash coding learning in a complete framework, and it uses pairwise image information. The FCHNN is our proposed method.

As we can see in Table 1 and Figure 3, the deep hash method had obvious performance advantages over the handcrafted-feature-based methods; compared with the DPSH method, the proposed FCHNN method obtained a higher retrieval accuracy, and the FCHNN had good generality, making it suitable for the hashing of both artificial design features and depth features. Among the five types of features, the features extracted from the fine-tuned VGG-VD16 model achieved the highest accuracy, which was better than that of the features extracted from the pre-trained VGG-VD16 model. So, it was verified that the fine tuning strategy could effectively improve the retrieval results.

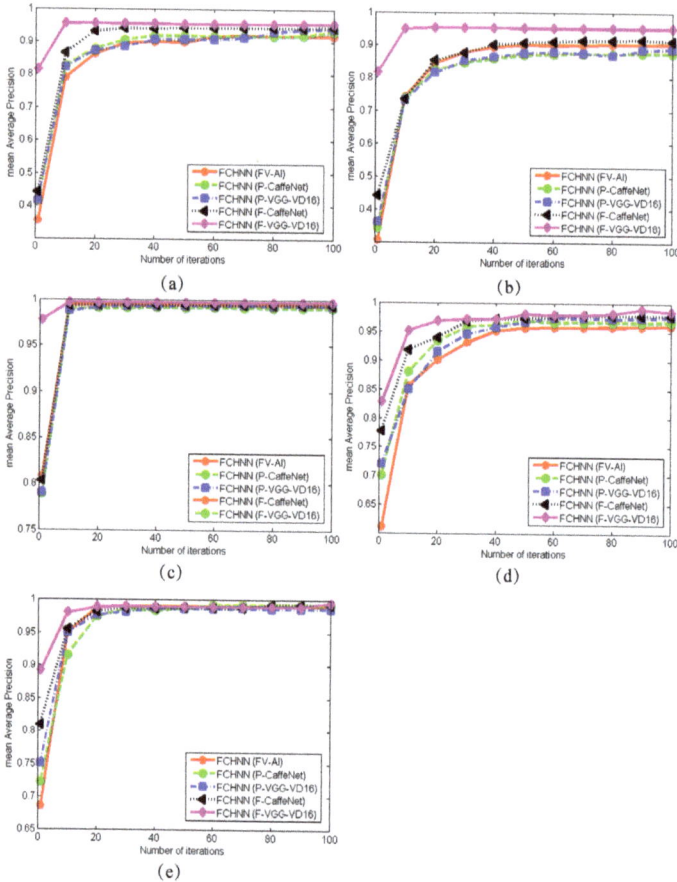

Figure 3. Comparison of five types of features in RSI retrieval based on five datasets. All results are given as the mean average precision (mAP). (**a**) AID dataset, (**b**) NWPU45 dataset, (**c**) PatternNet dataset, (**d**) RSI-CB128 dataset, and (**e**) RSI-CB256 dataset.

Table 1. Comparison of the hash retrieval performance (mAP) on the AID, NWPU45, PatternNet, RSI-CB128, and RSI-CB256 datasets.

Methods	Coding Length (bit)	AID	NWPU45	PatternNet	RSI-CB128	RSI-CB256
PRH (GIST) [8]	16	0.0712	0.0405	0.0872	0.0754	0.0836
	32	0.0541	0.0349	0.0968	0.0831	0.0978
	64	0.0559	0.0376	0.1304	0.0957	0.1072
PRH (BOVW) [8]	16	0.1052	0.0737	0.1746	0.1363	0.1677
	32	0.1244	0.0863	0.2604	0.1893	0.2158
	64	0.1561	0.1041	0.3077	0.2502	0.2969
PRH (FV-AI) [8]	16	0.1558	0.0955	0.3253	0.1957	0.2636
	32	0.1894	0.1310	0.4244	0.2631	0.3468
	64	0.2357	0.157	0.5336	0.3149	0.4525

Table 1. Cont.

Methods	Coding Length (bit)	AID	NWPU45	PatternNet	RSI-CB128	RSI-CB256
KULSH (GIST) [32]	16	0.0413	0.0241	0.0304	0.0293	0.0402
	32	0.0370	0.0232	0.0343	0.0289	0.0439
	64	0.0384	0.0233	0.0299	0.0313	0.0367
KULSH (BOVW) [32]	16	0.0410	0.0267	0.0431	0.0311	0.0373
	32	0.0378	0.0257	0.0329	0.0366	0.0447
	64	0.0394	0.0252	0.0356	0.0366	0.0447
KULSH (FV-AI) [32]	16	0.0933	0.0296	0.1323	0.0347	0.0410
	32	0.1458	0.0270	0.1874	0.0429	0.0457
	64	0.1983	0.0319	0.3366	0.0366	0.0539
KSLSH (GIST) [32]	16	0.1804	0.0744	0.3391	0.2573	0.3711
	32	0.2118	0.0816	0.4037	0.2885	0.4113
	64	0.2387	0.0904	0.4356	0.3122	0.4627
KSLSH (BOVW) [32]	16	0.2993	0.1734	0.5154	0.4342	0.4592
	32	0.3354	0.2527	0.6208	0.5163	0.5499
	64	0.3691	0.2861	0.6950	0.5546	0.5849
KSLSH (FV-AI) [32]	16	0.5343	0.3432	0.8351	0.6085	0.7372
	32	0.6115	0.4209	0.8851	0.6732	0.7936
	64	0.6531	0.4724	0.9281	0.7142	0.8279
DPSH [17]	16	0.6183	0.3656	0.5589	0.6061	0.7015
	32	0.8805	0.6066	0.8866	0.8106	0.8701
	64	0.9246	0.7481	0.9940	0.8438	0.9104
FCHNN (FV-AI)	16	0.6894	0.5713	0.7281	0.6066	0.7036
	32	0.9127	0.7320	0.9248	0.8961	0.9775
	64	0.9154	0.9035	0.9934	0.9593	0.9902
FCHNN (P-CaffeNet)	16	0.6733	0.6235	0.7299	0.6514	0.7272
	32	0.9181	0.7223	0.9077	0.9007	0.9769
	64	0.9300	0.8749	0.9901	0.9668	0.9918
FCHNN (F-CaffeNet)	16	0.7328	0.6793	0.8461	0.6812	0.7691
	32	0.9386	0.7463	0.9471	0.9141	0.9827
	64	0.9432	0.9131	0.9938	0.9782	0.9930
FCHNN (P-VGG-VD16)	16	0.6845	0.5905	0.7491	0.6551	0.7313
	32	0.9245	0.7366	0.8893	0.9016	0.9823
	64	0.9374	0.8890	0.9925	0.9756	0.9864
FCHNN (F-VGG-VD16)	16	**0.7825**	**0.7417**	**0.9264**	**0.7023**	**0.7666**
	32	**0.9568**	**0.8582**	**0.9689**	**0.9177**	**0.9820**
	64	**0.9583**	**0.9509**	**0.9963**	**0.9845**	**0.9950**

C. *The effect of the number of iterations in the process of network learning*

We compared the image retrieval accuracy (mAP) of five types of features for remote sensing image retrieval tasks on five large-scale datasets, and the mAP value was based on the result of 64-bit hash coding. We obtained the following conclusions: (1) The experiments on the five datasets showed that the proposed FCHNN method was able to obtain relatively stable precision in 40 iterations; (2) the features extracted by the fine-tuned VGG-VD16 model had the highest retrieval accuracy among the five types of features; the accuracy of the two fine-tuned CNN models was generally higher than that of the pre-trained model, which further validated the effectiveness of the fine-tuning strategy; (3) as the number of FCHNN iterations increased, the accuracy was improved.

D. *The effect of the training size*

Because Table 1 showed that features extracted from the fine-tuned VGG-VD16 model (i.e., F-VGG-VD16) were able to achieve the highest accuracy, we also employed the F-VGG-VD16 model to perform experiments on the five datasets in order to study the impacts of different training sizes on the training accuracy, as shown in Table 2. Clearly, as the training size increased, the performance of the model also gradually increased. This is consistent with the general knowledge in deep learning, which holds that larger datasets can lead to better performance of a model.

Table 2. Effects of the training size on the model performance.

Training Size [1]	Dataset				
	AID	NWPU45	PatternNet	RSI-CB128	RSI-CB256
20%	0.3723	0.3197	0.4503	0.3927	0.4103
40%	0.5564	0.5321	0.6057	0.5881	0.6117
60%	0.7927	0.7769	0.8122	0.8233	0.7975
80%	0.9583	0.9509	0.9963	0.9845	0.9950

[1] Training size: the percentage of the number of training samples with respect to the total number of samples.

E. *Comparison with other methods*

As shown in Figure 4, we compared the PR curves of the FCHNN and DPSH methods for the five datasets. The red curve represents the DPSH method and the green curve represents the FCHNN method. The input of the FCHNN was the best of the five features, that is, features extracted from the fine-tuned VGG-VD16 model (F-VGG-VD16). The results of the two methods used for the comparison were based on 64-bit hash coding. The experiments on the five datasets showed that the FCHNN was able to obtain better retrieval accuracy than that of DPSH.

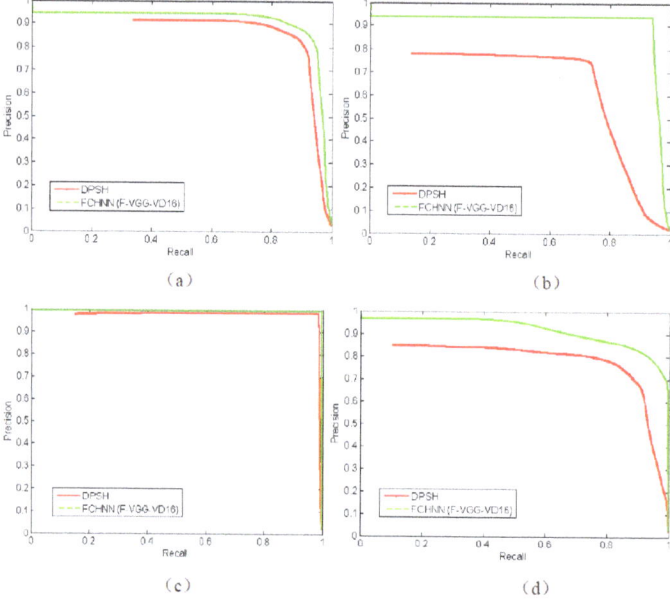

Figure 4. *Cont.*

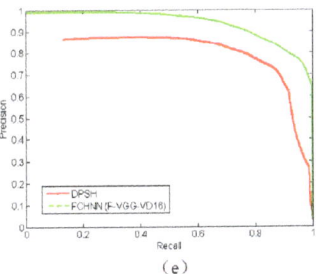

(e)

Figure 4. PR comparisons between the FCHNN and DPSH. (**a**) AID, (**b**) NWPU45, (**c**) PatternNet, (**d**) RSI-CB128, and (**e**) RSI-CB256.

5. Conclusions

We proposed a hash neural network model called the FCHNN that has three layers of fully connected layers in order to achieve efficient storage and retrieval of remote sensing images. The first two layers of the network contain 4096 neurons, and the last layer of the network contains N neurons. Through the supervised learning of pairwise images, hash coding mapping of different types of features, including mid-level representations based on low-level feature extraction, pre-trained deep features, and fine-tuned depth features, can be realized, and bit–bit binary can be achieved. The FCHNN is a network of features transmitted into binary code. In comparison with end-to-end networks of pixel-to-binary frameworks, the FCHNN has a higher learning efficiency and retrieval precision. Experiments on five large-scale remote sensing image datasets showed that the FCHNN has good versatility in the hash mapping of different types of features. The deep features extracted from the fine-tuned VGG-VD16 model achieved the best retrieval performance when used as input for the FCHNN.

In the face of massive amounts of remote sensing data, data storage and retrieval based on high-level features have a low efficiency and high computational complexity. In comparison with CNNH, DPSH, and other models, our proposed model (FCHNN) has great advantages. On the one hand, the FCHNN only contains three layers of fully connected layers, and it uses the supervised information of pairwise labels to learn the hash function. In comparison with the end-to-end deep hash learning method based on label pairs, its learning speed is faster; on the other hand, the FCHNN is a network based on feature-to-binary encoding, and it can obtain a higher retrieval precision. In addition, the FCHNN can not only learn artificially designed features, such as the Fisher vector encoding, but can also learn deep features, which have good universality. Importantly, in consideration of storage space, when mapping 4096-dimensional features to 64 bits, the FCHNN requires only eight bytes. Therefore, our model has good application prospects in the storage and retrieval of remote sensing images.

Author Contributions: N.L. and Y.Y. conceived the project and designed the experiments. N.L. performed the experiments and data analysis. H.M., J.T., L.W. and Q.L. contributed to the development of the concepts and helped write the manuscript. All authors have read and agreed to the published version of the manuscript

Funding: This study was supported by the National Natural Science Foundation of China (No. 92048205), the Pujiang Talents Plan of Shanghai (Grant No. 2019PJD035), and the Artificial Intelligence Innovation and Development Special Fund of Shanghai (No. 2019RGZN01041).

Institutional Review Board Statement: Not applicable.

Informed Consent Statement: Not applicable.

Data Availability Statement: The data generated for this study are available on request to the corresponding author.

Conflicts of Interest: The authors declare that the research was conducted without any commercial or financial relationships that could be construed as potential conflicts of interest.

References

1. Heppenstall, A.; Crooks, A.; Malleson, N.; Manley, E.; Ge, J.; Batty, M. Future developments in geographical agent-based models: Challenges and opportunities. *Geogr. Anal.* **2021**, *53*, 76–91. [CrossRef]
2. Singh, A.; Gupta, S. Learning to hash: A comprehensive survey of deep learning-based hashing methods. *Knowl. Inf. Syst.* **2022**, *64*, 2565–2597. [CrossRef]
3. Yao, T.; Wang, G.; Yan, L.; Kong, X.; Su, Q.; Zhang, C.; Tian, Q. Online latent semantic hashing for cross-media retrieval. *Pattern Recognit.* **2019**, *89*, 1–11. [CrossRef]
4. Song, G.; Tan, X.; Zhao, J.; Yang, M. Deep robust multilevel semantic hashing for multi-label cross-modal retrieval. *Pattern Recognit.* **2021**, *120*, 108084. [CrossRef]
5. Li, Y.; Ma, J.; Zhang, Y. Image retrieval from remote sensing big data: A survey. *Inf. Fusion* **2021**, *67*, 94–115. [CrossRef]
6. Gu, Y.; Wang, Y.; Li, Y. A survey on deep learning-driven remote sensing image scene understanding: Scene classification, scene retrieval and scene-guided object detection. *Appl. Sci.* **2019**, *9*, 2110. [CrossRef]
7. Bansal, M.; Kumar, M.; Kumar, M. 2D object recognition: a comparative analysis of SIFT, SURF and ORB feature descriptors. *Multimed. Tools Appl.* **2021**, *80*, 18839–18857. [CrossRef]
8. Li, P.; Ren, P. Partial randomness hashing for large-scale remote sensing image retrieval. *IEEE Geosci. Remote Sens. Lett.* **2017**, *14*, 464–468. [CrossRef]
9. Tan, X.; Zou, Y.; Guo, Z.; Zhou, K.; Yuan, Q. Deep Contrastive Self-Supervised Hashing for Remote Sensing Image Retrieval. *Remote Sens.* **2022**, *14*, 3643. [CrossRef]
10. Li, Y.; Zhang, Y.; Huang, X.; Zhu, H.; Ma, J. Large-scale remote sensing image retrieval by deep hashing neural networks. *IEEE Trans. Geosci. Remote Sens.* **2017**, *56*, 950–965. [CrossRef]
11. Shan, X.; Liu, P.; Wang, Y.; Zhou, Q.; Wang, Z. Deep hashing using proxy loss on remote sensing image retrieval. *Remote Sens.* **2021**, *13*, 2924. [CrossRef]
12. Zhao, Q.; Xu, Y.; Wei, Z.; Han, Y. Non-intrusive load monitoring based on deep pairwise-supervised hashing to detect unidentified appliances. *Processes* **2021**, *9*, 505. [CrossRef]
13. Zhang, Q.Y.; Li, Y.Z.; Hu, Y.J. A retrieval algorithm for encrypted speech based on convolutional neural network and deep hashing. *Multimed. Tools Appl.* **2021**, *80*, 1201–1221. [CrossRef]
14. Li, T.; Zhang, Z.; Pei, L.; Gan, Y. HashFormer: Vision Transformer Based Deep Hashing for Image Retrieval. *IEEE Signal Process. Lett.* **2022**, *29*, 827–831. [CrossRef]
15. Lai, H.; Pan, Y.; Liu, Y.; Yan, S. Simultaneous feature learning and hash coding with deep neural networks. In Proceedings of the IEEE Conference on Computer Vision and Pattern Recognition, Boston, MA, USA, 7–12 June 2015; pp. 3270–3278.
16. Lin, M.; Chen, Q.; Yan, S. Network in network. *arXiv* **2013**, arXiv:1312.4400.
17. Li, W.J.; Wang, S.; Kang, W.C. Feature Learning Based Deep Supervised Hashing with Pairwise Labels. In Proceedings of the Twenty-Fifth International Joint Conference on Artificial Intelligence, IJCAI'16, New York, NY, USA, 9–15 July 2016; pp. 1711–1717.
18. Vedaldi, A.; Fulkerson, B. VLFeat: An open and portable library of computer vision algorithms. In Proceedings of the 18th ACM International Conference on Multimedia, Firenze, Italy, 25–29 October 2010; pp. 1469–1472.
19. Vijayan, V.; Pushpalatha, K. A comparative analysis of RootSIFT and SIFT methods for drowsy features extraction. *Procedia Comput. Sci.* **2020**, *171*, 436–445. [CrossRef]
20. Dai-Hong, J.; Lei, D.; Dan, L.; San-You, Z. Moving-object tracking algorithm based on PCA-SIFT and optimization for underground coal mines. *IEEE Access* **2019**, *7*, 35556–35563. [CrossRef]
21. Vedaldi, A.; Lenc, K. Matconvnet: Convolutional neural networks for matlab. In Proceedings of the 23rd ACM International Conference on Multimedia, Brisbane, Australia, 26–30 October 2015; pp. 689–692.
22. Nogueira, K.; Penatti, O.A.; dos Santos, J.A. Towards better exploiting convolutional neural networks for remote sensing scene classification. *Pattern Recognit.* **2017**, *61*, 539–556. [CrossRef]
23. Gu, G.; Liu, J.; Li, Z.; Huo, W.; Zhao, Y. Joint learning based deep supervised hashing for large-scale image retrieval. *Neurocomputing* **2020**, *385*, 348–357. [CrossRef]
24. Chen, Y.; Lu, X. Deep discrete hashing with pairwise correlation learning. *Neurocomputing* **2020**, *385*, 111–121. [CrossRef]
25. Xia, G.S.; Hu, J.; Hu, F.; Shi, B.; Bai, X.; Zhong, Y.; Zhang, L.; Lu, X. AID: A benchmark data set for performance evaluation of aerial scene classification. *IEEE Trans. Geosci. Remote Sens.* **2017**, *55*, 3965–3981. [CrossRef]
26. Cheng, G.; Han, J.; Lu, X. Remote sensing image scene classification: Benchmark and state of the art. *Proc. IEEE* **2017**, *105*, 1865–1883. [CrossRef]
27. Zhou, W.; Newsam, S.; Li, C.; Shao, Z. PatternNet: A benchmark dataset for performance evaluation of remote sensing image retrieval. *ISPRS J. Photogramm. Remote Sens.* **2018**, *145*, 197–209. [CrossRef]
28. Li, H.; Tao, C.; Wu, Z.; Chen, J.; Gong, J.; Deng, M. Rsi-cb: A large scale remote sensing image classification benchmark via crowdsource data. *arXiv* **2017**, arXiv:1705.10450.

29. Zhou, W.; Newsam, S.; Li, C.; Shao, Z. Learning low dimensional convolutional neural networks for high-resolution remote sensing image retrieval. *Remote Sens.* **2017**, *9*, 489. [CrossRef]
30. Zhuo, Z.; Zhou, Z. Low dimensional discriminative representation of fully connected layer features using extended largevis method for high-resolution remote sensing image retrieval. *Sensors* **2020**, *20*, 4718. [CrossRef]
31. Zhang, X.; Zhou, L.; Bai, X.; Luan, X.; Luo, J.; Hancock, E.R. Deep supervised hashing using symmetric relative entropy. *Pattern Recognit. Lett.* **2019**, *125*, 677–683. [CrossRef]
32. Demir, B.; Bruzzone, L. Hashing-based scalable remote sensing image search and retrieval in large archives. *IEEE Trans. Geosci. Remote Sens.* **2015**, *54*, 892–904. [CrossRef]
33. Jafari, O.; Maurya, P.; Nagarkar, P.; Islam, K.M.; Crushev, C. A survey on locality sensitive hashing algorithms and their applications. *arXiv* **2021**, arXiv:2102.08942.
34. Zhou, W.; Liu, H.; Lou, J.; Chen, X. Locality sensitive hashing with bit selection. *Appl. Intell.* **2022**, *52*, 14724–14738. [CrossRef]
35. Shan, X.; Liu, P.; Gou, G.; Zhou, Q.; Wang, Z. Deep hash remote sensing image retrieval with hard probability sampling. *Remote Sens.* **2020**, *12*, 2789. [CrossRef]
36. Roy, S.; Sangineto, E.; Demir, B.; Sebe, N. Metric-learning-based deep hashing network for content-based retrieval of remote sensing images. *IEEE Geosci. Remote Sens. Lett.* **2020**, *18*, 226–230. [CrossRef]

Article

Self-Writer: Clusterable Embedding Based Self-Supervised Writer Recognition from Unlabeled Data

Zabir Mohammad [1], Muhammad Mohsin Kabir [1], Muhammad Mostafa Monowar [2,*], Md Abdul Hamid [2] and Muhammad Firoz Mridha [3]

1. Department of Computer Science and Engineering, Bangladesh University of Business and Technology, Dhaka 1216, Bangladesh
2. Department of Information Technology, Faculty of Computing and Information Technology, King AbdulAziz University, Jeddah 21589, Saudi Arabia
3. Department of Computer Science, American International University-Bangladesh (AIUB), Dhaka 1229, Bangladesh
* Correspondence: mmonowar@kau.edu.sa

Abstract: Writer recognition based on a small amount of handwritten text is one of the most challenging deep learning problems because of the implicit characteristics of handwriting styles. In a deep convolutional neural network, writer recognition based on supervised learning has shown great success. These supervised methods typically require a lot of annotated data. However, collecting annotated data is expensive. Although unsupervised writer recognition methods may address data annotation issues significantly, they often fail to capture sufficient feature relationships and usually perform less efficiently than supervised learning methods. Self-supervised learning may solve the unlabeled dataset issue and train the unsupervised datasets in a supervised manner. This paper introduces Self-Writer, a self-supervised writer recognition approach dealing with unlabeled data. The proposed scheme generates clusterable embeddings from a small fixed-length image frame such as a text block. The training strategy presumes that a small image frame of handwritten text should include the writer's handwriting characteristics. We construct pairwise constraints and nongenerative augmentation to train Siamese architecture to generate embeddings depending on such an assumption. Self-Writer is evaluated on the two most widely used datasets, IAM and CVL, on pairwise and triplet architecture. We find Self-Writer to be convincing in achieving satisfactory performance using pairwise architectures.

Keywords: writer recognition; self-supervised learning; embeddings; dimension reduction; clustering; twin network

MSC: 68TXX

1. Introduction

Handwriting is considered a distinctive human characteristic that can prove someone's authenticity through pattern recognition. Handwriting contains numerous distinctive features that exhibit the writer's unique handwriting characteristics, such as the slope of letters, shape of letters, rhythmic repetition of the letters, cursive or separated writing, spacing between letters, etc. [1]. Furthermore, handwriting techniques and features differ enormously from one individual to another, known as inter-class variance. The unique writing characteristics of an individual serve to make handwriting a behavioral biometric modality that authorizes recognition and verification of writers from handwritten scripts. The contemporary studies have indicated writing to be a remarkably reliable and helpful behavioral biometric mechanism that is used in diverse application disciplines, including forensic analysis [2], analysis of historical documents [3,4] and security [5].

There are two modes to implement writer identification: verification and recognition. The writer verification system performs a one-to-one comparison and determines whether the same person has written two different texts or not. At the same time, the writer recognition system performs a one-to-many search with handwriting data of known authors in an extensive database. The system should display a list of possible authors for the unknown text samples following the comparison. Due to the enormous variety of human handwriting, writer recognition is more complicated than writer verification.

Furthermore, these two modes can be executed both online and offline. The online technique uses the spatial characteristics of the writing, which are taken in real time by using digitizing acquisition equipment (e.g., Anoto pen). These characteristics are sent for further processing and analysis via a particular transducer device. Then, the processing device converts dynamic writing movement characteristics such as stroke order, altitude, velocity, trajectory, pen pressure, writing duration, etc., into a signal sequence. Offline-based recognition, however, is a static technique that commonly uses digitized handwritten images as input data. Because online techniques utilize a good number of features, it is likely to perform better than the offline approach. However, online recognition methods require additional devices that are costly and unavailable in most scenarios. This triggers us to exploit the offline recognition approach, knowing that it poses significant research challenges due to the availability of only digitized handwritten text images.

Deep learning (DL) frameworks have been intensively explored in supervised writer recognition and have been shown to outperform several benchmark datasets [1,6,7]. However, supervised writer recognition methods require a significant amount of labeled data. Additionally, obtaining manual labeling is costly compared to obtaining unlabeled data, which is readily available in abundance. Unsupervised writer recognition may solve the data annotation label issue. So far, unsupervised algorithms are not particularly effective at training neural networks because of their inability to capture the visual semantics needed to tackle real-world problems the way strongly supervised methods do. However, self-supervised learning may convincingly address the unlabeled dataset issue by training the unsupervised dataset in a supervised manner.

Self-supervised learning is a variant of the unsupervised learning method wherein the supervised task is performed from the unlabelled data. To learn from self-supervision, the technique must go through two stages: initialization of the network weights using pseudolabels [8,9], and completion of the actual task by using supervised learning [10,11]. Self-supervised learning allows us to take advantage of a range of labels provided for free with the data. Producing a handwritten document dataset with clean labels is costly. In addition, unlabeled handwritten text is constantly generated. One strategy to take advantage of this considerably more significant amount of unlabeled data is to appropriately define the learning objectives so that the data itself provides supervision. Self-supervised learning has been quite successful in the field of speech recognition for a long time, and includes processes such as Wav2vec [12] and natural language processing (NLP), as evidenced by Collobert–Weston 2008 model [13], Word2Vec [14], GloVE [15], and, more recently, BERT [16], RoBERTa [17], and others.

This paper introduces Self-Writer: a clusterable embedding-based, self-supervised writer recognition directly from unlabeled data. The term "embedding" refers to the process of creating vectors of continuous values. Currently, triplet [18], and pairwise loss [19] techniques can be used to generate embeddings in the context of DL. Three parallel inputs pass across the network in a triplet loss architecture: anchor, positive, and negative. Concerning the anchor, the positive input has an identical class, whereas the negative input has a distinct class. A pair of information flows across the network in pairwise architecture belonging to the same or separate classes. Furthermore, we insist on making the training process for DL architecture self-supervised. The system, however, requires manuscripts of handwritten text and needs to ensure that the manuscripts comprise only one individual's handwritten text. The manuscripts come in lines of handwritten text and are further windowed into smaller frames, such as a word or text block, for training the DL framework. The construction of the training approach is illustrated in Figure 1. To the best of our knowledge, this is the first attempt that exploits self-supervised learning strategy in writer recognition. In this paper, we make the following contributions.

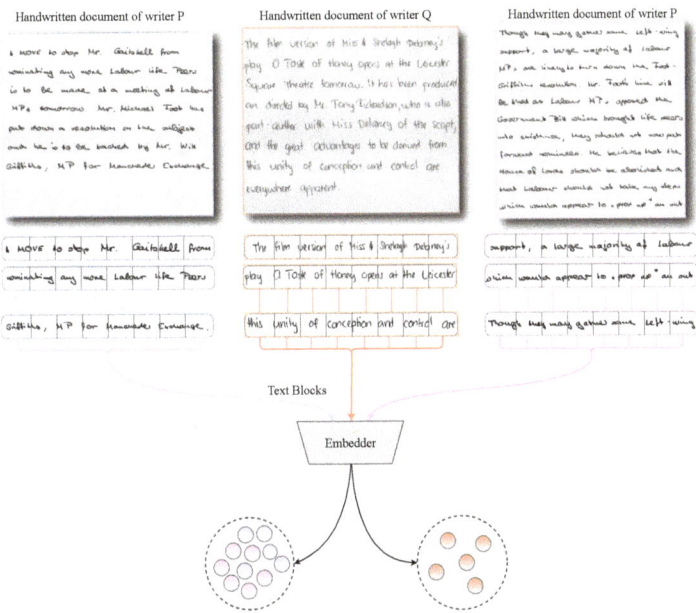

Figure 1. The figure demonstrates a set of handwritten documents with an unknown number of writers (in the example, two writers, p and q). Handwritten documents are segmented into a form of line, and further line-segmented images are windowed into smaller image frames, considering that all the frames of a single document belong to a single class. A DL-based embedding method also identifies feature similarities and relationships in handwritten documents. Clusterable embeddings are generated as a result of the technique.

- We introduce a self-supervised strategy of writer recognition based on generating clusterable embeddings, named Self-Writer. The training procedure learns directly from the unlabeled data.
- To train the Siamese architecture, we use a hypothesis-based pairwise constraint and nongenerative augmentation. The AutoEmbedder framework and nongenerative augmentation concentrate on the actual feature relationship instead of the hypothetical constraints.
- Two intercluster-based strategies—triplet and pairwise architectures—evaluate the proposed policy and conclude that a DL architecture can distinguish writers from pseudolabels depending on feature similarity.

We write the rest of the paper as follows. The recent literature regarding writer identification tasks is presented in Section 2. Section 3 explains the structure of the training strategy as well as the challenges and adaptations. Empirical setup regarding the evaluation of the proposed pipeline, datasets, and the investigation of the architectures' performance is outlined in Section 4. In Section 5, we sketch the pros and cons of the proposed approach. Finally, Section 6 concludes the paper.

2. Related Work

Writer recognition utilizing deep learning strategies has gained profound attention by researchers to address distinctive writer recognition and verification tasks. Over the past few years, significant research has been done on offline writer recognition, and many decent solutions are available in this domain. Among them, the techniques exploiting the hidden Markov model (HMM), Gaussian mixture model (GMM), deep neural networks

(DNNs), convolutional neural networks (CNNs), and recurrent neural networks (RNNs) were the most prominent. The robustness of modern deep learning architectures provides an excellent structure for the latest writer recognition systems [20].

Before the proliferation of neural network approaches, Gabor filters and XGabor filters, and scale-invarient feature transform (SIFT) were mostly used to extract feature data. The majority of the research efforts applied wavelets [21], graph relations [22], statistical analysis [23,24], and HMM-based [25] models after feature extraction. By exploiting the weighted histogram of GMM scores and a similarity and dissimilarity Gaussian mixture model technique, Khan et al. [1] introduced an offline writer recognition system. Because the weighting process penalizes irrelevant descriptors, this technique achieves substantially better performance than the traditional averaging of negative loglikelihood values. In [26], a novel approach for writer identification is presented, based on the LDA model with n-grams of author texts and cosine similarity. For language-independent writer recognition, Sulaiman et al. [7] presented a mixture of handcrafted and in-depth features, extracting both LBP and convolutional neural network (CNN) features from overlapped frames and encoding the local information by using the VLAD technique. However, these methods showed a decent performance but were less accurate than modern neural network architectures because of their weak feature-extraction capability. Due to deep learning, various complex computer vision tasks such as visual reasoning are developed [27,28].

With the improvement of neural network architectures, more accurate approaches have been proposed in the writer recognition domain. Christlein et al. [29] presented a three-step pipeline for writer recognition: feature extraction with CNN, aggregating local features into one global descriptor and normalizing the descriptor. The authors aimed to investigate complicated and deep CNN architectures and some new findings such as the advantage of Lp-pooling over max pooling, and the normalization of activation following convolutional layers of the network. Zhang et al. [30] suggested a writer recognition framework by using the recurrent neural network (RNN) model for directly dealing with online handwriting raw data. Their framework outperforms the handcrafted feature-based and CNN-based techniques due to its robustness. In [31], Semma et al. employ FAST key points and the Harris corner detector to identify points of interest in the handwriting and extract key points from handwriting and feeding small patches around these key points to a CNN for feature learning and classification. Xing et al. [6] proposed DeepWriter, a text-independent writer recognition based on a deep, multistream CNN. The main drawback of the paper is that when the number of writers is increased, the model's accuracy is significantly reduced. Fiel et al. [32] presented the feature vector generation for each writer by using a CNN to identify writers by analyzing their handwritten texts. The feature vector approach uses preprocessing techniques such as binarization, text line segmentation, and sliding windows, and extracts images from the ICDAR 2011, 2013 dataset. However, this study shows poor results on the other datasets. Sheng He et al. [33] proposed multitask learning to provide a deep adaptive learning method for writer recognition based on single word pictures. This method improved the existing features of CNN by recognizing the content to analyze a writer's recognition, and exploited deep features. In the evaluation, they used the CVL and IAM datasets that contain segmented word pictures with labels for both word and writer. Furthermore, the authors proposed FragNet [34], a two-pathway network defined by a feature pyramid, which is used to extract feature maps, and fragment pathway, which is trained to predict the writer identity based on fragments extracted from the input image and the feature maps on the feature pyramid. The main drawback of the FragNet model is that it requires word image or region segmentation, which is challenging on highly cursive script documents. Nevertheless, writer recognition based on single-word images has not yet shown satisfactory performance. Deep learning achieves few-shot learning through meta-learning by using previous experience. In [35], the authors proposed a deep learning method that uses meta-learning to learn and generalize from a small sample size in image classification.

The attention mechanism has been widely used in recent years and has overcome few-shot learning. This technique was typically used with CNN or RNN to improve deep feature extractions in writer identification. Zhang et al. [36] introduce a new residual Swin transformer classifier (RSTC) that integrates both local and global handwriting styles and produces robust feature representations with single-word pictures. The transformer block models local information with interacting strokes while holistically encoding with the identity branch and global block features' global information. Chen et al. [37] proposed the letters and styles adapters (LSA) to encode different letters, which were inserted between CNN and LSTM. To aggregate features, they also introduced hierarchical attention pooling (HAP).

Apart from the aforementioned methodologies, unsupervised writer recognition is still an underresearched domain. Very few researchers have worked on this and achieved significant results. Christlein et al. [38] trained a residual network by using deep surrogate classes, and the learned activation features without supervision outperformed the descriptors of cutting-edge methods for writer recognition. To study the impact of interlinear spacing, the authors wanted to evaluate single handwritten lines rather than whole paragraphs. In addition, a few semisupervised learning methods have been introduced as well for writer recognition. With the aim of improving writer recognition performance, Chen et al. [39] suggested a semisupervised feature learning. Their method trains both unlabeled and labeled data at the same time. The authors also proposed a data augmentation method called weighted label smoothing regularization (WLSR). The proposed WLSR method depends on the similarity of the sample space between the original labeled samples and additional unlabeled samples and can regularize the baseline of a CNN to enable the learning of more discriminated features.

Due to the difficulties of extensive data labeling for supervised deep neural networks as well as the ineffectiveness of unsupervised learning, self-supervised learning has become a promising research area for deep neural networks. Deep neural networks are usually trained through backpropagation by utilizing some objective function. However, it is challenging to estimate what objective function extracts suitable feature relations that could guide good neural networks without labels. Self-supervised learning addresses this issue by presenting different self-supervision tasks for networks to solve. Using self-supervision makes it easier to measure the performance captured by using an objective function similar to those used in supervised learning without requiring any labels. Many such tasks have been proposed in the last few years. For example, in the case of NLP, one can hide a word from a sentence and ask the network to predict the missing word. In addition, many computer vision-based self-supervised learning tools have been proposed in the last few years [10,40]. In [41,42], the authors use time as a source of supervision in videos, simply predicting the frames in a video. Self-supervision can also operate with a single image. One can hide a portion of the image given the task to the network to generate pixels of the hidden part [43,44] or recover color after grayscale conversion [40,45]. Another approach is to create a synthetic categorization task where one can create a surrogate class by altering a single image multiple times through translations, color shifts, and rotations [46]. Furthermore, in [47], in order to detect 3D symmetry from single-view RGB-D images, the author uses weak supervision to detect objects.

In recent years, self-supervised learning has shown great success in NLP such as BERT [16], RoBERTa [17], and Glove [15]; in the field of speech recognition, Wav2Vec [12] has had success, and in the field of computer vision [10,48] has worked well. However, none of the research was conducted on writer recognition in a self-supervised manner. Moreover, the generation of abundant, unlabeled, handwritten text from different individuals drives us to solve the writer recognition problem in a self-supervised manner based on the interfeature relationships of data, all without relying on the labels.

3. Methodology

This section presents the proposed self-supervised writer recognition pipeline in more detail. The generation of clusterable embeddings, in this paper, is established on selfsupervised learning. First, a self-supervision task is created depending on the following assumption: in most cases, whenever a writer starts writing, he/she writes on a blank manuscript. As a result, most manuscripts include one individual's handwriting. However, some individuals might contain multiple manuscripts, or some may be impure, i.e., a manuscript might contain the writings of numerous individuals. Nevertheless, the impurity ratio would be sufficiently low in the most general handwritten manuscripts. As a result, one of the most prevalent neural network pipelines, the Siamese network [43], is used to investigate such a strategy. To extract embeddings, we use the AutoEmbedder framework [19] as a DL architecture. These generated embedding points work to extract features of the writer's handwriting characteristics, which helps to recognize the writer. The basic workflow of Self-Writer is illustrated in Figure 2.

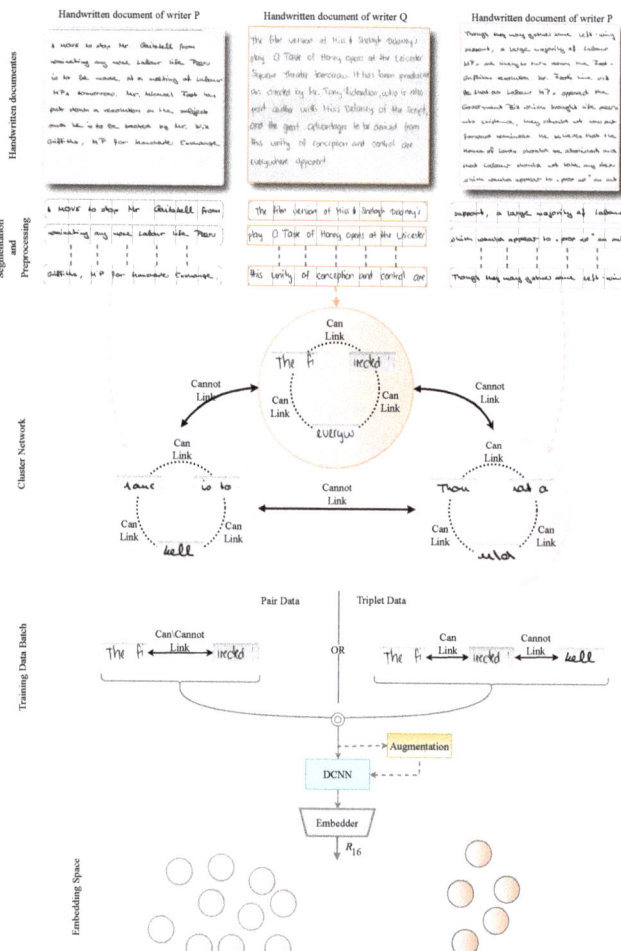

Figure 2. Overall procedure of Self-Writer. First, each manuscript is segmented into lines and assigned a pseudo label for each script. Additionally, an OpenCV-based Python script is used to preprocess the line images. Furthermore, a cluster network is constructed from the manuscript's line segments, using a nonoverlapping sliding window approach to generate smaller text blocks. Finally, depending on the requirements of the Siamese network, the cluster network is used to construct training data batches. The pairwise architecture receives two input data; either a can-link pair or a cannot-link pair. However, it demands an equal number of can-link and cannot-link pairs in a batch of training data. On the other hand, triplet architecture receives three input data; a pair of can-link data and cannot-link data, and then the DL architecture or the embedder is trained on randomly augmented training data.

The methodology section is organized as follows. First, we explain the preprocessing step in Section 3.1. In Section 3.2, the self-supervision task is discussed, followed by the problem formulation and assumptions in Section 3.3. Furthermore, the construction of pairwise constraints is defined in Section 3.4. In Section 3.5, uncertainties in the pairwise constraints are discussed. Finally, a detailed description of the DL framework, training procedure, and data augmentation schema is presented in Sections 3.6 and 3.7.

3.1. Data Preprocessing

In our experiment, handwritten texts are considered to be manuscripts. Furthermore, we require line segmentation of the handwritten scripts. Researchers, such as [49–51], have introduced different line segmentation techniques. However, the IAM [52], and CVL [53] datasets already provide line segmentation schema. However, some lighting, background, and noise issues are observed in the line images. First, we apply a supplementary OpenCV-based Python script [54] to eliminate unwanted data such as noise removal, background elimination, etc. Figure 3 represents (i) the raw version of the image and (ii) the enhanced version. The preprocessing part aims to enhance image quality and improve image readability information. Afterward, we resize line-segmented images with a height of 112 pixels while maintaining the aspect ratio. Note that the fixed-size representation of line images may distort the writer's handwriting characteristics. Then, we segment the line images into smaller text blocks by using a non-overlapping sliding window approach. Finally, we have scaled the dataset in the range [0,1].

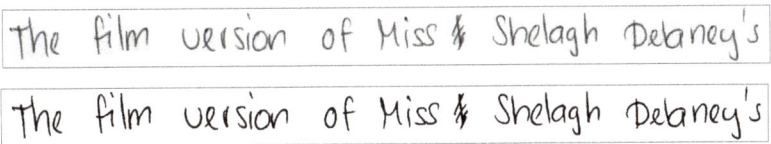

Figure 3. Raw line segmented images of the IAM dataset and an enhanced version of the image after applying a supplementary OpenCV-based python script.

3.2. Self-Supervision Task

Self-supervised learning has various forms based on the domain. Self-Writer aligns with contrastive self-supervised learning strategies [55]. In order to learn from self-supervised learning, the system must define a self-supervision task. In general, self-supervised learning receives supervision signals by utilizing the underlying structure of the data. Self-supervised learning takes advantage of the data's structure. As a result, it can leverage a wide variety of supervisory signals across large datasets based on cooccurring modalities without relying on labels. Because our proposed writer recognition method is based on self-supervised learning, we require handwritten scripts to get the supervision signals from the data by considering each manuscript as a different individual assigning a pseudo label. Furthermore, the documents are windowed into smaller text blocks to train the DL architecture in a supervised manner based on the pseudo label. The self-supervised task of the DL architecture is to generate clusterable embedding of the text block of manuscripts. The self-supervision task leads us to a supervised loss function. However, the final performance of the self-supervision task is usually unimportant to us. Instead, we are more interested in learning the intermediate representation of data. We validate in Section 4.3 that the self-supervision task holds excellent semantic or structural meanings and be helpful for the DL framework to recluster data based on feature similarities instead of the hypothetical assumption.

3.3. Paper's Assumptions

The proposed strategy aims to resolve handwriting recognition in a self-supervised manner depending on some hypothetical assumptions. Table 1 illustrates the mathematical notations employed in this work to make it easier for readers. To understand the problem statement, consider D as a dataset of handwritten text in manuscripts, where X_k represents a single manuscript containing an individual's handwriting. Consider x_i to be a smaller text block of the manuscript, with $x_i \in X_k$. M number of nonoverlapping text blocks are extracted from a specific manuscript, X_k. Because a manuscript is associated with a single person, the smaller text blocks are also associated with that person. Based on this criterion, we created a cluster network known as pairwise constraints between two text blocks. If two text blocks are from the same script, they are considered in the same cluster. On the contrary, two text blocks from different scripts are considered different clusters. A set of clusters C can be formed based on the pairwise relationship, where each cluster $c_i \in C$ belongs to a particular manuscript.

Considering most manuscripts contain one person's handwriting, we can consider that most clusters c_i hold a single person's data. However, a single individual can have multiple manuscripts, and the individual's data may be spread across multiple clusters. As a result, the challenge is to find optimal cluster relationships such that no two clusters contain data from the same individual.

Table 1. A summary of the mathematical notations used in the paper is provided.

Notation	Description
D	A set of manuscripts of handwritten text. We assume that most manuscripts contain handwriting of an individual.
X	A single handwritten manuscript, $X \in D$.
x_i	A text block, generated by taking non-overlapping sliding window approach from a line segmented images of a manuscripts, $x_i \in X_k$.
M	The numbers of possible text blocks in a manuscript. Therotically, $M \times |x_i| = |X_k|$
C	A set of clusters. Those clusters are constructed by utilizing the hypothetical cluster network. Because cluster correlation is established on manuscripts relations, it can consider $|X| = |C|$
c_i	Represents a subset of the entire set of clusters. c_i illustrates a cluster constructed by the interrelationship of text blocks on the document X_k.
N	The number of writers in X, considering the ground truth.
α	The pairwise [19] architecture's distance hyperparameter. In other architectures, may denote the state of connectivity between any two cluster nodes.

The DL framework aggregates numerous clusters into a single cluster that holds all of an individual's embeddings. We imply that if a DL function may accurately extract features from text blocks, it can provide an optimal reasoning of similarities and dissimilarities between text blocks. Furthermore, a suitably trained DL architecture can successfully recluster the data based on feature relationships rather than the number of hypothetical clusters.

3.4. Pairwise Constraints

The proposed approach uses a cluster network to train the DL embedding architecture, also known as pairwise constraints. A pairwise constraint specifies a pairwise relation between input pairs. Let us consider two input data x_i and x_j as two random text blocks. There are two possibilities: (i) text blocks may belong to the same manuscript (can-link constraints), or (ii) text blocks may belong to different manuscripts (cannot-link constraints). Mathematically, we can represent it as follows,

$$\forall x_i \in X_k \text{ and } \forall x_j \in X_k; \; x_i, x_j \in c_k \\ \forall x_i \in X_k \text{ and } \forall x_j \notin X_k; \; x_i, x_j \notin c_k, \quad (1)$$

where c_k is a separate cluster of the same class and X_k is a specific manuscript.

In the problem's current state, the writer's label or ground truth is unknown for all handwritten scripts, considering each document belongs to a distinct individual. As a result, the number of manuscripts, $|D|$ is the same as the number of unique pseudolabels.

The cluster constraints defined in (1) are used to train the DL framework. We define a ground regression function based on pairwise criteria derived in Equation (1) to properly introduce the intercluster and intracluster relation to a DL framework. The function is described as follows:

$$P(x_i, x_j) = \begin{cases} 0 & \text{if } x_i, x_j \in c_k \\ \alpha & \text{if } x_i \in c_p \text{ and } x_j \in c_q. \end{cases} \quad (2)$$

In Equation (2), the $P_c(.,.)$ function returns the distance constraints between embedding (generated from text blocks) pair. In general, the function implies that embedding pairs belong to the same cluster when their distance is zero; otherwise, they must be separated by α. However, embedding pairs from distinct clusters may be separated away by a distance greater than α, as defined in the AutoEmbedder framework in Equation (4). The pairwise constraints described in Equation (2) are used to train a DL framework.

3.5. Uncertainty of Pairwise Constraints

The cluster assignment of writers is uncertain due to two primary concerns: (i) the cluster assignment is unspecified concerning ground truth, and (ii) the manuscript X_k might be impure. Impurity, with regard to manuscripts, refers to a script that includes the handwriting of more than one writer. Theoretically, the number of writers considered ground truth labels, defined as $|N|$, is less than the number of cluster assignments according to the pseudo label, where $|N| < |C|$ and $|C| = |X|$. Due to such circumstances, the training dataset established on pairwise attributes often perceives an "error in can-link constraints" and "impurity in can-link constraints", as defined below,

- Error in cannot-link constraints: Consider that the input pair x_i and x_j belong to two different classes, $x_i \in c_p$ and $x_j \in c_q$, where $c_p \neq c_q$. Because the cluster assignment is based on manuscripts, the number of manuscripts outnumbers the actual number of writers. In consideration of the ground values, the hypothesis $c_p \neq c_q$ might be incorrect, and the input pair could belong to the same author.
- Impurity in can-link constraints: The main idea of the dataset is that a handwritten manuscript X_k comprises only one person's writing. In general, a manuscript may incorrectly identify writing and contain the writing of numerous individuals in a single manuscript. Let the input pair x_i and x_j belong to same script, $x_i, x_j \in c_i$. The manuscript might be impure, so the cluster assignment c_i may be wrong, and the input pair may belong to different individuals.

As our handwritten manuscripts contain a single individual's handwriting, the task of DL is to eliminate the error in cannot-link constraints based on the feature space relationship. As a result, if the features can be prioritized to a DL architecture, it may apparently combine appropriate clusters from inaccurate cannot-link constraints. However, impurity in can-link constraints can be considerably reduced in further segmentation procedures, such as sentence segmentation.

3.6. AutoEmbedder Architecture

We employ a pairwise constraint-based AutoEmbedder architecture as a DL framework to recluster handwritten text blocks. Moreover, we present further improvements to the network's overall training procedure to enhance learning progress. To train AutoEmbedder architecture, we use pairwise constraints specified by function $P(.,.)$ in Equation (2). The architecture adheres to Siamese network constraints, which can be stated as follows:

$$S(x_i, x_j) = ReLU(||M(x_i) - M(x_j)||, \alpha). \quad (3)$$

In Equation (3), $S(.,.)$ denotes a Siamese neural network (SNN) with a pair of inputs. The architecture shares a single DCNN, $M(.,.)$, which maps higher-dimensional input into meaningful lower-dimensional clusterable embeddings. The distance between generated embedding pair is calculated by using Euclidean distance and passed through a thershold ReLU activation fuction, which is derived in Equation (4):

$$ReLU(x) = \begin{cases} x & \text{if } 0 \leq x < \alpha \\ \alpha & \text{if } x \geq \alpha. \end{cases} \quad (4)$$

The threshold value α in Equation (4) indicates the cluster margin of the network. As a consequence of the cluster margin α, $S(.,.)$ function produces output in range $[0,\alpha]$. Figure 4 illustrates the overall architecture of AutoEmbedder using a Siamese neural network. The generic AutoEmbedder framework is trained by using the L2 loss function. The AutoEmbedder framework is trained for each data batch with an equal amount of can-link and cannot-link constraints. However, the problem is easily handled in a triplet architecture because each triplet includes a combination of cannot-link (anchor-negative) and can-link (anchor-positive) pairs.

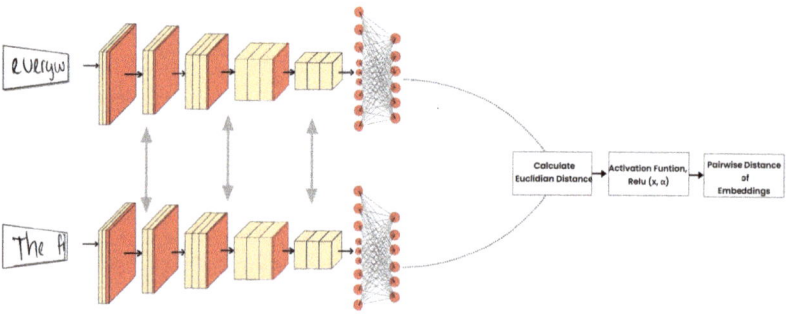

Figure 4. The training architecture of AutoEmbedder using a Siamese neural network (SNN). The subnetwork of SNN is weight-sharable, and the activation function is Relu, which is described in Equation (4). The architecture calculates pairwise distance output based on the generated embeddings pair.

3.7. Augmenting Training Data

In terms of the ground truth, both can-link and cannot-link cluster connections may include faulty assumptions. Therefore, a simple augmentation schema is applied to prevent the DL framework from overfitting faulty cluster associations. Even though there are a variety of augmentation approaches available, we prefer to combine the augmentation process described in Table 2.

Here, the augmentation pipeline includes the nongenerative online augmentation of half of the training batch data with an augmentation probability of 0.5. However, in a "Oneof" block, the transformations are defined along with their probabilities. The block normalizes the probability of all transformations within the block and applies one transformation on the image based on normalization. In this way, there is more efficiency in applying suitable transformations. The block also has a probability parameter, which indicates the probability of undertaking the block or not. Furthermore, all the transformations are defined according to their probabilities, and they are illustrated in Table 2.

Table 2. The table presents the augmentation pipeline associated with transformation definitions along with their probabilities.

Oneof Blocks	Transformations	Description	Probability of Transformations	Probability of Oneof Blocks	Augmentation Probability
Oneof	Flip	Flip the input either horizontally, vertically	0.5	0.5	0.5
	Crop and Pad	Randomly crop input image and pad images based on image size fractions.	0.5		
Oneof	Downscale	Decreases image quality by downscaling and upscaling back.	0.3	0.5	
	Gaussian Blur	Apply a Gaussian filter with a random kernel size to blur the input image	0.3		
	Motion Blur	Apply motion blur to the input image using a random-sized kernel.	0.3		
Oneof	Multiplicative Noise	Multiply images to a random number or array of numbers.	0.3	0.5	
	Random Brightness Contrast	Randomly change brightness and contrast of the input image.	0.3		
	Gaussian Noise	Apply gaussian noise to the input image.	0.3		
Oneof	Pixel Dropout	Set pixels to 0 with some probability.	0.5	0.5	
	CoarseDropout	Coarse drop out of the rectangular regions in the image	0.5		

In the case of erroneous data pairs, augmenting image frames makes the AutoEmbedder network less confusing. The architecture may be enhanced by augmenting it while disregarding erroneous data pairs caused by different transformations. Furthermore, augmenting data causes data variation, which allows the network to extract more useful features from the data. Algorithm 1 presents the pseudocode of the pairwise training process.

Algorithm 1: Self-Writer training algorithm

Input: Subset of training dataset X, DL model with initial weights M, Number of iterations $epochs$, Training batch size $batchSize$, Distance hyperparameter α
Output: Trained Embedding DL model.
Initialize a siamese network with ,$ReLU(S(.,.),\alpha)$;
$iter \leftarrow 0$;
while $iter < epochs$ **do**
  foreach $X_{batch} \in X$ **do**
    Initialize empty lists, $I, I', Y \leftarrow \{\}, \{\}, \{\}$;
    $counter \leftarrow 0$;
    foreach $x \in X_{batch}$ **do**
      $I \leftarrow$ append x in I, ;
      if $counter$ **mod** 2 **then**
        $I' \leftarrow$ randomly choose and append a can-link text block from X;
        $Y \leftarrow$ append 0 in Y;
      else
        $I' \leftarrow$ randomly choose a cannot-link text block from X;
        $Y \leftarrow$ append α in Y;
      $counter \leftarrow counter + 1$;
    $I \leftarrow$ randomly choose half of data and augment them;
    $I' \leftarrow$ randomly choose half of data and augment them;
    $S \leftarrow$ Train S with I, I', Y

4. Results

This section evaluates the proposed self-supervised writer recognition method called Self-Writer. As the architecture objective is to generate clusterable embedding, the K-means algorithm is used to measure the purity of the embedding clusters. In Section 4.1, we present the evaluation metrics. A brief description of the dataset is provided in Section 4.2. Section 4.3 discusses the implementation details and the training procedure of our proposed Self-Writer. Finally, the result analysis is presented in Section 4.3.

4.1. Evaluation Metrics

To measure the clustering effectiveness of generated embeddings of the Self-Writer schema, three well-known metrics, normalized mutual information (NMI), accuracy (ACC), and adjusted rand index (ARI), are used. The evaluation metrics are discussed below.

- Normalized Mutual Information: The normalized mutual information can be mathematically defined as

$$NMI(c,c') = \frac{I(c,c')}{max(H(c),H(c'))}, \quad (5)$$

where c and c' are the ground truth and predicted cluster, respectively. $I(.)$ define the mutual information between c and c', and $H(.)$ denotes the entropy.

- Accuracy: Accuracy refers to the unsupervised clustering accuracy, expressed as

$$ACC(c,c') = \left(max \frac{\sum_{i=1}^{n} 1(c_i = m(c'_i))}{2} \right), \quad (6)$$

where l_i defines the ground truth labels, c_i denotes the cluster assignment produced by Self-Writer, and $m(.)$ ranges over all possible one-to-one mapping of the labels and clusters, from which the best mapping is taken.

- Adjusted Rand Index: The adjusted rand index is calculated by using the contengency [56]. The ARI can be expressed as

$$ARI = \frac{\sum_{ij} \binom{n_{ij}}{2} - \left[\sum_i \binom{a_i}{2} \sum_j \binom{b_j}{2} \right] / \binom{n}{2}}{\frac{1}{2} \left[\sum_i \binom{a_i}{2} + \sum_j \binom{b_j}{2} \right] - \left[\sum_i \binom{a_i}{2} \sum_j \binom{b_j}{2} \right] / \binom{n}{2}}. \quad (7)$$

Here, n_{ij}, a_i, and b_j are the values of the contingency table produced by the Self-Writer.

All three metrics produce a result in between the [0, 1] range. The higher value of these indices indicates a better correlation between ground truth and cluster prediction.

4.2. Datasets

4.2.1. IAM

The IAM is one of the most prominent and renowned English handwritten datasets, containing 1539 scanned handwritten scripts with 657 distinct writers using various pens. The manuscripts are scanned at 300 dots per inch (DPI) with 256 gray levels. However, the dataset comes with different forms such as manuscripts, sentences, words, and lines that provide different handwriting and word-recognition protocols. Out of 657 writers, 356 writers contribute only a single handwritten script. Each writer provided a number of documents ranging from one document (356 writers) to the most oversized (59 documents from one writer). Due to the variance of patterns of each writer, we consider the writers who provided more than equal four manuscripts and conducted the experiment with the first four manuscripts of the writers.

4.2.2. CVL

Another recent handwriting dataset for writer recognition is the CVL [53] handwriting dataset containing 1606 handwritten scripts with 310 distinct writers using different color pens. A total of 282 writers contributed five manuscripts samples (four in English and one in German), and the rest contributed seven manuscripts (six in English and one in German). The dataset is also different from the IAM dataset. However, unlike the IAM dataset, the CVL dataset is well distributed. In this experiment, we also consider all the manuscripts for each writer.

4.3. Results and Comparison

To analyze the embeddings based on the proposed strategy, AutoEmbedder (pairwise architecture) and a triplet architecture are implemented. Except for these two techniques, the most popular DL approaches for writer recognition do not adhere to the training characteristics discussed in the study. They often operate supervised learning strategies. Hence, they are omitted in this experiment.

For both DL frameworks, we use DenseNet121 [57] as baseline architecture. Furthermore, both DL architectures are connected with a dense layer containing 16 nodes. As a result, both architectures generate 16-dimensional embedding vectors. For the triplet network, we have added l2-normalization on the output layer, as it is suggested to increase the framework's accuracy [58], and valid triplet is generated manually. The pairwise architecture is trained by using default L2-loss also known as the mean square error (MSE), while semihard triplet loss [18] is used to train the triplet architecture. The training pipeline is illustrated in Figure 5.

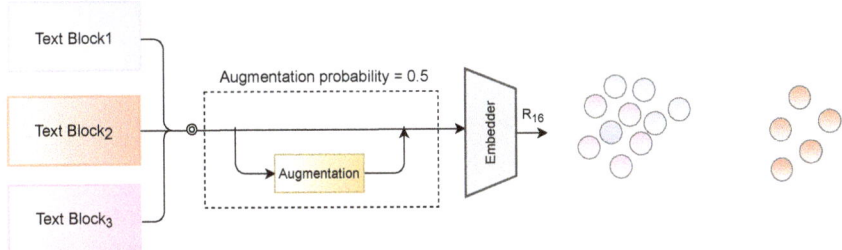

Figure 5. The same data processing pipeline is used to train both pairwise and triplet frameworks. The DL frameworks receive half of the inputs randomly augmented with an augmentation probability of 0.5.

The evaluation phase ensures that both frameworks are trained by using an identical dataset. Because the proposed approach is self-supervised and deals with unlabeled datasets, the frameworks get the exact dataset for training and testing purposes. However, the labels for the training process are unspecified and initiated on the paper's hypothetical premises. A dataset such as this is referred to as a training dataset. Considering the ground truth values of writers with the same dataset is referred to as the ground dataset. We used a batch size of 64 to train both frameworks. The training is carried out with the Adam [59] optimizer with a learning rate of 0.0005.

The training phase of Self-Writer includes high computational complexity, including online data augmentation. In addition, computing NMI, ACC, and ARI metrics required quadratic time complexity. As a result, we have decided to restrict the number of writers to 150. We trained on a subset of the dataset rather than the entire dataset. In order to test the ground truth data, two random samples of each text segment are chosen. The model was trained over 400 epochs.

Figure 6 compares the triplet and pairwise networks during training on two distinct datasets, with writers equal to 25 and impurity equal to 0. The triplet architecture learns from the training dataset in a seamless manner and overfits immensely on the augmented training data. The benchmark of the ground dataset is also anticipated because the metrics of triplet architecture increase at first and then drop dramatically due to overfitting. From

Figure 6's triplet architecture on two different datasets, it can be conceded that it only remembers the features related to the hypothetical labels.

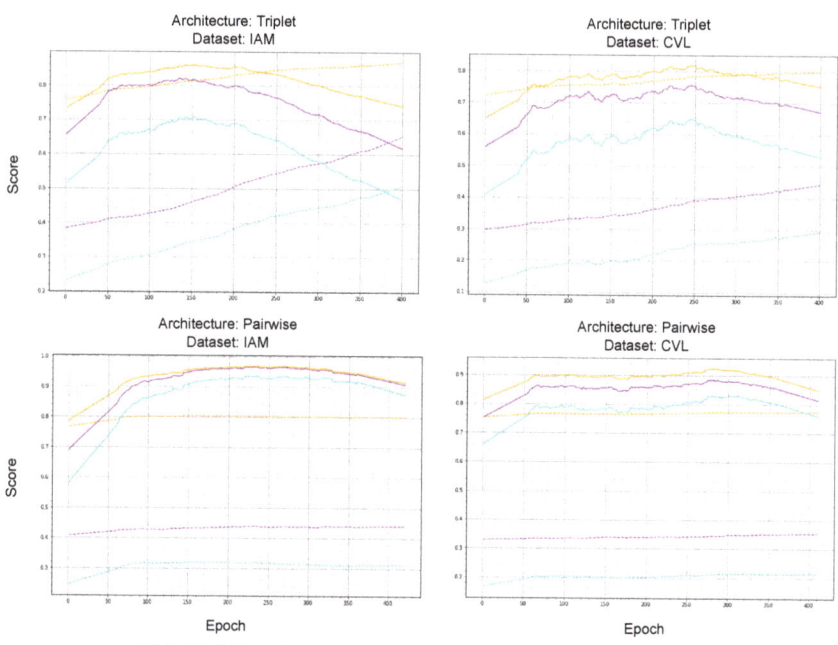

Figure 6. Graphs illustrating the metrics of the training and ground dataset containing 25 writers with an impurity of 0. The first row represents the triplet network and the second row represents the pairwise network, respectively.

In contrast, the pairwise framework produces an adequate performance with some inconsistencies. Generally, DL frameworks generate more accuracy on training data than validation data. However, the performance of the ground dataset is mostly superior to the training data in our method. Nevertheless, after 300 epochs, the performance on the ground dataset started to decrease gradually. The architecture started getting overfitted on training data due to the limited number of writers. Furthermore, for reducing overfit on training data, we increase the number of writers to 50, shown in Figure 7. The triplet framework still gradually overfits training data. Furthermore, the ground dataset's accuracy started to drop due to memorizing feature relationships based on hypothetical labels. However, the pairwise framework performed a steady performance on ground datasets.

The performance of the training method comprehensively depends on the impurity of training data. Increasing the impurity ratio reduces the architecture's performance. Benchmarks were conducted with impurity = 0.1 and 0.05, while considering writers = 50, as shown in Figures 8 and 9. The training architecture continues to overfit the triplet architecture. On the other hand, pairwise architecture gradually memorizes the training dataset based on feature relation.

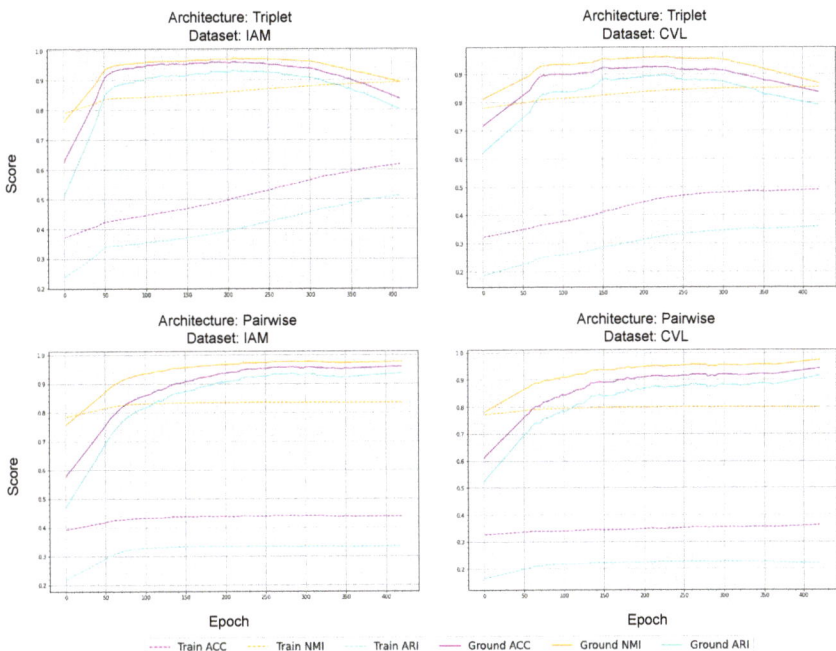

Figure 7. Graphs illustrating the metrics of pretext task and ground dataset containing 50 writers with the purity of 0. The first row represents the triplet network and the second row represents the pairwise network, respectively.

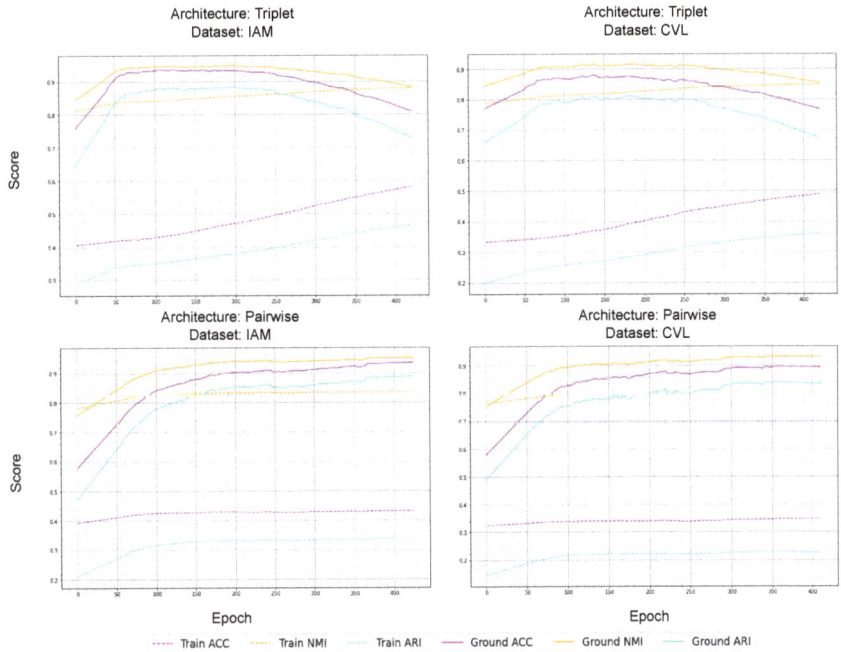

Figure 8. Graphs illustrating the metrics of the pretext task and ground dataset containing 50 writers with a purity of 0.05. The first row represents the triplet network and the second row represents the pairwise network, respectively.

The semihard triplet loss function is designed to minimize the embedding distance between positive and anchor data and strictly distance the embeddings of negative and anchor data. As the triplet architecture is trained over semihard triplet loss and heavily adheres to the aforementioned criteria, the architecture overfits hypothetical constraints while ignoring the real feature-dependent relationships.

In contrast, instead of overfitting training data, the pairwise architecture learns to extract features. The reason lies in AutoEmbedder's training strategy as L2-loss does not take into consideration the pseudolabel; instead, it learns aggregately from a batch of data. Therefore, the framework can obtain feature similarities because it is not precisely supervised using L2-loss. As a result, the architecture can recluster the data in hyperspace depending on the feature similarities.

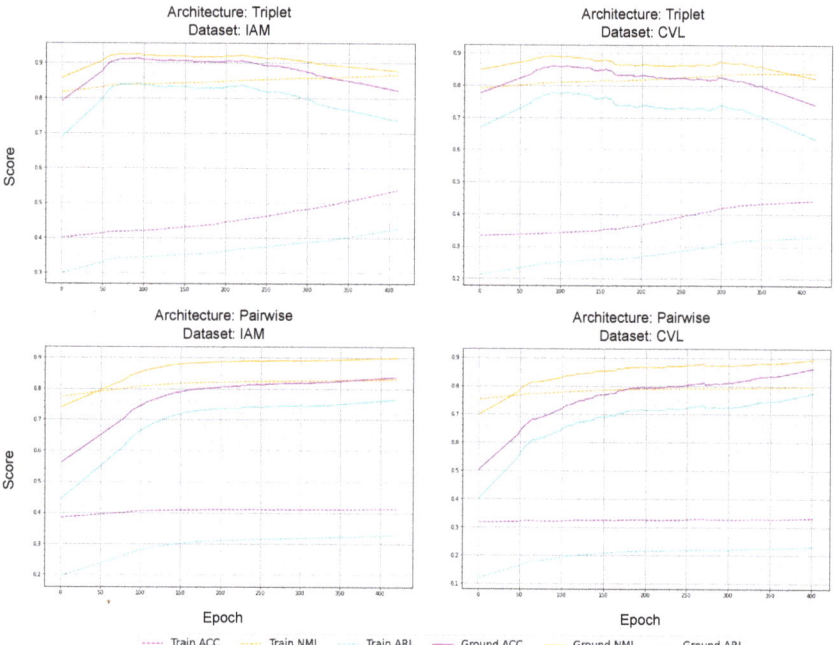

Figure 9. Graphs illustrating the metrics of the pretext task and the ground dataset containing 50 writers with impurity 0.1. The first row represents the triplet network and the second row represents the pairwise network, respectively.

With pairwise architecture-based AutoEmbedder, we further investigate several writers and impurity conditions. Tables 3 and 4 show the IAM and CVL datasets' evaluation metrics on the training and ground datasets. The table represents a comprehensive summary of the performance variance in the training dataset depending on the number of writers and impurity. On any dataset, the AutoEmbedder-based paired architecture retains a marginal performance with impurity = 0. Furthermore, increasing the number of writers and the impurity ratio causes a reduction in the architecture's performance. Although the number of writers is held constant at 25 and 50, a slight fluctuation is observed in both datasets. Increasing the number of writers by 50 resulted in an inconsistent improvement in performance.

Table 3. The table illustrates the pairwise architecture in the IAM dataset across four-speaker groups: 25, 50, 100, and 127. The table also analyzes two segmentation impurities, 0 and 0.1, for each group of writers to illustrate the shortcomings of the faulty assumption.

		Impurity = 0			Impurity = 0.05			Impurity = 0.1		
		NMI	ACC	ARI	NMI	ACC	ARI	NMI	ACC	ARI
25 writers	Pretext task	0.801	0.463	0.334	0.791	0.422	0.352	0.778	0.430	0.372
	Ground task	0.956	0.948	0.912	0.898	0.854	0.848	0.856	0.807	0.792
50 writers	Pretext task	0.849	0.452	0.351	0.845	0.432	0.348	0.834	0.424	0.345
	Ground task	0.988	0.969	0.934	0.958	0.943	0.897	0.903	0.861	0.801
100 writers	Pretext task	0.841	0.419	0.309	0.7895	0.394	0.310	0.731	0.398	0.312
	Ground task	0.901	0.841	0.813	0.876	0.823	0.801	0.851	0.816	0.794
127 writers	Pretext task	0.836	0.404	0.301	0.779	0.396	0.294	0.711	0.382	0.299
	Ground task	0.898	0.817	0.798	0.847	0.794	0.776	0.816	0.787	0.741

Table 4. The table illustrates the pairwise architecture in the CVL dataset across four-speaker groups: 25, 50, 100, and 150. The table also analyzes two segmentation impurities, 0 and 0.1, for each group of writers to illustrate the shortcomings of the faulty assumption.

		Impurity = 0			Impurity = 0.05			Impurity = 0.1		
		NMI	ACC	ARI	NMI	ACC	ARI	NMI	ACC	ARI
25 writers	Pretext task	0.786	0.372	0.228	0.811	0.384	0.246	0.771	0.368	0.250
	Ground task	0.943	0.910	0.908	0.899	0.862	0.857	0.907	0.850	0.810
50 writers	Pretext task	0.800	0.368	0.231	0.800	0.362	0.246	0.800	0.374	0.268
	Ground task	0.974	0.941	0.919	0.930	0.901	0.845	0.914	0.867	0.816
100 writers	Pretext task	0.786	0.352	0.228	0.764	0.340	0.219	0.744	0.336	0.214
	Ground task	0.908	0.871	0.819	0.894	0.846	0.770	0.861	0.811	0.784
150 writers	Pretext task	0.753	0.337	0.216	0.727	0.312	0.178	0.703	0.297	0.154
	Ground task	0.846	0.793	0.764	0.824	0.781	0.743	0.816	0.775	0.725

In order to investigate the appropriate feature relationship between text blocks, the architecture requires a significant amount of handwriting characteristics variations from users. Limiting the number of writers to 25, the architecture struggles to find more appropriate feature relationships and observes a reduction in performance. By increasing the number of writers to 50, the feature variances in training data are balanced and observed a performance improvement.

5. Discussion

The pairwise architecture with training strategy performs well in the writer recognition process. However, throughout the study, the architecture has several difficulties that must be addressed. First, training the architecture with less handwriting variation results in overfitting, as observed while the number of writers' dataset is 25. Secondly, as the system is fully segmentation-dependent, the target lies in developing an optimal audio segmentation procedure. Resolving these challenges would benefit the architecture for a wide range of writer recognition and evaluation usage. Furthermore, due to the use of Siamese architecture, the architecture has an identical subnetwork, increasing the computation throughout the process. Thus, the training strategy required a long period of time.

Apart from the limitations, the self-writer strategy requires no pretraining on large handwritten datasets, which is often observed in other writer recognition methods. Furthermore, the Self-Writer strategy requires comparatively less per-writer data than the other writer recognition methods. From an overall perspective, the Self-Writer keeps the requirement of labeled data to a minimum.

6. Conclusions

This paper presents Self-Writer, a self-supervised writer recognition system that generates clusterable embeddings depending on the writers' unique handwriting characteristics. Self-Writer deals with unlabeled data and is trained with pseudolabels. Self-supervised learning has its various forms based on the domain; self-writer aligns with contrastive self-supervised learning strategies. We evaluate such a strategy with two relevant DL architectures, pairwise and triplet. The empirical results demonstrate that the pairwise architecture-based AutoEmbedder, as an embedding architecture, performs better than triplet architecture for our proposed self-supervised writer recognition. Furthermore, the architecture performs well regarding the number of writers and handwritten text segmentation errors in unlabeled data. However, depending on the writers' variations, the method requires clean documents and robust line segmentation techniques to generate clusterable embeddings. Therefore, a segmentation technique and VLAD encoding might be an extended version of the proposed work. In addition, to evaluate the clusterable embedding, we use the K-means algorithm. However, locally weighted and multidiversified ensemble clustering, which enhances the clustering robustness by fusing the information of multiple-based clusterings, might be an extended version of the proposed work. Nevertheless, we firmly believe that such a comprehensive and hypothetical technique for generating hypothetical labels to train writer recognition systems will assist researchers in developing new strategies.

Author Contributions: Conceptualization, Z.M.; formal analysis, Z.M. and M.M.K.; funding acquisition, M.M.M.; investigation, M.A.H. and M.F.M.; methodology, Z.M. and M.F.M.; project administration, M.M.M. and M.A.H.; resources, M.M.M. and M.A.H.; supervision, M.F.M.; writing—original draft, Z.M. and M.M.K.; writing—review & editing, M.M.M. and M.A.H. All authors have read and agreed to the published version of the manuscript.

Funding: This research work was funded by Institutional Fund Projects under grant no. (IFPIP: 320-611-1443). The authors gratefully acknowledge technical and financial support provided by the Ministry of Education and King AbdulAziz University, DSR, Jeddah, Saudi Arabia.

Conflicts of Interest: The authors declare no conflict of interest.

References

1. Khan, F.A.; Khelifi, F.; Tahir, M.A.; Bouridane, A. Dissimilarity Gaussian mixture models for efficient offline handwritten text-independent identification using SIFT and RootSIFT descriptors. *IEEE Trans. Inf. Forensics Secur.* **2018**, *14*, 289–303. [CrossRef]
2. Tapiador, M.; Gómez, J.; Sigüenza, J.A. Writer identification forensic system based on support vector machines with connected components. In Proceedings of the International Conference on Industrial, Engineering and Other Applications of Applied Intelligent Systems, Berlin/Heidelberg, Germany, 17 May 2004; pp. 625–632.
3. Fornés, A.; Lladós, J.; Sánchez, G.; Bunke, H. Writer identification in old handwritten music scores. In Proceedings of the 2008 the Eighth IAPR International Workshop on Document Analysis Systems, Nara, Japan, 16–19 September 2008; pp. 347–353.
4. Fornés, A.; Lladós, J.; Sánchez, G.; Bunke, H. On the use of textural features for writer identification in old handwritten music scores. In Proceedings of the 2009 10th International Conference on Document Analysis and Recognition, Catalonia, Spain, 26–29 July 2009; pp. 996–1000.
5. Ballard, L.; Lopresti, D.; Monrose, F. Evaluating the security of handwriting biometrics. In Proceedings of the Tenth International Workshop on Frontiers in Handwriting Recognition, La Baule, France, 23–26 October 2006.
6. Xing, L.; Qiao, Y. Deepwriter: A multi-stream deep CNN for text-independent writer identification. In Proceedings of the 2016 15th International Conference on Frontiers in Handwriting Recognition (ICFHR), Shenzhen, China, 23–26 October 2016; pp. 584–589.
7. Sulaiman, A.; Omar, K.; Nasrudin, M.F.; Arram, A. Length independent writer identification based on the fusion of deep and hand-crafted descriptors. *IEEE Access* **2019**, *7*, 91772–91784. [CrossRef]
8. Doersch, C.; Zisserman, A. Multi-task self-supervised visual learning. In Proceedings of the IEEE International Conference on Computer Vision, Venice, Italy, 22–29 October 2017; pp. 2051–2060.
9. Zhai, X.; Oliver, A.; Kolesnikov, A.; Beyer, L. S4l: Self-supervised semi-supervised learning. In Proceedings of the IEEE/CVF International Conference on Computer Vision, Seoul, Korea, 27 October–2 November 2019; pp. 1476–1485.
10. Doersch, C.; Gupta, A.; Efros, A.A. Unsupervised visual representation learning by context prediction. In Proceedings of the IEEE International Conference on Computer Vision, Santiago, Chile, 7–13 December 2015; pp. 1422–1430.

11. Gidaris, S.; Bursuc, A.; Komodakis, N.; Pérez, P.; Cord, M. Boosting few-shot visual learning with self-supervision. In Proceedings of the IEEE/CVF International Conference on Computer Vision, Seoul, Korea, 27 October–2 November 2019; pp. 8059–8068.
12. Baevski, A.; Zhou, H.; Mohamed, A.; Auli, M. wav2vec 2.0: A framework for self-supervised learning of speech representations. *arXiv* **2020**, arXiv:2006.11477.
13. Collobert, R.; Weston, J. A unified architecture for natural language processing: Deep neural networks with multitask learning. In Proceedings of the 25th International Conference on Machine Learning, Helsinki, Finland, 5–9 July 2008; pp. 160–167.
14. Mikolov, T.; Chen, K.; Corrado, G.; Dean, J. Efficient estimation of word representations in vector space. *arXiv* **2013**, arXiv:1301.3781.
15. Pennington, J.; Socher, R.; Manning, C.D. Glove: Global vectors for word representation. In Proceedings of the 2014 Conference on Empirical Methods in Natural Language Processing (EMNLP), Doha, Qatar, 25–29 October 2014; pp. 1532–1543.
16. Devlin, J.; Chang, M.W.; Lee, K.; Toutanova, K. Bert: Pre-training of deep bidirectional transformers for language understanding. *arXiv* **2018**, arXiv:1810.04805.
17. Liu, Y.; Ott, M.; Goyal, N.; Du, J.; Joshi, M.; Chen, D.; Levy, O.; Lewis, M.; Zettlemoyer, L.; Stoyanov, V. Roberta: A robustly optimized bert pretraining approach. *arXiv* **2019**, arXiv:1907.11692.
18. Schroff, F.; Kalenichenko, D.; Philbin, J. Facenet: A unified embedding for face recognition and clustering. In Proceedings of the IEEE Conference on Computer Vision and Pattern Recognition, Boston, MA, USA, 7–12 June 2015; pp. 815–823.
19. Ohi, A.Q.; Mridha, M.F.; Safir, F.B.; Hamid, M.A.; Monowar, M.M. Autoembedder: A semi-supervised DNN embedding system for clustering. *Knowl.-Based Syst.* **2020**, *204*, 106190. [CrossRef]
20. Janiesch, C.; Zschech, P.; Heinrich, K. Machine learning and deep learning. *Electron. Mark.* **2021**, *31*, 685–695. [CrossRef]
21. He, Z.; Fang, B.; Du, J.; Tang, Y.Y.; You, X. A novel method for offline handwriting-based writer identification. In Proceedings of the Eighth International Conference on Document Analysis and Recognition (ICDAR'05), Seoul, Korea, 29 August–1 September 2005; pp. 242–246.
22. Helli, B.; Moghaddam, M.E. A text-independent Persian writer identification based on feature relation graph (FRG). *Pattern Recognit.* **2010**, *43*, 2199–2209. [CrossRef]
23. He, Z.; Tang, Y. Chinese handwriting-based writer identification by texture analysis. In Proceedings of the 2004 International Conference on Machine Learning and Cybernetics (IEEE Cat. No. 04EX826), Shanghai, China, 26–29 August 2004; Volume 6, pp. 3488–3491.
24. Zhu, Y.; Tan, T.; Wang, Y. Biometric personal identification based on handwriting. In Proceedings of the 15th International Conference on Pattern Recognition, ICPR-2000, Barcelona, Spain, 3–8 September 2000; Volume 2, pp. 797–800.
25. Schlapbach, A.; Bunke, H. A writer identification and verification system using HMM based recognizers. *Pattern Anal. Appl.* **2007**, *10*, 33–43. [CrossRef]
26. Anwar, W.; Bajwa, I.S.; Ramzan, S. Design and implementation of a machine learning-based authorship identification model. *Sci. Program.* **2019**, *2019*, 9431073. [CrossRef]
27. Zheng, W.; Liu, X.; Ni, X.; Yin, L.; Yang, B. Improving visual reasoning through semantic representation. *IEEE Access* **2021**, *9*, 91476–91486. [CrossRef]
28. Zheng, W.; Yin, L.; Chen, X.; Ma, Z.; Liu, S.; Yang, B. Knowledge base graph embedding module design for Visual question answering model. *Pattern Recognit.* **2021**, *120*, 108153. [CrossRef]
29. Christlein, V.; Bernecker, D.; Maier, A.; Angelopoulou, E. Offline writer identification using convolutional neural network activation features. In Proceedings of the German Conference on Pattern Recognition, Hannover, Germany, 12–15 September 2015; pp. 540–552.
30. Zhang, X.Y.; Xie, G.S.; Liu, C.L.; Bengio, Y. End-to-end online writer identification with recurrent neural network. *IEEE Trans. Hum.-Mach. Syst.* **2016**, *47*, 285–292. [CrossRef]
31. Semma, A.; Hannad, Y.; Siddiqi, I.; Djeddi, C.; El Kettani, M.E.Y. Writer identification using deep learning with fast keypoints and harris corner detector. *Expert Syst. Appl.* **2021**, *184*, 115473. [CrossRef]
32. Fiel, S.; Sablatnig, R. Writer identification and retrieval using a convolutional neural network. In Proceedings of the International Conference on Computer Analysis of Images and Patterns, Valletta, Malta, 2–4 September 2015; pp. 26–37.
33. He, S.; Schomaker, L. Deep adaptive learning for writer identification based on single handwritten word images. *Pattern Recognit.* **2019**, *88*, 64–74. [CrossRef]
34. He, S.; Schomaker, L. Fragnet: Writer identification using deep fragment networks. *IEEE Trans. Inf. Forensics Secur.* **2020**, *15*, 3013–3022. [CrossRef]
35. Zheng, W.; Tian, X.; Yang, B.; Liu, S.; Ding, Y.; Tian, J.; Yin, L. A few shot classification methods based on multiscale relational networks. *Appl. Sci.* **2022**, *12*, 4059. [CrossRef]
36. Zhang, P. RSTC: A New Residual Swin Transformer For Offline Word-Level Writer Identification. *IEEE Access* **2022**, *10*, 57452–57460. [CrossRef]
37. Chen, Z.; Yu, H.X.; Wu, A.; Zheng, W.S. Level online writer identification. *Int. J. Comput. Vis.* **2021**, *129*, 1394–1409. [CrossRef]
38. Christlein, V.; Gropp, M.; Fiel, S.; Maier, A. Unsupervised feature learning for writer identification and writer retrieval. In Proceedings of the 2017 14th IAPR International Conference on Document Analysis and Recognition (ICDAR), Kyoto, Japan, 9–15 November 2017; Volume 1, pp. 991–997.

39. Chen, S.; Wang, Y.; Lin, C.T.; Ding, W.; Cao, Z. Semi-supervised feature learning for improving writer identification. *Inf. Sci.* **2019**, *482*, 156–170. [CrossRef]
40. Zhang, R.; Isola, P.; Efros, A.A. Colorful image colorization. In Proceedings of the European Conference on Computer Vision, Amsterdam, The Netherlands, 11–14 October 2016; pp. 649–666.
41. Walker, J.; Gupta, A.; Hebert, M. Dense optical flow prediction from a static image. In Proceedings of the IEEE International Conference on Computer Vision, Santiago, Chile, 7–13 December 2015; pp. 2443–2451.
42. Walker, J.; Doersch, C.; Gupta, A.; Hebert, M. An uncertain future: Forecasting from static images using variational autoencoders. In Proceedings of the European Conference on Computer Vision, Amsterdam, The Netherlands, 11–14 October 2016; pp. 835–851.
43. Guo, Q.; Feng, W.; Zhou, C.; Huang, R.; Wan, L.; Wang, S. Learning dynamic siamese network for visual object tracking. In Proceedings of the IEEE International Conference on Computer Vision, Venice, Italy, 22–29 October 2017; pp. 1763–1771.
44. Pathak, D.; Krahenbuhl, P.; Donahue, J.; Darrell, T.; Efros, A.A. Context encoders: Feature learning by inpainting. In Proceedings of the IEEE Conference on Computer Vision and Pattern Recognition, Las Vegas, NV, USA, 27–30 June 2016; pp. 2536–2544.
45. Larsson, G.; Maire, M.; Shakhnarovich, G. Learning representations for automatic colorization. In Proceedings of the European Conference on Computer Vision, Amsterdam, The Netherlands, 11–14 October 2016; pp. 577–593.
46. Dosovitskiy, A.; Springenberg, J.T.; Riedmiller, M.; Brox, T. Discriminative unsupervised feature learning with convolutional neural networks. *Adv. Neural Inf. Process. Syst.* **2014**, *27*, 766–774. [CrossRef]
47. Shi, Y.; Xu, X.; Xi, J.; Hu, X.; Hu, D.; Xu, K. Learning to detect 3D symmetry from single-view RGB-D images with weak supervision. *IEEE Trans. Pattern Anal. Mach. Intell.* **2022**, 1-15. [CrossRef]
48. Noroozi, M.; Favaro, P. Unsupervised learning of visual representations by solving jigsaw puzzles. In Proceedings of the European Conference on Computer Vision, Amsterdam, The Netherlands, 11–14 October 2016; pp. 69–84.
49. Li, Y.; Zheng, Y.; Doermann, D.; Jaeger, S. Script-independent text line segmentation in freestyle handwritten documents. *IEEE Trans. Pattern Anal. Mach. Intell.* **2008**, *30*, 1313–1329. [CrossRef] [PubMed]
50. Malik, S.; Sajid, A.; Ahmad, A.; Almogren, A.; Hayat, B.; Awais, M.; Kim, K.H. An efficient skewed line segmentation technique for cursive script OCR. *Sci. Program.* **2020**, *2020*, 8866041. [CrossRef]
51. Zheng, W.; Liu, X.; Yin, L. Sentence representation method based on multi-layer semantic network. *Appl. Sci.* **2021**, *11*, 1316. [CrossRef]
52. Marti, U.V.; Bunke, H. The IAM-database: An English sentence database for offline handwriting recognition. *Int. J. Doc. Anal. Recognit.* **2002**, *5*, 39–46. [CrossRef]
53. Kleber, F.; Fiel, S.; Diem, M.; Sablatnig, R. Cvl-database: An off-line database for writer retrieval, writer identification and word spotting. In Proceedings of the 2013 12th International Conference on Document Analysis and Recognition, Washington, DC, USA, 25–28 August 2013; pp. 560–564.
54. Mridha, M.F.; Ohi, A.Q.; Ali, M.A.; Emon, M.I.; Kabir, M.M. BanglaWriting: A multi-purpose offline Bangla handwriting dataset. *Data Brief* **2021**, *34*, 106633. [CrossRef]
55. Jaiswal, A.; Babu, A.R.; Zadeh, M.Z.; Banerjee, D.; Makedon, F. A survey on contrastive self-supervised learning. *Technologies* **2020**, *9*, 2. [CrossRef]
56. Santos, J.M.; Embrechts, M. On the use of the adjusted rand index as a metric for evaluating supervised classification. In Proceedings of the International Conference on Artificial Neural Networks, Limassol, Cyprus, 14–17 September 2009; pp. 175–184.
57. Huang, G.; Liu, Z.; Van Der Maaten, L.; Weinberger, K.Q. Densely connected convolutional networks. In Proceedings of the IEEE Conference on Computer Vision and Pattern Recognition, Honolulu, HI, USA, 21–26 July 2017; pp. 4700–4708.
58. Hermans, A.; Beyer, L.; Leibe, B. In defense of the triplet loss for person re-identification. *arXiv* **2017**, arXiv:1703.07737.
59. Kingma, D.P.; Ba, J. Adam: A method for stochastic optimization. *arXiv* **2014**, arXiv:1412.6980.

Article

Application of Artificial Intelligence for Better Investment in Human Capital

Mohammed Abdullah Ammer [1], Zeyad A. T. Ahmed [2,*], Saleh Nagi Alsubari [2], Theyazn H. H. Aldhyani [3,*] and Shahab Ahmad Almaaytah [3]

1. Department of Finance, School of Business, King Faisal University, Al-Ahsa 31982, Saudi Arabia
2. Department of Computer Science, Dr Babasaheb Ambedkar Marathwada University, Aurangabad 431004, India
3. Applied College in Abqaiq, King Faisal University, Al-Ahsa 31982, Saudi Arabia
* Correspondence: zeyad.ahmed2019@yahoo.com (Z.A.T.A.); taldhyani@kfu.edu.sa (T.H.H.A.)

Abstract: Selecting candidates for a specific job or nominating a person for a specific position takes time and effort due to the need to search for the individual's file. Ultimately, the hiring decision may not be successful. However, artificial intelligence helps organizations or companies choose the right person for the right job. In addition, artificial intelligence contributes to the selection of harmonious working teams capable of achieving an organization's strategy and goals. This study aimed to contribute to the development of machine-learning models to analyze and cluster personality traits and classify applicants to conduct correct hiring decisions for particular jobs and identify their weaknesses and strengths. Helping applicants to succeed while managing work and training employees with weaknesses is necessary to achieving an organization's goals. Applying the proposed methodology, we used a publicly available Big-Five-personality-traits-test dataset to conduct the analyses. Preprocessing techniques were adopted to clean the dataset. Moreover, hypothesis testing was performed using Pearson's correlation approach. Based on the testing results, we concluded that a positive relationship exists between four personality traits (agreeableness, conscientiousness, extraversion, and openness), and a negative correlation occurred between neuroticism traits and the four traits. This dataset was unlabeled. However, we applied the K-mean clustering algorithm to the data-labeling task. Furthermore, various supervised machine-learning models, such as random forest (RF), support vector machine (SVM), K-nearest neighbor (KNN), and AdaBoost, were used for classification purposes. The experimental results revealed that the SVM attained the highest results, with an accuracy of 98%, outperforming the other classification models. This study adds to the current literature and body of knowledge through examining the extent of the application of artificial intelligence in the present and, potentially, the future of human-resource management. Our results may be of significance to companies, organizations and their leaders and human-resource executives, in addition to human-resource professionals.

Keywords: Big Five personality test; artificial intelligence; human resources; employee selection; teamwork; machine learning

MSC: 68T01

1. Introduction

Recently, the world has witnessed tremendous developments in artificial intelligence (AI) techniques, which are necessary for management science because of their predictive accuracy, classification, ease of analysis, and time-saving features. Traditional methods were used in the past, based on handwriting as an analytical tool for personality or the manual observation of some personal traits [1].

The application of artificial intelligence (AI) for human-resource management through the use of the Big Five personality test can be a powerful tool for making data-driven decisions and improving efficiency. By analyzing the results of the Big Five personality test, human-resources professionals can identify patterns and trends in personality traits and predict which candidates will be likely to be successful in specific job roles. Additionally, AI algorithms can be used to identify training-and-development needs, analyze employee-performance data, and identify factors that contribute to high levels of employee engagement and retention. Overall, the use of AI in human-resource management has the potential to greatly enhance decision-making and improve the overall effectiveness of HR processes [2,3].

When candidates submit their applications for a specific job to a company, the first expectation of the human-resources manager is that they select the right candidate for potential placement. A common approach is to require a certificate and experience from the applicant. Most organizations focus on specific criteria, including creativity, communication, the ability to analyze, speed of intuition, and the ability to overcome the types of challenges associated with the position. In addition, leadership skills are often sought. These include firmness, administrative discipline, and the ability to direct others toward the organization's goals [4–6].

The Big Five model, sometimes referred to as the five-factor model, is currently the theory of personality that has the greatest level of acceptance among psychologists. According to this idea, an individual's personality may be broken down into five primary components, sometimes known by the acronym OCEAN (openness, conscientiousness, extraversion, agreeableness, and neuroticism) [7].

The Big Five personality test may be carried out by any organization. However, the test does not exclude or withhold some jobs from some people; the goal is more significant and profound. Some organizations are interested in developing a team with a high capacity for carrying out specific tasks to achieve company goals [8–10]. Figure 1 shows Big Five personality traits.

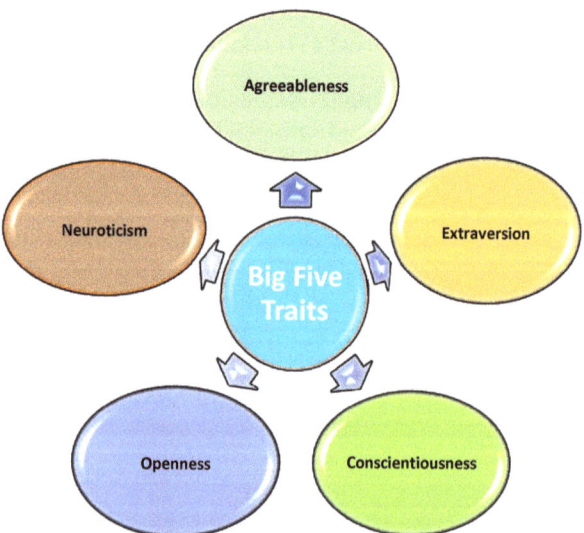

Figure 1. Big Five personality traits.

In modern psychology, the Big Five personality test examines the essential categories of individual personality included in OCEAN [11], which determine individuals' personalities and explain their behaviors. The OCEAN categories include the following:

- Openness to new experiences: This trait characterizes people who enjoy the arts and new adventures. People with a high score on this characteristic are often inquisitive, less traditional, and more inventive.

- Conscientiousness measures people who are organized, productive, and accountable. High-scoring results for this trait are often obtained by meticulous and highly reliable individuals. Low scores are given to people who exhibit low performance and are uninterested in their jobs.
- Extraversion evaluates sociability and an individual's source of energy and excitement. Furthermore, in a manner that could be compared with a spotlight, those who score well on this characteristic often inspire others to succeed.
- Agreeableness measures trustworthiness, candor, and getting along with people. Low scores for this trait are often indicative of less trustworthy and more dissatisfied individuals. These tend to be more argumentative, which may reduce their chances of being hired [12].
- Neuroticism assesses an individual's emotional stability, impulsivity, and anxiety in the face of pressure. People who go absent without leave (AWOL) from work, use harsh language, or behave negatively after an intense meeting will likely have a higher score for this trait.

This approach, which is recommended in this study, has two advantages:

1. A quicker and less expensive way to determine job applicants' personalities.
2. A faster process means there is no need to spend significant time determining applicants' behavior, reducing the need to spend significant money on interviews [13,14].

It was mentioned in [15] that it is necessary to investigate personality with more focus and with a fuller consideration of the particulars of expansion and revolution than have been employed hitherto. To highlight the issue in this study, it is indicated by Verma and Bandi [16] that 69% of employees' inadequate qualities are due to poor hiring decisions. The explanations for this include deficiencies in the understanding of candidates' profiles and their alignment with companies' cultures, in addition to the subjective assessment of candidates' hard and soft skills. This is because the employment process is typically conducted by human recruiters, who individually check CVs and other sources to find applicants. As individuals have narrow capabilities, performing all the necessary tasks is not easy, and generally entails more time from each individual recruiter. Other issues include human limitations, such as prejudices, biases, and time constraints, which can influence how a recruitment procedure operates [17] and may lead a company to lose applicants who are better suited [18]. Indeed, AI and machine learning may help to solve this problem by making human-capital management more smart and effective. Thus, the purpose of study is to enlarge upon and fill the gap in the current research by examining how AI will help organizations to select their human capital to increase the effectiveness of their recruitment.

The rest of the article is broken up into the following sections. The next part presents a literature review of the existing studies. Section 3 provides the methodology, which examines the data collection and sources, as well as the technique used for the analysis. The results are discussed in Section 4, while the discussion of these results and their connection to the motivation behind the study are presented in Section 5. The conclusion and potential directions for future research are presented in Section 5.

2. Literature Review

In the current era, technological advancements have made it possible to obtain and analyze data to acquire information about human behavior [19]. For example, the analysis of the Big Five personality traits has been applied in different fields, such as health care, education, online-behavior analysis, and human-resource management. Alamsyah et al. [20] identified prospective employment applicants based on a personality measurement using an ontology model with the help of social-media data. They selected five Twitter users whose data were available on social media as samples.. Furthermore, through their approach, they found that the personality measurement using this model revealed that each job applicant had different personality traits, such as openness, extraversion, agreeableness, and conscientiousness.

Another study, presented by Laleh et al. [21], analyzed the behavior of users and customers on social-media platforms such as Twitter and Facebook. The users' text data, such as likes, follow-ups, and online posts were collected in order to track their activities. The aim was to determine which customers were targeted and attracted by the promotion of particular companies' products, thus increasing these companies' profits. Some companies also use online social media posts for behavioral and psychological analysis. Qin et al. [22] presented a deep-learning model based on an artificial neural network, BP, to predict OCEAN personality traits. The textual analysis and deep-learning model were trained and tested on a dataset collected from the Sina Weibo website. The results showed that the model can predict the efficiency of the OCEAN personality test, achieving an accuracy of 74%.

Some studies have been conducted on the academic field. For instance, John et al. [23] used questionnaires to test students' performances. Another study, by Curtis et al. [24], tested the relationship between personality traits and employee aging. The study found that neuroticism may be negatively related to the tested individuals' general cognitive ability, capacity, and smooth thinking.

In health care, Dymecka et al. [25] tested the influence of self-efficacy and the Big Five personality characteristics on emergency-telephone-number operators' stress during the COVID-19 epidemic. One hundred emergency-telephone operators participated in the research and provided the data. The authors discovered that the operators of emergency telephone numbers suffered from a considerable amount of stress. All the Big Five personality characteristics and self-efficacy were linked to the amount of stress experienced. Self-efficacy and emotional stability were significant predictors of reported stress in a sample of emergency-telephone-number operators using stepwise regression.

Furthermore, Muntean et al. [26] tested doctors' stress. The authors tested doctors exposed daily to several stressors; their levels of occupational stress were thoroughly examined. In mental health, Chavoshi et al. [27] studied the relationship between depressive symptoms and the Big Five personality traits. The results showed an association between neuroticism and depressive symptoms that was significantly positive, whereas the link between extraversion, conscientiousness, and openness was significantly negative [28].

Xu et al. [29] studied how the geographic environment influences human personality at the provincial level. The authors studied the association between the Big Five personality characteristics and the measurement of mountainous areas. They investigated the differences in the personalities of inhabitants of mainland China in relation to geographical region by exploring the relationships between the Big Five personality characteristics and indices of mountainous areas. Priyadharshini et al. [30] applied the Big Five personality test in the selection of decision makers and leaders in various investment, military, and government sectors, in which decisions determine the fates of countries or other sectors, and the failure or success of their projects.

There are some similarities between the Big Five test and the Myers–Briggs Type Indicator (MBTI).. The MBTI is a personality model that is rarely used in personality computing. Unlike the Big Five and HEXACO, the MBTI defines personality according to types rather than traits; in other words, the human personality is solely defined by a specific personality type or class, rather than through different scores for multiple traits. The Myers-Briggs Type Indicator (MBTI) classifies people into one of four categories: extraversion or introversion, sensing or intuition, thinking or feeling, and judging or perceiving. This is a technique that is usually used in the process of assisting persons in better comprehending their personal communication preferences, as well as the manner in which they engage with other people. Knowledge of the Myers-Briggs Type Indicator (MBTI) may assist individuals in adapting their interpersonal styles to suit a variety of settings and audiences. In psychology, the MBTI applies four binary criteria and categorizes individuals into one of 16 distinct personality types. The MBTI has long since been replaced by approaches such as the Big Five traits, which are more reliable, valid, and complete. These approaches are considerably more descriptive of the underlying reality (e.g., most individuals are neither drastically introverted nor extroverted, but rather somewhere in the center) than categorical characteristic dimensions such as those deployed by the MBTI. The Big Five is not the only contemporary theory of personality. Its most notable rivals are the honesty–humility, emotionality, extraversion, agreeableness, conscientiousness, and openness-to-experience (HEXACO) model. However, HEXACO and the Big Five are relatively similar; HEXACO's additional honesty–humility element is the primary distinguishing feature [28], which adds a sixth dimension to personality analysis, [31].

3. Methodology

Many modern psychologists who study personality point to the Big Five personality traits as evidence that there are at least five fundamental aspects of human nature [32]. Extraversion, agreeableness, openness, conscientiousness, and neuroticism are the five main characteristics of a person's character. In modern management methods, knowledge of personality traits is essential. Therefore, career professionals and psychologists use this information in a personality career test for recruitment and candidate assessment [33]. This study developed a machine-learning approach to Big Five personality test dataset to give decision makers in organizations or businesses detailed information on the personalities of applicants and more insight into how they react in different situations, which can help in selecting occupations for employees. The proposed methodology has seven phases, as follows:

1. Dataset collection.
2. Data preprocessing.
3. Feature selection.
4. Clustering algorithms.
5. Data splitting.
6. Training machine-learning models.
7. Evaluation of the results.

Figure 2 shows the structure of the methodology.

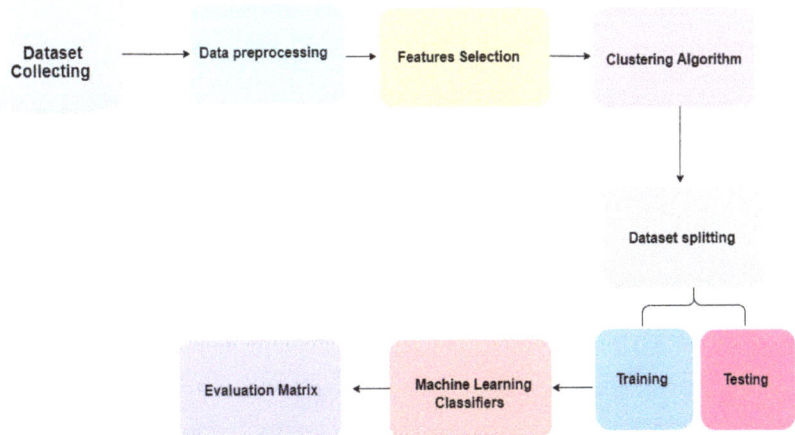

Figure 2. Architecture of the proposed methodology.

3.1. Dataset Collection

Open Psychometrics collected this dataset from participants worldwide through an online model [34]. This dataset contains information from 1,015,342 individuals who answered the questionnaire, which comprised 50 questions. It is publicly available on Kaggle [35]. Figure 3 shows the countries with 10,000 or more participants. A large number of participants were from the following countries: USA, with 545,912 participants; the UK, with 66,487; Canada, with 61,805; Australia, with 49,753; the Philippines, with 19,844; and India, with 17,482. Some countries had few participants. These included Yemen, with 14 participants, and Burundi, with one participant.

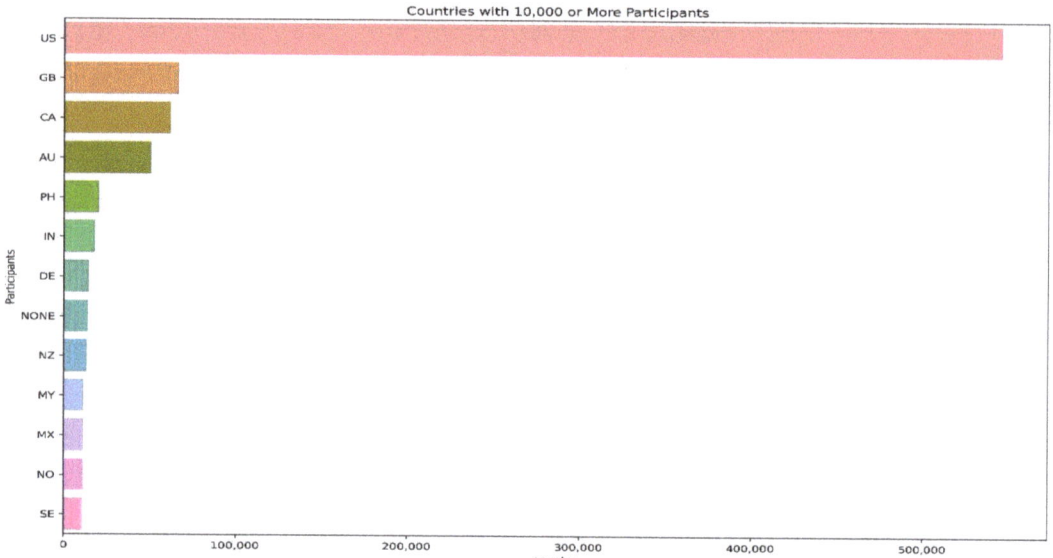

Figure 3. The distribution of participants on the dataset.

3.2. Data Preprocessing

This dataset needed processing because it had missing values. When no value was stored for a particular feature in the dataset, the "dropna" method was used to clean the dataset. The dataset also contained some unwanted features; therefore, we focused on the responses to questions that only related to personal traits. Next, MinMaxScaler was used to scale the data. It modifies attributes by scaling each attribute to a specified range. The default range is between 0 and 1. Subsequently, principal-component analysis (PCA) was used to reduce the dimensionality of the data and k-means for clustering to label the data. The following sections explain the rest of the preprocessing.

3.2.1. Correlation Testing Using Pearson's Approach

The Pearson correlation coefficient (named after Karl Pearson) can be used to summarize the strength of the linear relationship between data samples. Python software 3.9 was used to find correlations between features. It is expressed by Equation (1), below.

$$r = \frac{\sum (x - m_x)(y - m_y)}{\sqrt{\sum (x - m_x)^2 \sum (y - m_y)^2}} \tag{1}$$

The range of the correlation is between −1 and +1. When the correlation value is closer to zero, there is no linear trend between the two variables. When the correlation is close to 1, the correlation is more positive, which means that a change in one variable affects the other variable. A correlation closer to −1 is similar, but instead of increasing, one variable decreases as the other increases [36]. The heatmap shows that the diagonals are all "1," dark blue, because these squares correlate each variable with itself (indicating a perfect correlation). For the rest of the values, the larger the number and the darker the color, the stronger the correlation between the two variables. The plot is also symmetrical about the diagonal, since the same two variables are paired together in these squares. To make the heatmap in Figure 4 more comprehensible, we combined the personality traits into five variables using the mean value of 50 variables and tested the correlations. Figure 4 shows a positive relationship between conscientious personality (CSN) and open personality (OPN), of 0.4. Furthermore, there was a positive relationship between extraversion personality (EXT) and agreeableness personality (AGR), of 0.4. In addition, there was a positive relationship between the AGR and the CSN, of 0.36. When we compared the correlations between any personality trait and neuroticism personality traits, we found a weak correlation, as shown in Figure 4.

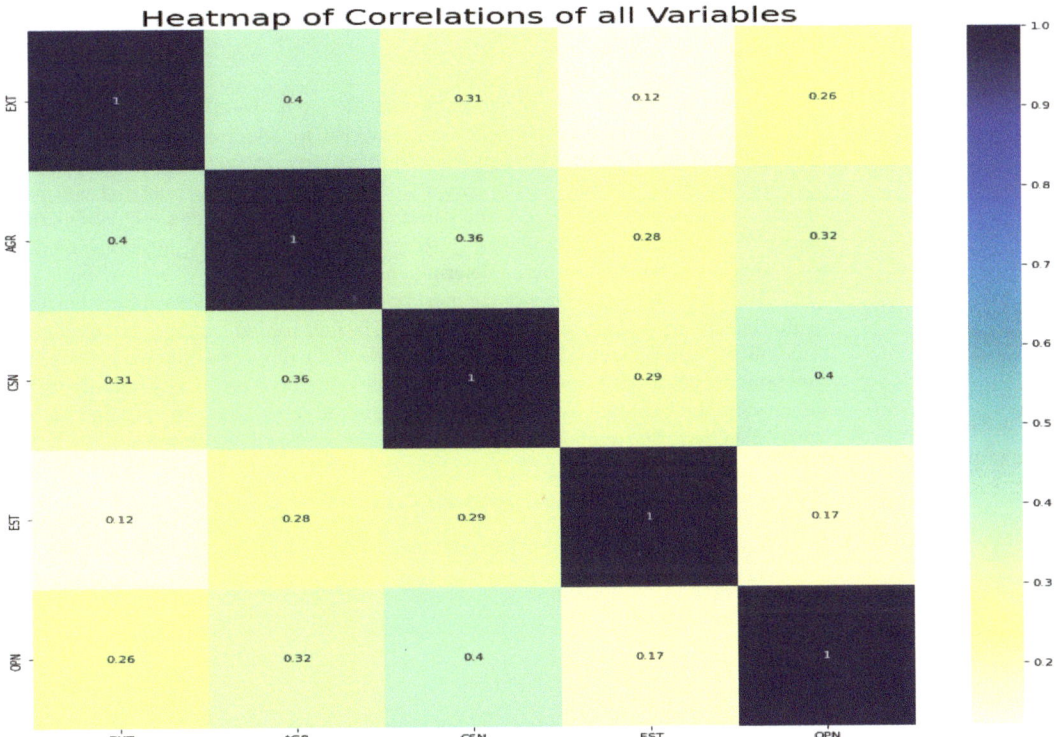

Figure 4. Correlations between personality traits.

3.2.2. Feature Selection

The dataset used in this study had 50 features, and each group of personal traits had 10 positive and negative questions. These groups had strong internal correlations. To develop our model, we used a subset from the dataset of 20,000 (20 k) samples, because of the limitations of computer configurations. However, PCA was applied. Principal-component analysis is an unsupervised learning approach used to decrease the dimensionality of data features and is extensively employed as a dimensionality-reduction algorithm [37–39]. Reducing the dimensionality of input dataset features used to train and test a predictive model achieves a higher performance level. From another perspective, it makes large datasets easy to process and classify in less calculation time. The main objective of the PCA algorithm is to wrap high-dimensional features into a set of lower-dimensional spaces and then reconstruct them. The PCA can be calculated by Equation (2), where $\bar{x}$ is the mean and x_i a set of input features. Table 1 shows results of PCA method when selecting significant features.

$$x_j = x_i - \bar{x} \tag{2}$$

where i and j are simply index variables that are used to refer to different data features within a dataset.

Table 1. Results of PCA.

Extraversion	Neuroticism	Agreeableness	Conscientiousness	Openness	Clusters
0.60	0.48	0.62	0.64	0.66	4
0.68	0.42	0.64	0.62	0.54	0
0.58	0.52	0.56	0.56	0.62	0
0.52	0.54	0.64	0.54	0.62	3
0.70	0.46	0.60	0.64	0.72	4

3.2.3. Clustering Algorithm

Clustering is the process of gathering data into groups based on patterns of similarity and distance. In this study, the dataset was not labeled; for this reason, we applied clustering to label the data. The use of k-means clustering is a simple way to divide a dataset into K groups that do not overlap. To implement k-means clustering, we must first assume how many clusters we require [40,41]. The k-means algorithm then locates each observation in one of the K clusters. The number of clusters was determined using the Elbow method.

Elbow method for clustering determination

The Elbow method is one of the most popular methods for determining the optimal value of k, referring to the number of clusters. The idea behind the Elbow method is based on how the arm is made. However, the structure of the Elbow method may change based on how the parameter "metric" is set. The Elbow method used a k-means algorithm to determine the k number of clusters by setting in the range (k = 2 to 9) to find groups in unlabeled data. The method detected five clusters, as shown in Figure 5.

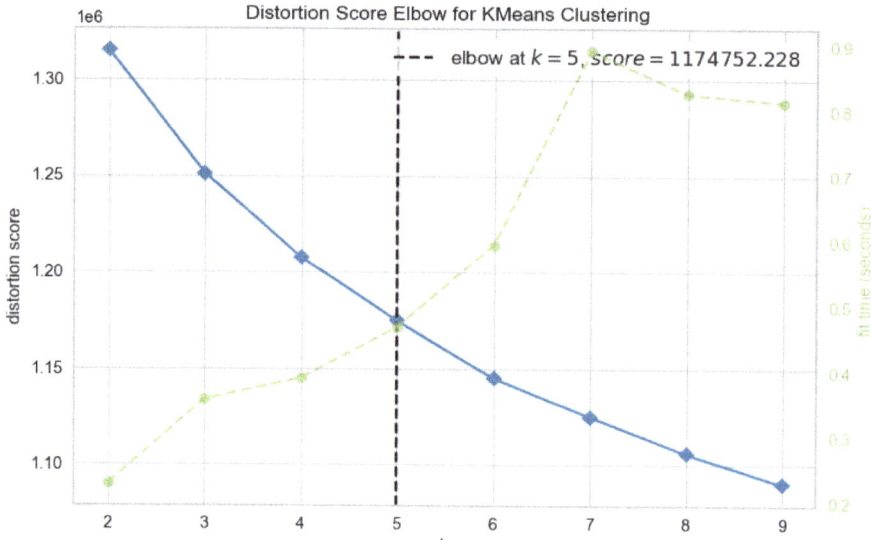

Figure 5. Elbow-method plot.

The k-means algorithm grouped the data by dividing the samples into n groups with the same degree of variation. This was achieved by minimizing what is called inertia, or within-cluster sum-of-squares. The aim was to discover a centroid with the least amount of inertia or within-cluster sum-of-squares. The following is an explanation of how k-means works:

- Step 1: Calculate the value "K," which denotes the number of clusters. In this instance, we chose K = 5 (agreeableness, extraversion, openness, conscientiousness, neuroticism).
- Step 2: Initialize a cluster by choosing, for instance, five different centroids at random from fresh data points. If "K" is equal to 5 and there are five centroids, cluster initialization occurs.
- Step 3: Calculate the distance between each point and the centroid. For instance, calculate the distance between the first point and the centroid.
- Step 4: Assign each point to the closest cluster and then measure the distance between the initial point and the centroid.
- Step 5: As the new centroid, compute the mean of each cluster. Each cluster's mean should be used to update the centroid.
- Step 6: Repeat steps 3–5 with the new cluster center. Repeat until reaching a halt, indicating convergence (no more changes), as well as the maximum number of repetitions. The process is complete when the clustering does not change during the preceding round.

The algorithm created groups based on the similarity between the answers, and it was arranged in five clusters. The next step was training and testing output-cluster data based on machine-learning models.

3.3. Machine-Learning Models

Supervised learning is a machine-learning method that is applied using labeled datasets. The models based on this method must determine the mapping function connecting the input variable (X) to the output variable (Y). After the data were labeled, using a k-means clustering algorithm, we trained and tested several machine-learning algorithms to obtain a high-accuracy model to predict measurements of different personality traits. Random forest (RF), linear support vector machine (LSVM), K-nearest neighbor (KNN), and AdaBoost algorithms were applied to divide the dataset into the following classes: Class 0, Class 1, Class 2, Class 3, and Class 4.

3.3.1. Support Vector Machine (SVM) Method

Support-vector-machine classification is a supervised-learning algorithm that uses support-vector machines to classify feature values into different categories. This algorithm is particularly useful for linearly separable data, meaning the feature values can be easily separated into distinct categories based on their features. One of the main advantages of SVM classification is its ability to handle high-dimension data and large datasets. It can also handle cases in which the data are not linearly separable by using kernel functions to transform the data into a higher-dimensional space, in which they become separable.

Support-vector-machine classification works by finding the hyperplane in a high-dimensional space that maximally separates different classes. In predicting personality traits, SVM classification can be used to identify patterns in the data indicative of specific traits. For example, a hyperplane separating individuals high in openness from those low in openness may be identified through SVM classification, allowing for accurate predictions of an individual's openness level. In this research, the radial basis function (RBF) was employed to classify the data [42].

$$K(X, X') = exp\left(-\frac{\|X - X'\|^2}{2\sigma^2}\right) \qquad (3)$$

where $\|X - X'\|^2$ is Euclidean distance between the input variables.

3.3.2. AdaBoost Method

AdaBoost (adaptive boosting) classification is a machine-learning technique. It works by iteratively training weak classifiers, which are models that perform slightly better than chance, and then combining them into a single strong classifier (Freund and). The weak classifiers are trained on different subsets of the data, with a greater weight given to misclassified samples in order to focus on improving their classification. One of the key benefits of AdaBoost classification is that it can be applied to a wide range of classification problems, including binary and multi-class classification. It has also been shown to perform well in cases in which the data are unbalanced.

AdaBoost classification can be used to predict personality traits in order to identify patterns in the data indicative of specific traits. For example, a classifier combining multiple weak learners that can accurately predict an individual's openness level may be identified through AdaBoost classification.

3.3.3. K-Nearest Neighbors (KNN)

K-nearest neighbors (KNN) is a classification technique that is both one of the easiest and one of the most essential in ML. In the fields of pattern recognition, data mining, and intrusion detection, supervised learning is one of the strategies that is used the most often. Because it does not make any fundamental assumptions about the manner in which data are distributed, it is entirely superfluous in the context of real-world scenarios [43,44]. The KNN algorithm's goal is to determine the class label that should be applied to a particular query point by locating the points that are geographically the most similar to that location. We determined that the k value should be set to 3.

$$A_i = \sqrt{(c_1 - c_2) + (d_1 - d_2)} \qquad (4)$$

The k value is employed to locate and compute the points in the feature vectors that are closest to each other. As a result, the value must stand out. Furthermore, $c_1 - c_2$ and $d_1 - d_2$ are feature vectors for finding the closest point

3.4. Evaluation Metrics

A model was evaluated by testing an algorithm on an unseen dataset that was not used during the training step to analyze the model performances. In these experiments, we used several standard micro averages of a metric, such as confusion matrix, accuracy, f1-score, precision, and recall. The classification results were also quantified using the ROC metric, which calculated the false-positive and false-negative samples, as illustrated in the representation graph below. A confusion matrix shows four categories of results: (1) true positive (*TP*), (2) false negative (*FN*), (3) false positive (*FP*), and (4) true negative (*TP*). The equations for these metrics are as follows:

$$Accuracy = \frac{TP + TN}{FP + FN + TP + TN} \times 100 \qquad (5)$$

$$Precision = \frac{TP}{TP + FP} \times 100 \qquad (6)$$

$$Recall = \frac{TP}{TP + FN} \times 100 \qquad (7)$$

$$F1 - score = 2 * \frac{precision \times Sensitivity}{precision + Sensitivity} \times 100 \qquad (8)$$

3.5. Experimental Results

This section presents the empirical results from experiments conducted to classify participants' personal traits into Class _0, Class_1, Class _2, Class _3, and Class_4. The participants belonging to Class_0 were identified as having the same medium score measurements for three traits, extraversion, agreeableness, and openness, and low scores for conscientiousness and neuroticism. Class_1 means the participant has a high score for neuroticism and a low score for conscientiousness, openness, extraversion, and agreeableness. Class_2 means the participant has a high agreeableness score and a medium score for other traits. Class_3 means that the participant has a low conscientiousness score and similar scores for other traits. Class_4 means that the participant has identical scores for openness and agreeableness and the same medium scores for the other three traits. We used 20,000 samples as a subset of the Big Five personality-test dataset.

The training and testing of the used dataset were carried out by using two different data-split approaches: traditional data splitting and cross-validation splitting.

3.5.1. Traditional Data Spilt

The samples were split as follows. In total, 70% were placed in the training set and 30% were used to test various machine-learning models to detect and classify participants' personal traits. These models included KNN, SVM, RF, and AdaBoost. Performance evaluation of each model was conducted using weighted-measurement metrics, such as precision, recall, f1-score, and accuracy. In addition to these metrics, a confusion matrix was also applied. Figure 6 shows the confusion matrix for the best model-classification results.

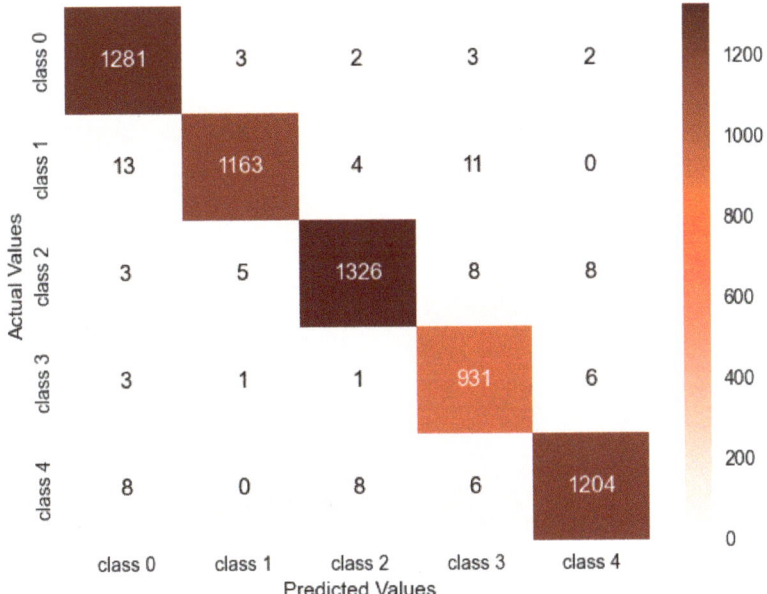

Figure 6. Confusion matrix for the SVM model.

Based on the results of the confusion metric, the SVM model obtained 95 misclassified samples out of the 6000, which were used as a testing set. The model's performance was reliable and could be applied to classify the participants' personality traits accurately. Table 2 summarizes the classification results of the traditional data-splitting models.

Table 2. Testing results of the proposed machine-learning models using traditional data splitting.

Classifier Name	Precision %	Recall %	F1-Score %	Testing Accuracy %	Training Accuracy %
KNN	92.88	92.85	92.85	92.85	96.1
RF	95.7	95.7	95.7	95.7	1.00
SVM	98.42	98.41	98.41	98.41	98.73
AdaBoost	68.69	68.35	68.17	68.35	69.00

Table 1 and the confusion matrix in Figure 6 analyze the performances of the proposed models. By comparing the results of the evaluation metrics, we found that the SVM classifier proved its effectiveness and efficiency with an accuracy of 98%. Furthermore, it outperformed the other classifiers in classifying and predicting participants' personality traits using different categories, as described in the previous section. Furthermore, poor performance was observed using the AdaBoost model. The ROC curve for the SVM classifier is shown in Figure 7 shows ROC of SVM method in the training and testing evaluation method.

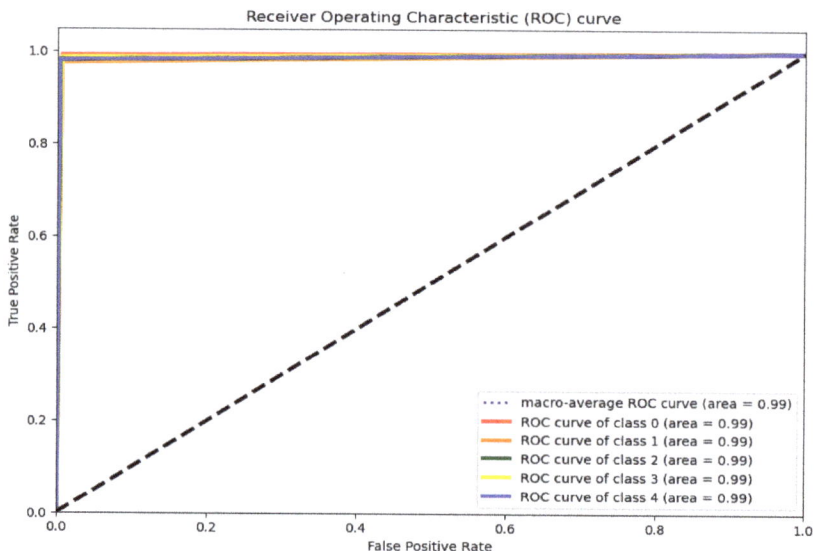

Figure 7. The ROC of the SVM model using traditional data split.

3.5.2. Cross-Validation Spilt

Cross-validation is a statistical method used to evaluate the performances of machine-learning models. It involves dividing a dataset into separate training and testing subsets and using the training subset to fit the model. The model is then evaluated on the testing subset to assess its performance. This process is repeated multiple times, with different subsets of the data used as the training and testing sets each time. In this study, we implemented a common k-fold cross-validation method to ensure the accuracy of our results, as shown in Table 1.

In this experiment, we used five-fold cross-validation, which is a resampling procedure used to evaluate the performance of our proposed machine-learning models. It involves dividing the dataset into five subsets (folds), training the model on four folds, and evaluating its performance on the remaining fold. This process is repeated five times, with a different fold used as the test set in each iteration. The performance measure is then averaged across all five iterations to estimate the model's performance with unseen data. The testing results of the KNN, RF, SVM, and AdaBoost classifiers using the five-fold cross-validation are presented in Tables 3–6. The experiential results clearly show that SVM classifier provided the best performance and outperformed other classifiers.

Table 3. The results of KNN classifier using five-fold cross-validation.

K-Fold Iteration	Precision %	Recall %	F1-Score %	Testing Accuracy %	Training Accuracy %
Fold 1	92.9	92.9	92.9	92.9	96.1
Fold 2	93.5	93.5	93.5	93.5	96.0
Fold 3	93.4	93.4	93.4	93.4	95.9
Fold 4	92.1	92.1	92.1	92.1	96.4
Fold 5	93.3	93.3	93.3	93.3	96.0
Mean	93.0	93.0	93.0	93.0	96.1

Table 4. The results of the RF classifier using five-fold cross-validation.

K-Fold Iteration	Precision %	Recall %	F1-Score %	Testing Accuracy %	Training Accuracy %
Fold 1	96.1	96.1	96.1	96.1	1.0
Fold 2	95.7	95.7	95.7	95.7	1.0
Fold 3	96.1	96.1	96.1	96.1	1.0
Fold 4	95.6	95.6	95.6	95.6	1.0
Fold 5	95.3	95.3	95.3	95.3	1.0
Mean	95.8	95.8	95.8	95.8	1.0

Table 5. The results of the SVM classifier using five-fold cross-validation.

K-Fold Iteration	Precision %	Recall %	F1-Score %	Testing Accuracy %	Training Accuracy %
Fold 1	98.3	98.3	98.3	98.3	98.9
Fold 2	98.5	98.5	98.5	98.5	98.8
Fold 3	98.7	98.7	98.7	98.7	98.9
Fold 4	98.5	98.5	98.5	98.5	98.8
Fold 5	98.1	98.1	98.1	98.1	99.0
Mean	98.4	98.4	98.4	98.4	98.9

Table 6. The results of the AdaBoost classifier using five-fold cross-validation.

K-Fold Iteration	Precision %	Recall %	F1-Score %	Testing Accuracy %	Training Accuracy %
Fold 1	68.3	68.3	68.3	68.3	67.6
Fold 2	66.2	66.2	66.2	66.2	67.5
Fold 3	73.6	73.6	73.6	73.6	73.5
Fold 4	63.8	63.8	63.8	63.8	64.3
Fold 5	69.1	69.1	69.1	69.1	69.5
Mean	68.2	68.2	68.2	68.2	68.5

4. Discussion

In this study, we presented a personal-traits-testing model based on machine-learning techniques that can help organizations and government agencies to select appropriate employees for specific jobs or to form a working team to perform a specific task. The compatibility of team qualities contributes significantly to the success of large businesses and the achievement of their strategic goals. The model was designed based on a standard dataset collected from the responses of individuals worldwide. Machine-learning techniques were used in the data analysis, clustering, and classification. For the clustering task, the k-means algorithm successfully sorted the data into five clusters, each containing similar personal patterns from the participants. These clusters were agreeableness, conscientiousness, extraversion, openness, and neuroticism. To the best of our knowledge, no other study has applied the same idea and dataset. However, some previous studies were identified in the literature review, such as social-identity personality traits based on social-media data [15,21], and in other domains, such as healthcare (using questionnaires [24]) and education [22]. Table 7 shows a comparison of the proposed system's results with those of previous studies. Figure 8 shows ROC of SVM method in cross validation method.

Table 7. Comparison of results and those of previous systems.

References	Method	Accuracy %
Ref. [45]	ANN	85.06
Ref. [46]	ANN	71
Proposed system	SVM	98

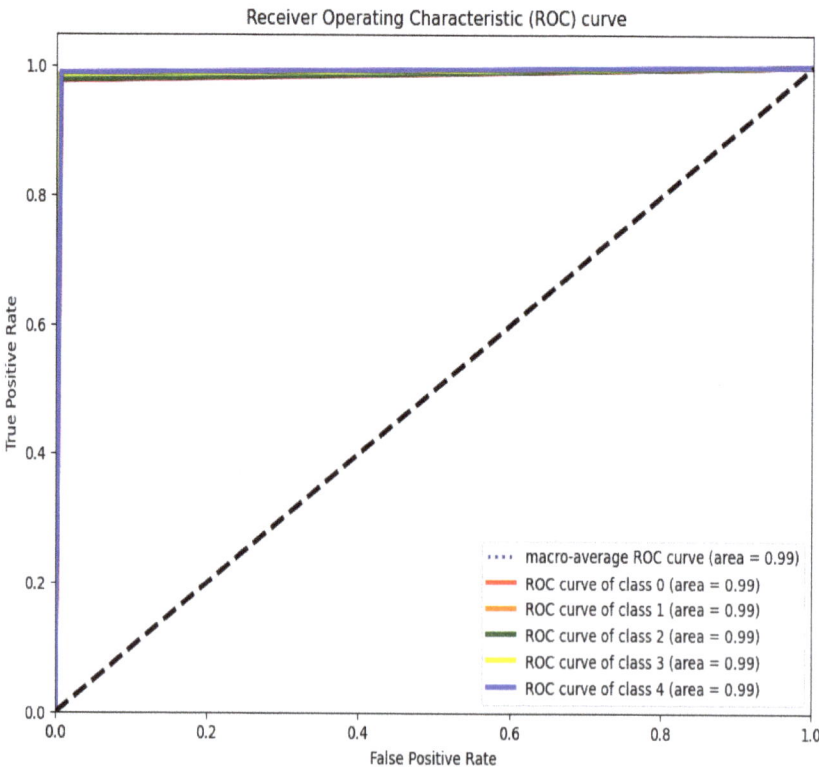

Figure 8. The ROC of the SVM model using five-fold cross-validation.

The application of information technology in the management of human resources has developed steadily in different countries, along with the level of information technology. Human-resource-management information systems have the potential to reduce the amount of information transmitted, as well as the amount of time this requires. Additionally, it has the potential to release human-resource personnel from mundane administrative tasks, and change the mode of service that human-resources departments provide, transforming into a management role involving the provision of decision-making support and solutions

5. Conclusions

This study concluded that behavioral tests must be applied in human-resources management and performance management to motivate qualified employees toward achieving organization's strategic goals. The study analyzed behavioral data collected from 20,000 participants through a publicly available dataset on the Kaggle platform. We obtained the Big Five personality-test results to cluster the participants by type of behavior. Supervised machine-learning models were used to analyze the responses to the questions according to personal traits. The algorithm was able to divide the individuals into a group of clusters; each cluster was a set of similar personality traits.

The findings of the study were as follows:

- The internal correlation test of the groups for every ten questions showed a positive correlation.
- There was a positive relationship between the following four traits: agreeableness, conscientiousness, extraversion, and openness.
- The relationship between one personality trait, neuroticism, and the other four personality traits was negative.
- This test helps to identify participants' psychological and behavioral traits in any domain.
- Companies and organizations prefer participants who can integrate and adapt to their work teams.
- This test can be a source of safety for organizations in preventing violent behavior.

Machine-learning models, such as SVM, RF, KNN, and AdaBoost, were used to classify personalities based on psychological traits, derived from the participants' responses, with satisfactory results. By comparing the evaluation-metrics results, we found that the SVM classifier proved effective and efficient, with an accuracy of 98%. Furthermore, it outperformed the other classifiers in classifying and predicting the participants' personality traits using different categories. Finally, poor performance was evident when using the AdaBoost model.

The proposed personal-traits-testing model can be adopted. Its accuracy rate is high, and it can save time and effort compared to personal interviews and direct questions to determine the characteristics of the candidates. The answers to these questions may be untrue and hide aspects of a candidate's true personality. Organizations can apply this proposed methodology to evaluate employees' personality traits during their work on strategic plans. Achieving the goals that maintain an organization's image requires people with specific personal and behavioral skills. Analyses of user preferences and behavioral predictions based on user data may provide some useful reference points for optimizing information structure and improving service accuracy. These can be learned from the data. However, the OCEAN user-personality-model-identification algorithms still have certain limitations. The machine-learning algorithm is one modern approach with a comparative advantage. This algorithm may be quickly adapted to meet a broad range of directional issues, which makes it a competitive option. When we began to write this paper, one of our primary objectives was to improve the identification process used by the OCEAN personality model via the application of a neural-network approach. The plan for advancing this direction of study is to develop a model based on deep-learning algorithms.

Author Contributions: Conceptualization, M.A.A., Z.A.T.A., S.N.A. and T.H.H.A.; methodology, M.A.A., Z.A.T.A. and S.N.A.; software, Z.A.T.A. and T.H.H.A.; validation, M.A.A., Z.A.T.A., S.A.A. and T.H.H.A.; formal analysis, Z.A.T.A. and S.N.A.; investigation, M.A.A., S.N.A. and T.H.H.A.; resources, M.A.A., Z.A.T.A., S.A.A. and T.H.H.A.; data curation, M.A.A., Z.A.T.A., S.N.A. and

T.H.H.A.; writing—original draft preparation, M.A.A., Z.A.T.A., S.N.A. and T.H.H.A.; writing—review and editing, Z.A.T.A., S.N.A. and T.H.H.A.; visualization, Z.A.T.A., S.N.A. and T.H.H.A.; supervision, Z.A.T.A., S.N.A. and T.H.H.A.; project administration, M.A.A. and T.H.H.A.; funding acquisition, M.A.A. and T.H.H.A. All authors have read and agreed to the pubished version of the manuscript.

Funding: This research and the APC were funded by the Deanship of Scientific Research, Vice Presidency for Graduate Studies and Scientific Research, King Faisal University, Saudi Arabia [Grant No. GRANT2713].

Data Availability Statement: Not applicable.

Acknowledgments: The authors acknowledge the Deanship of Scientific Research, Vice Presidency for Graduate Studies and Scientific Research, King Faisal University, Saudi Arabia [Grant No. GRANT2713].

Conflicts of Interest: The authors declare no conflict of interest.

References

1. Alnamrouti, A.; Rjoub, H.; Ozgit, H. Do Strategic Human Resources and Artificial Intelligence Help to Make Organisations More Sustainable? Evidence from Non-Governmental Organisations. *Sustainability* **2022**, *14*, 7327. [CrossRef]
2. Robbins, S.; van Wynsberghe, A. Our New Artificial Intelligence Infrastructure: Becoming Locked into an Unsustainable Future. *Sustainability* **2022**, *14*, 4829. [CrossRef]
3. Wang, M.; Pan, X. Drivers of Artificial Intelligence and Their Effects on Supply Chain Resilience and Performance: An Empirical Analysis on an Emerging Market. *Sustainability* **2022**, *14*, 16836. [CrossRef]
4. Carmichael, L.; Poirier, S.-M.; Coursaris, C.K.; Léger, P.-M.; Sénécal, S. Users' Information Disclosure Behaviors during Interactions with Chatbots: The Effect of Information Disclosure Nudges. *Appl. Sci.* **2022**, *12*, 12660. [CrossRef]
5. Mahlasela, S.; Chinyamurindi, W.T. Technology-related factors and their influence on turnover intentions: A case of government employees in South Africa. *Electron. J. Inf. Syst. Dev. Ctries.* **2020**, *86*, e1. [CrossRef]
6. Bamiatzi, V.; Bozos, K.; Cavusgil, S.T.; Hult, G.T.M. Revisiting the firm, industry, and country effects on profitability under recessionary and expansion periods: A multilevel analysis. *Strateg. Manag. J.* **2016**, *37*, 1448–1471. [CrossRef]
7. Otero-López, J.M.; Santiago, M.J.; Castro, M.C. Big Five Personality Traits, Coping Strategies and Compulsive Buying in Spanish University Students. *Int. J. Environ. Res. Public Health* **2021**, *18*, 821. [CrossRef]
8. Fernández-Mesa, A.; Alegre, J. Entrepreneurial orientation and export intensity: Examining the interplay of organisational learning and innovation. *Int. Bus. Rev.* **2015**, *24*, 148–156. [CrossRef]
9. Zhu, C.; Liu, A.; Wang, Y. Integrating organisational learning with high-performance work system and entrepreneurial orientation: A moderated mediation framework. *Front. Bus. Res. China* **2019**, *13*, 1–24. [CrossRef]
10. North, K.; Kumta, G. *Knowledge Management: Value Creation through Organizational Learning*; Springer: Cham, Switzerland, 2018.
11. De Raad, B. *The Big Five Personality Factors: The Psycholexical Approach to Personality*; Hogrefe & Huber Publishers: Göttingen, Germany, 2000.
12. John, O.P.; Srivastava, S. The Big-Five Trait Taxonomy: History, Measurement, and Theoretical Perspectives. 1999. Available online: https://personality-project.org/revelle/syllabi/classreadings/john.pdf (accessed on 10 November 2022).
13. Benet-Martínez, V.; John, O.P. Los Cinco Grandes across Cultures and Ethnic Groups: Multitrait-Multimethod Analyses of the Big Five in Spanish and English. *J. Pers. Soc. Psychol.* **1998**, *75*, 729–750. [CrossRef]
14. John, O.P.; Donahue, E.M.; Kentle, R.L. *The Big Five Inventory*; Versions 4a and 54; University of California: Berkeley, CA, USA, 1991.
15. Digman, J.M. Personality Structure: Emergence of the Five Factor Model. *Annu. Rev. Psychol.* **1990**, *41*, 417–440. [CrossRef]
16. Verma, R.; Bandi, S. Challenges of artificial intelligence in human resource management in Indian IT sector. In Proceedings of the XXI Annual International Conference, New Delhi, India, 4–5 January 2020; Available online: https://www.internationalconference.in/XXI_AIC/TS5E/MsRichaVerma.pdf (accessed on 20 November 2022).
17. McRobert, C.J.; Hill, J.C.; Smale, T.; Hay, E.M.; Van der Windt, D.A. A multi-modal recruitment strategy using social media and internet-mediated methods to recruit a multidisciplinary, international sample of clinicians to an online research study. *PLoS ONE* **2018**, *13*, e0200184. [CrossRef]
18. Baron, I.S.; Mustafa; Agustina, H. The challenges of recruitment and selection systems in Indonesia. *J. Manag. Ment Mark. Rev.* **2018**, *3*, 185–192. [CrossRef]
19. Arpaci, I.; Kocadag Unver, T. Moderating Role of Gender in the Relationship between Big Five Personality Traits and Smartphone Addiction. *Psychiatr. Q.* **2020**, *91*, 577–585. [CrossRef]
20. Alamsyah, A.; Dudija, N. Identifying Personality of the New Job Applicants using the Ontology Model on Twitter Data. In Proceedings of the 2nd International Conference on ICT for Rural Development (IC-ICTRuDev), Jogjakarta, Indonesia, 27–28 October 2021; pp. 1–5.
21. Laleh, A.; Shahram, R. Analyzing Facebook activities for personality recognition. In Proceedings of the 16th IEEE international conference on machine learning and applications (ICMLA), Cancun, Mexico, 18–21 December 2017; pp. 960–964.

22. Qin, X.; Liu, Z.; Liu, Y.; Liu, S.; Yang, B.; Yin, L.; Zheng, W. User OCEAN Personality Model Construction Method Using a BP Neural Network. *Electronics* **2022**, *11*, 3022. [CrossRef]
23. John, R.; John, R.; Rao, Z.R. The Big Five personality traits and academic performance. *J. Law Soc. Stud.* **2020**, *2*, 10–19. [CrossRef]
24. Curtis, R.G.; Windsor, T.D.; Soubelet, A. The relationship between Big-5 personality traits and cognitive ability in older adults–a review. *Aging Neuropsychol. Cogn.* **2015**, *22*, 42–71. [CrossRef]
25. Dymecka, J.; Tarczyński, R.; Gerymski, R. Stress in emergency telephone number operators during the COVID-19 pandemic: The role of self-efficacy and Big Five personality traits. *Health Psychol. Rep.* **2022**. Available online: https://www.researchgate.net/publication/361843686_Stress_in_emergency_telephone_number_operators_during_the_COVID-19_pandemic_the_role_of_self-efficacy_and_Big_Five_personality_traits (accessed on 20 December 2022).
26. Muntean, L.M.; Nireștean, A.; Mărușteri, M.; Sima-Comaniciu, A.; Lukacs, E. Occupational Stress and Personality in Medical Doctors from Romania. *Healthcare* **2022**, *10*, 1612. [CrossRef]
27. Chavoshi, P. The Relationship Between the Big-Five Personality Traits and Depressive Symptoms: A Meta-Analysis. Master's Thesis, The University of Western Ontario, London, ON, Canada, 2022. Available online: https://ir.lib.uwo.ca/cgi/viewcontent.cgi?article=11546&context=etd (accessed on 10 November 2022).
28. Aghabayk, K.; Rejali, S.; Shiwakoti, N. The Role of Big Five Personality Traits in Explaining Pedestrian Anger Expression. *Sustainability* **2022**, *14*, 12099. [CrossRef]
29. Xu, L.; Luo, Y.; Wen, X.; Sun, Z.; Chao, C.; Xia, T.; Xu, L. Human Personality Is Associated with Geographical Environment in Mainland China. *Int. J. Environ. Res. Public Health* **2022**, *19*, 10819. [CrossRef] [PubMed]
30. Priyadharshini, S.U. Influence of Big 5 personality traits on the investment decisions of retail investors-an empirical approach. *PalArch's J. Archaeol. Egypt/Egyptol.* **2020**, *17*, 9725–9736.
31. Ludeke, S.G.; Bainbridge, T.F.; Liu, J.; Zhao, K.; Smillie, L.D.; Zettler, I. Using the Big Five Aspect Scales to translate between the HEXACO and Big Five personality models. *J. Personal.* **2019**, *87*, 1025–1038. [CrossRef] [PubMed]
32. Mueller, A.; Claes, L.; Mitchell, J.E.; Wonderlich, S.A.; Crosby, R.D.; de Zwaan, M. Personality Prototypes in Individuals with Compulsive Buying Based on the Big Five Model. *Behav. Res. Ther.* **2010**, *48*, 930–935. [CrossRef] [PubMed]
33. Big Five personality traits. Available online: https://www.123test.com/big-five-personality-theory/ (accessed on 2 November 2022).
34. Big Five Personality Test. Available online: https://openpsychometrics.org/tests/IPIP-BFFM/ (accessed on 28 October 2022).
35. Big Five Personality Test. Available online: https://www.kaggle.com/datasets/tunguz/big-five-personality-test (accessed on 24 October 2022).
36. Almaiah, M.A.; Almomani, O.; Alsaaidah, A.; Al-Otaibi, S.; Bani-Hani, N.; Hwaitat, A.K.A.; Al-Zahrani, A.; Lutfi, A.; Awad, A.B.; Aldhyani, T.H.H. Performance Investigation of Principal Component Analysis for Intrusion Detection System Using Different Support Vector Machine Kernels. *Electronics* **2022**, *11*, 3571. [CrossRef]
37. Al-Nefaie, A.H.; Aldhyani, T.H.H. Bitcoin Price Forecasting and Trading: Data Analytics Approaches. *Electronics* **2022**, *11*, 4088. [CrossRef]
38. Ibrahim, S.; Nazir, S.; Velastin, S.A. Feature Selection Using Correlation Analysis and Principal Component Analysis for Accurate Breast Cancer Diagnosis. *J. Imaging* **2021**, *7*, 225. [CrossRef]
39. Aldhyani, T.H.H.; Alkahtani, H. Artificial Intelligence Algorithm-Based Economic Denial of Sustainability Attack Detection Systems: Cloud Computing Environments. *Sensors* **2022**, *22*, 4685. [CrossRef]
40. Granato, D.; Santos, J.S.; Escher, G.B.; Ferreira, B.L.; Maggio, R.M. Use of principal component analysis (PCA) and hierarchical cluster analysis (HCA) for multivariate association between bioactive compounds and functional properties in foods: A critical perspective. *Trends Food Sci. Technol.* **2018**, *72*, 83–90. [CrossRef]
41. Aldhyani, T.H.; Alshebami, A.S.A.; Alzahrani, M.Y. Soft Computing Model to Predict Chronic Diseases. *J. Inf. Sci. Eng.* **2020**, *36*, 365–376.
42. Al-Adhaileh, M.H.; Aldhyani, T.H.H. Artificial intelligence framework for modeling and predicting crop yield to enhance food security in Saudi Arabia. *PeerJ Comput. Sci.* **2022**, *2022*, e1104. [CrossRef]
43. Alkahtani, H.; Aldhyani, T.H.H. Developing Cybersecurity Systems Based on Machine Learning and Deep Learning Algorithms for Protecting Food Security Systems: Industrial Control Systems. *Electronics* **2022**, *11*, 1717. [CrossRef]
44. Ahmed, M.; Seraj, R.; Islam, S.M.S. The k-means Algorithm: A Comprehensive Survey and Performance Evaluation. *Electronics* **2020**, *9*, 1295. [CrossRef]
45. Kodinariya, T.M.; Makwana, P.R. Review on determining number of Cluster in K-Means Clustering. *Int. J. Adv. Res. Comput. Sci. Manag. Stud.* **2013**, *1*, 90–95.
46. Zeng, Z.; Qi, L. "Internet + Artificial Intelligence" Human Resource Information Management System Construction Innovation and Research. *Math. Probl. Eng.* **2021**, *2021*, 5585753. [CrossRef]

Disclaimer/Publisher's Note: The statements, opinions and data contained in all publications are solely those of the individual author(s) and contributor(s) and not of MDPI and/or the editor(s). MDPI and/or the editor(s) disclaim responsibility for any injury to people or property resulting from any ideas, methods, instructions or products referred to in the content.

Article

MRBERT: Pre-Training of Melody and Rhythm for Automatic Music Generation

Shuyu Li [1] and Yunsick Sung [2],*

[1] Department of Multimedia Engineering, Graduate School, Dongguk University–Seoul, Seoul 04620, Republic of Korea
[2] Department of Multimedia Engineering, Dongguk University–Seoul, Seoul 04620, Republic of Korea
* Correspondence: sung@dongguk.edu; Tel.: +82-2-2260-3338

Abstract: Deep learning technology has been extensively studied for its potential in music, notably for creative music generation research. Traditional music generation approaches based on recurrent neural networks cannot provide satisfactory long-distance dependencies. These approaches are typically designed for specific tasks, such as melody and chord generation, and cannot generate diverse music simultaneously. Pre-training is used in natural language processing to accomplish various tasks and overcome the limitation of long-distance dependencies. However, pre-training is not yet widely used in automatic music generation. Because of the differences in the attributes of language and music, traditional pre-trained models utilized in language modeling cannot be directly applied to music fields. This paper proposes a pre-trained model, MRBERT, for multitask-based music generation to learn melody and rhythm representation. The pre-trained model can be applied to music generation applications such as web-based music composers that includes the functions of melody and rhythm generation, modification, completion, and chord matching after being fine-tuned. The results of ablation experiments performed on the proposed model revealed that under the evaluation metrics of HITS@k, the pre-trained MRBERT considerably improved the performance of the generation tasks by 0.09–13.10% and 0.02–7.37%, compared to the usage of RNNs and the original BERT, respectively.

Keywords: automatic music generation; generative pre-training; embedding; representation learning

MSC: 68T99

1. Introduction

In the past decade, artificial intelligence has made breakthroughs due to the introduction of deep learning, which allows the use of various artificial intelligence models in different fields. Representation learning has been in the spotlight because it significantly reduces the amount of data required to train a model through semi-supervised and self-supervised learning, and, more importantly, it overcomes the limitations of traditional supervised learning that requires annotated training data. Representation learning has achieved excellent results in computer vision [1], natural language processing [2], and music generation [3,4].

Deep learning-based music technology has been extensively studied for its potential in music. This includes music generation [3,4], music classification [5,6], melody recognition [7,8], and music evaluation [9,10]. These functions rely on learning and summarizing knowledge from music corpus, rather than obtaining it from music theory. Among them, music generation research is notable because it involves performing a creative task. Music generation tasks can be categorized into three categories, namely autoregressive [11], conditional [12], and sequence-to-sequence (Seq2Seq) generation [13]. In autoregressive generation, the current value is predicted based on the information from previous values. For music, each predicted note becomes a consideration when predicting the following notes, and a piece of music can be generated by looping this process. In conditional generation, contextual information is used to predict the missing value. When predicting the missing values in random positions of music, contextual information from both left and right directions should be considered. Thus, music completion can be realized. In Seq2Seq generation, a novel sequence based on the given sequence is generated. Seq2Seq generation involves two processes: understanding the given sequence and then generating a new sequence subsequently using the understood content. Seq2Seq generation can be applied in music to generate matching chords based on a given melody.

The above-mentioned traditional music generation models are typically designed to accomplish only one of the aforementioned three categories and cannot be generalized to other tasks. Inspired by natural language modeling, music generation requires a model that can be applied to multitasking without requiring large training resources [2]. Bidirectional encoder representations from transformers (BERT) [14] is a language representation model in natural language modeling that is used to pre-train deep directional representations from unlabeled text by jointly conditioning on both left and right contextual information in all layers. The pre-trained model can be fine-tuned with only an additional output layer to create state-of-the-art models for numerous tasks without substantial task-specific architecture modifications. Therefore, this paper will also focus on the application of representation models in music generation.

Compared to traditional music generation models, pre-trained model-based automatic music generation models exhibit several advantages. First, pre-trained models can learn better representations of music than traditional music generation models. Traditional music generation models utilize PianoRoll [15] as the representation, which is similar to one-hot encoding. Therefore, PianoRoll exhibits the same sparse matrix problem as one-hot encoding, and contextual information is ignored. However, music in the pre-trained model is mapped into n-dimensional spaces, which is a non-sparse representation by considering the contextual information from two directions [14]. Second, pre-trained models can handle long-distance dependencies. Traditional models [16–18] of music generation typically utilize recurrent neural networks (RNNs) and their variants, such as long short-term memory (LSTM) and gate recurrent unit (GRU), to generate music because of their ability to memorize temporal information. However, RNNs exhibit vanishing gradients caused by backpropagation through time (BPTT) and cannot handle long-distance dependences. Although LSTM and GRU alleviate the long-distance dependency problem by adding memory cells and gates, their effect is limited because of BPTT [19]. BERT, based on the multihead attention mechanism, can link long-distance notes and consider global features [20]. Finally, pre-trained models can process data in parallel, whereas RNN-like models run recurrently, which not only causes vanishing gradients but also wastes computing resources. Because the transformers in BERT run in parallel mode, all tokens in the sequence are embedded into them without waiting for the data of the previous time step to be processed [20]. However, applying traditional natural language pre-trained models directly for music representation learning cannot provide the desired results. The problem is that there is no concept of rhythm in natural language, but the rhythm is as important as the melody in music. Therefore, an approach for learning musical representation that takes into account both the melody and rhythm is needed for use in music generation.

In this paper, a modification of BERT, namely MRBERT, is proposed for the pre-training of the melody and rhythm for fine-tuning music generation. In pre-training, the melody and rhythm are embedded separately. For exchanging the information of the melody and rhythm, semi-cross attention instead of merging, as performed in traditional methods, is used, which prevents features loss. In fine-tuning, the following three generation tasks are designed: autoregressive, conditional, and Seq2Seq. Thus, a pre-trained model is fine-tuned with the output layers corresponding to the three types of generation tasks to realize multitask music generation.

The contributions of this paper are as follows: (1) A novel generative pre-trained model based on melody and rhythm, namely MRBERT, is proposed for multitask music generation, including autoregressive and conditional generation, as well as Seq2Seq generation. (2) In pre-training for representation learning, the melody and rhythm are considered separately, based on the assumption that they have strong dependencies on themselves and weak dependencies between each other. Experimental results have also shown that this assumption is reasonable and can be widely applied to related research. (3) The proposed MRBERT with three generation tasks allows users to generate melodies and rhythms from scratch through interaction with the user, or to modify or complete existing melodies and rhythms, or even to generate matching chords based on existing melodies and rhythms.

2. Related Work

This section describes BERT [14] first as a well-known representation learning model and then two music representation learning studies, MusicBERT [21] and MidiBERT [22], based on BERT are introduced.

BERT is a language representation model that is designed to learn deep bidirectional representations from unlabeled text. It did this by conditioning on both the left and right context in all layers of the model. BERT is able to achieve state-of-the-art results on a wide range of natural language processing tasks, including question answering and language inference, by being fine-tuned with only one additional output layer. It has been shown to perform particularly well on a number of benchmarks, including the GLUE benchmark, the MultiNLI dataset, and the SQuAD question answering dataset. The main contribution of BERT is that it proves the importance of bidirectional pre-training for representation learning. Unlike previous language modeling approaches that used a unidirectional language model for pre-training [2] and used a shallow concatenation of independently trained left-to-right and right-to-left language modeling (LM) [23], BERT used a masked language model (MLM) to enable pre-trained deep bidirectional representations.

Due to BERT's success in natural language processing tasks, researchers have started to apply representation learning to music data. Two representative studies in this area are MusicBERT and MidiBERT.

MusicBERT is a large-scale pre-trained model for music understanding and consists of large symbolic music corpus containing more than 1 million pieces of music and songs. MusicBERT designed several mechanisms, including OctupleMIDI encoding and a bar-level masking strategy, to enhance the pre-training of symbolic music data. Furthermore, four music understanding-based tasks were designed, two of which were generation tasks, melody completion and accompaniment suggestion; the other two were classification tasks, genre and style classification.

MidiBERT used a smaller corpus than MusicBERT and focused on piano music. For the token representation, it used the beat-based revamped MIDI-derived events [24] token representation and borrowed Compound words [25] representation to reduce the length of the token sequences. Furthermore, MidiBERT established a benchmark for symbolic music understanding, including not only note-level tasks, melody extraction, and velocity prediction but also sequence-level tasks, composer classification, and emotion classification.

Unlike these two studies, the proposed MRBERT model is a pre-trained model that can be used for music generation tasks. In the MRBERT, a music corpus called OpenEWLD [26], which is a leadsheet-based corpus that contains the necessary information for music generation, such as the melody, rhythm, and chords, is used. The MRBERT differs from other models in that melody and rhythm are divided into separate token sequences. Additionally, the embedding layer of the traditional BERT and the attention layer in its transformer are modified to better fit the pre-training of the melody and rhythm. Finally, the MRBERT was designed to differentiate from the prediction and classification tasks of traditional methods by using three generation tasks, which are used to evaluate the performance of the pre-trained model for music generation.

3. Automatic Music Generation Based on MRBERT

In this paper, the MRBERT is proposed to learn the representations of the melody and rhythm for automatic music generation. First, the token representation is described. The structure and the pre-training of the MRBERT is explained and, finally, the strategies of fine-tuning are described.

3.1. Token Representation

The melody, rhythm, and chords are extracted from OpenEWLD [26] music corpus for pre-training and fine-tuning. The OpenEWLD music corpus consists of songs in the leadsheet, as displayed in Figure 1A. In Figure 1B, the leadsheet is converted from MusicXML to events through Python library music21. Figure 1C reveals that events include Instruments, Keys, Timesignatures, Measures, ChordSymbols, and Notes, where only information related to the melody, rhythm, and chords are extracted. For example, "G4(2/4)" indicates that the pitch of the note is G in the fourth octave, and the duration of the note is 2/4. The next step is to separate the melody and rhythm sequences, as displayed in Figure 1D. The chord sequences are extracted from ChordSymbols to prepare for the Seq2Seq generation task in the fine-tuning, as presented in Figure 1E. For example, "C" represents the chord that continues with the melody until the next chord occurs.

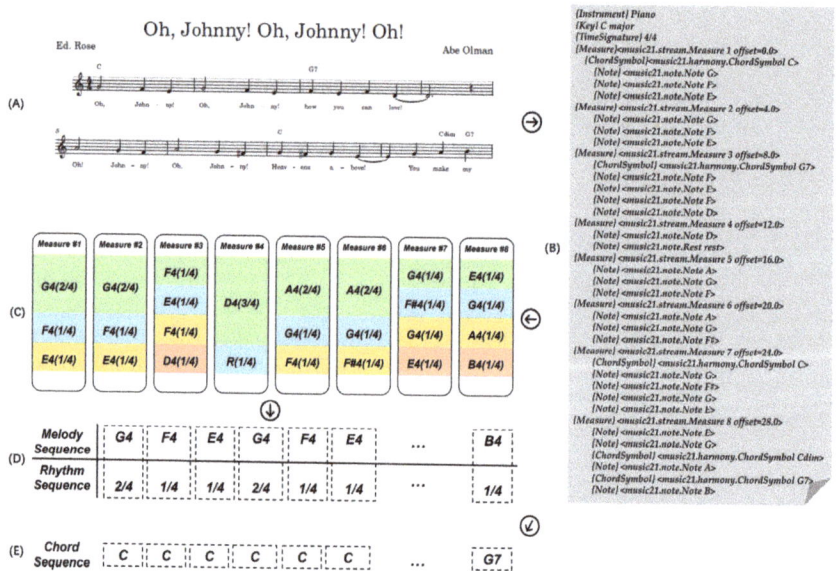

Figure 1. Pipeline of token representation. (**A**) A example leadsheet in music corpus; (**B**) The events converted from MusicXML; (**C**) Extracted events related to the melody, rhythm and chords; (**D**) Generated melody sequence and rhythm sequence; (**E**) Generated chord sequence.

3.2. Pre-Training of MRBERT

The MRBERT is a pre-trained model for the learning representations of the melody and rhythm. As displayed in Figure 2, the melody ($m_1, m_2, \_, \ldots, m_n$) and rhythm ($r_1, r_2, \_, \ldots, r_n$) sequences are input to the embedding layers, where the "$\_$" represents the random masked tokens. The tokens of the melody sequences and rhythm sequences are embedded by the corresponding token embedding layer. The position embedding layer, which is shared by the melody and rhythm, adds the position feature on them. Through the embedding layers, the melody embedding e^M and the rhythm embedding e^R are obtained. Next, e^M and e^R are input to the corresponding transformer, which exchanges information through semi-cross attention. Semi-cross attention is proposed to realize the information exchange between the melody and rhythm. As presented in formula (1), the cross query of e^M is obtained from the dot-production of the query of the melody q^M with the activated query of the rhythm q^R by using softmax. The use of the key k^M and value v^M is similar to that of the self-attention. For the rhythm, the query of the melody q^M is required for calculating the cross query of e^R. Finally, the melody hidden states h^M and rhythm hidden states h^R output by the transformers are passed through the melody prediction layer and rhythm prediction layer to predict the masked melody m' and rhythm r'.

$$Semi\ Cross\ Attention^M = softmax\left(\frac{q^M \cdot (softmax(q^R))k^{MT}}{\sqrt{d_k}}\right)v^M$$

and (1)

$$Semi\ Cross\ Attention^R = softmax\left(\frac{q^R \cdot (softmax(q^M))k^{RT}}{\sqrt{d_k}}\right)v^R$$

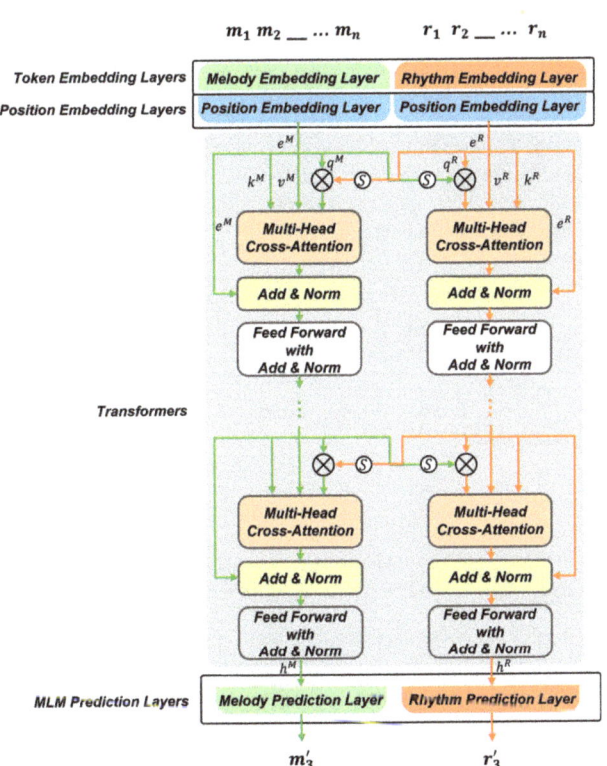

Figure 2. Pipeline of pre-training of MRBERT.

The pre-training strategy of this paper refers to the MLM proposed by BERT, which follows that 15% of the tokens in the sequence are randomly masked: (1) 80% of the selected tokens are replaced by MASK; (2) 10% are replaced by randomly selected tokens; (3) the remaining 10% remain unchanged. Furthermore, to enhance the performance of the pre-training, this paper refers to BERT-like models and other related studies, drops the next sentence prediction pre-training task, and uses dynamic masking [27].

3.3. Fine-Tuning of Generation Tasks

To address the diverse generation tasks, the MRBERT is fine-tuned with three downstream tasks, namely autoregressive, conditional, and Seq2Seq generation. Furthermore, after fine-tuning for each task, joint generation can be achieved by executing the three generation methods simultaneously.

3.3.1. Autoregressive Generation Task

To accomplish the autoregressive generation task, its generation pattern should be known, which can be summarized as a unidirectional generation similar to a Markov chain [28] $P(t_i|t_1, t_2, t_3, \ldots, t_{i-1})$, where the probability of the token t_i depends on t_1 to t_{i-1}. Autoregressive generation reveals that the tokens are predicted in order from left to right, and the current token is predicted based on the previous tokens. First, <BOS> (the beginning of the sequence, which is a special token in vocabulary) is passed into the MRBERT. Next, the output layers, which are a pair of fully connected layers, predict the melody and rhythm based on the hidden state from the MRBERT. Finally, the predicted melody and rhythm are used to calculate the cross-entropy loss for backpropagation. When backpropagation ends, the input token sequences are incremented by one time step, and the model predicts the melody and rhythm of the next time step until <EOS> (the end of the sequence, a special token corresponding to <BOS>) is generated. The ground truth label data are easily obtained by shifting the input sequences to the right by one time step. The pre-trained model and output layer continuously shorten the gap between the prediction and the label data through fine-tuning. After fine-tuning, whenever the melody and rhythm are generated, generations are added to the end of the sequence to form a new input, as displayed in Figure 3.

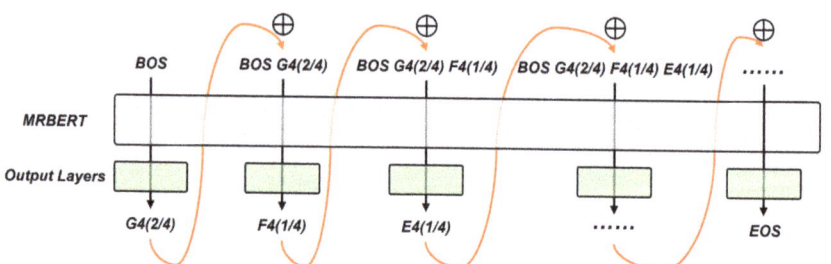

Figure 3. Pipeline of autoregressive generation. The orange arrows represent the predicted melody and rhythm should be continuously added to the end of the input.

3.3.2. Conditional Generation Task

Unlike in autoregressive generation, in conditional generation, not only previous tokens but also future tokens are considered when predicting unknown tokens. The model should consider the bidirectional contextual information of the unknown tokens. To realize this task, a generation pattern such as a denoising autoencoder [29] is used, $P(t_j|t_1, t_2, \ldots, t_{j-1}, t_{j+1}, \ldots, t_i)$, where the unknown token t_j should be predicted based on the known tokens. Fine-tuning for conditional generation is highly similar to pre-training. However, since multiple tokens are masked, when predicting one of the tokens, it is assumed to be independent of the other masked tokens. To address this problem, shorter sequences are used and only a pair of melody and rhythm tokens is masked in fine-tuning. The cross-entropy loss is calculated by the predictions (melody or rhythm) and ground truth labels, which are then used for fine-tuning. After fine-tuning, the MRBERT and the output layer of the conditional generation fill in the missing parts according to the contextual information obtained from the given melody and rhythm as displayed in Figure 4.

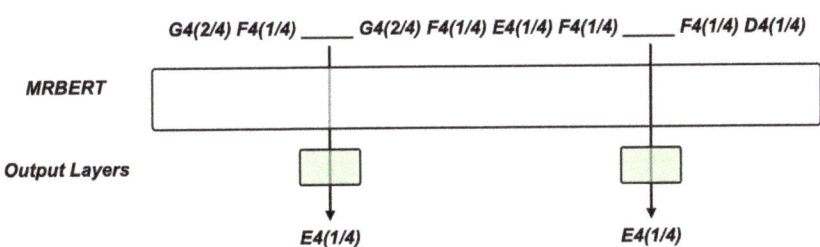

Figure 4. Pipeline of conditional generation. The underline represents the missing part of the music.

3.3.3. Seq2Seq Generation Task

When the melody and rhythm are created, chords should be added to make it sound less monotonous. This generation pattern can be summarized as $P(t_1, t_2, \ldots, t_i \mid t'_1, t'_2, \ldots, t'_i)$, where t' represents the given tokens, and t represents the tokens that should be predicted. The probability of t for the position 1 to i is based on the given t' of 1 to i. In fine-tuning, the melody and rhythm sequences are input into the MRBERT, and the chords of the corresponding position are predicted by the output layer of the Seq2Seq generation. The cross-entropy loss calculated from the predicted chords and ground truth label data is used for fine-tuning. After fine-tuning, the MRBERT can accept the melody and rhythm, and subsequently generate chords through the output layer of the Seq2Seq generation, as displayed in Figure 5. The continuous output of the same chord symbol indicates that the same chord is continuing until a different symbol appears.

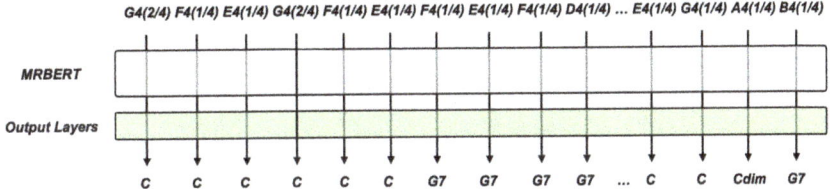

Figure 5. Pipeline of Seq2Seq generation. Melody and rhythm can be of any length, and the length of the generated chords vary accordingly.

3.3.4. Joint Generation

Users can use the MRBERT with three generation tasks interactively, as displayed in Figure 6. A simulated use case reveals how the three generation approaches operate simultaneously. First, the melody and rhythm can be generated under the autoregressive generation task. Next, the user can adjust the tokens in the generated melody and rhythm through conditional generation. Finally, the chords are matched to the generated melody and rhythm through the Seq2Seq generation task.

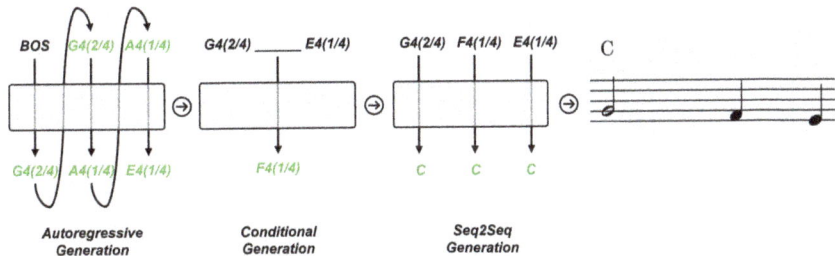

Figure 6. Human–interactive use case of automatic music generation.

Among the predictions provided under the aforementioned three tasks, in addition to the prediction with the highest probability, other candidates and their corresponding probabilities are also given because, in music, a fixed answer rarely exists. Although the high-probability prediction is the most reasonable for analyzing after the model has learned the music corpus, it may not be the most appropriate. Users can choose the candidate they think is the most suitable.

4. Experiments

The MRBERT was first trained to convergence through the pre-training task MLM. Next, ablation experiments were conducted on three generation tasks based on the pre-trained MRBERT. BERT, which is a traditional language pre-trained model, was used as the baseline for the ablation experiments.

4.1. Dataset

The EWLD (Enhanced Wikifonia Leadsheet Dataset) is a dataset of music leadsheets containing various metadata about composers, works, lyrics, and features. It is designed specifically for musicological and research purposes. OpenEWLD [26] is a dataset extracted from EWLD, containing only public domain leadsheets, which is used as the dataset for training in this paper. As shown in Figure 1, each leadsheet contains the melody, rhythm, and chords required for training. A total of 502 leadsheets from different composers are included in OpenEWLD, and 90% of these were selected for training, with the remaining 10% used for evaluation.

4.2. Experimental Environment

The ablation experiment includes *w/o cross-attn.* (BERT + separate embedding), which used separate embedding and original self-attention instead of semi-cross attention; *w/o separate embed.* (BERT), that is, the melody and rhythm shared a common embedding layer and only used self-attention (*w/o* means "without"). Furthermore, experimental results on RNNs (and BiRNNs) without any pre-training techniques were also listed to detail the effect of pre-training. HITS@k [21] (k = 1, 3, 5, and 10), which can calculate the proportion of the correct answer included in the k candidates, was used as the evaluation metrics. HITS@k was calculated as shown in formula (2), where n represents the number of samples; $\mathbb{I}(\cdot)$ is an indicator function that returns 1 if the rank of the correct answer is less than k, and 0 otherwise.

$$HITS@k = \frac{1}{n}\sum_{i=1}^{n}\mathbb{I}(rank_i \leq k) \qquad (2)$$

Table 1 presents the hyperparameters of the MRBERT (with ablation model) in pre-training and fine-tuning. During pre-training, most of the hyperparameters were set to the same values as those in RoBERTa-base [27], with slight differences in the *Number of Layers*, *Learning Rate Decay*, *Batch Size*, *Max Steps*, and *Warmup Steps*. The *Number of Layers* in the MRBERT was set to 6×2 because it has two sets of transformer blocks corresponding to the melody and rhythm separately, while ensuring that the number of parameters in the model is on the same level as in the ablation experiments. In terms of the *Learning Rate Decay*, *power* was used rather than linear, that is to make the change in the learning rate smoother and more conducive to convergence. While the settings of the *Batch Size*, *Max Steps*, and *Warmup Steps* were adjusted according to the music corpus used.

Table 1. Hyperparameters for pre-training and fine-tuning of MRBERT (with ablation model).

Parameters	MRBERT	w/o Cross-Attn.	w/o Separate Embed.
[1] Number of Layers	6×2 [3]	12	12
Hidden size	768	768	768
FFN inner hidden size	3072	3072	3072
Attention heads	12	12	12
Attention head size	64	64	64
Dropout	0.1	0.1	0.1
Batch Size	32	32	32
Weight Decay	0.01	0.01	0.01
Max Steps	10 k	10 k	10 k
Warmup Steps	1 k	1 k	1 k
Learning Rate Decay	power	power	power
Adam ϵ	1×10^{-6}	1×10^{-6}	1×10^{-6}
Adam β_1	0.9	0.9	0.9
Adam β_2	0.98	0.98	0.98
[2] Melody Vocab Size	68 + 4 = 72 [4]	68 + 4 = 72	-
Rhythm Vocab Size	17 + 4 = 21	17 + 4 = 21	-
Melody + Rhythm Vocab Size	-	-	68 + 17 + 4 = 89
Chord Vocab Size	795 + 4 = 799	795 + 4 = 799	795 + 4 = 799

[1] Hyperparameters for pre-training. [2] Hyperparameters for fine-tuning. [3] 6 transformer layers of melody and 6 transformer layers of rhythm. [4] 4 represents the number of special tokens: <BOS>, <EOS>, <UNK>, <PAD>.

In fine-tuning, the *Melody Vocab Size*, *Rhythm Vocab Size*, and *Chord Vocab Size* determine the dimension of the probability distribution given by the output layer. The melody and rhythm have 72 and 21 candidates, respectively, which contain four special tokens (<BOS>, <EOS>, <UNK>, <PAD>). In the ablation experiment of *w/o separate embed.*, since the melody and rhythm share an embedding layer, the number of candidates is 89. Furthermore, the number of chord candidates reached 799.

4.3. Results of Autoregressive Generation

When evaluating autoregressive generation, the pre-trained MRBERT with the output layer of the autoregressive generation task predicts the next melody and rhythm at each time step based on the previous. Figure 7 displays the generated melody and rhythm.

Figure 7. Leadsheets of the generated melody sequence.

Table 2 presents the generated melody and rhythm, and the probabilities of the predictions at each time step. The top prediction of the rhythm occupies a higher proportion, whereas the probabilities of all the melody predictions are balanced. The model is more confident in the rhythm prediction. This result is consistent with the analysis results of the music data. Music typically has obvious rhythm patterns, whereas the progression of the melody is complex and changeable.

Table 2. Details of autoregressive generation.

Time Step	Pitch	Probabilities of Melody				Rhythm	Probabilities of Rhythm			
1	<BOS>					<BOS>				
2	Rest	Rest:0.100	G4: 0.098	F4: 0.092	D4: 0.089	1/4	1/4: 0.309	1/8: 0.263	1/2: 0.146	1/16: 0.054
3	A4	A4: 0.111	G4:0.104	D4: 0.095	Rest: 0.095	1/4	1/4: 0.519	1/8: 0.205	1/2: 0.114	3/4: 0.046
4	G4	G4: 0.127	E4: 0.114	A4: 0.087	F4: 0.079	1/4	1/4: 0.501	1/8: 0.202	1/4: 0.104	3/4: 0.054
5	E4	E4: 0.132	A4: 0.098	F4: 0.081	D4: 0.072	1/8	1/8: 0.364	1/4: 0.364	1/2: 0.097	3/4: 0.070
6	G4	G4: 0.161	A4: 0.153	D4: 0.079	B4: 0.069	1/8	1/8: 0.427	1/4: 0.356	1/2: 0.073	3/8: 0.042
7	A4	A4: 0.187	E4: 0.146	B4: 0.080	D4: 0.077	1/4	1/4: 0.423	1/8: 0.398	1/2: 0.065	3/8: 0.037
8	E4	E4: 0.152	A4: 0.136	G4: 0.125	D4: 0.104	1/8	1/8: 0.465	1/4: 0.308	1/2: 0.076	3/4: 0.049
9	G4	G4: 0.157	E4: 0.147	A4: 0.118	D4: 0.112	1/8	1/8: 0.412	1/4: 0.313	1/2: 0.072	3/8: 0.061
10	A4	A4: 0.164	D4: 0.100	E4: 0.089	C5: 0.066	1/8	1/8: 0.355	1/4: 0.344	1/2: 0.110	3/8: 0.056
11	C5	C5: 0.125	G4: 0.107	D4: 0.093	F4: 0.087	1/8	1/8: 0.385	1/4: 0.370	1/2: 0.112	3/8: 0.038
12	G4	G4: 0.177	A4: 0.148	E4: 0.139	D4: 0.088	1/8	1/8: 0.569	1/4: 0.267	1/2: 0.056	3/8: 0.045
13	A4	A4: 0.163	E4: 0.113	D4: 0.106	Rest: 0.086	1/8	1/8: 0.405	1/4: 0.338	1/2: 0.071	3/8: 0.048
14	E4	E4: 0.131	A4: 0.108	F4: 0.085	D4: 0.074	1/4	1/4: 0.453	1/8: 0.319	1/2: 0.082	3/8: 0.029
15	F4	F4: 0.148	A4: 0.102	G4: 0.090	C5: 0.086	1/8	1/8: 0.497	1/4: 0.263	1/2: 0.075	3/4: 0.046
16	G4	G4: 0.212	A4: 0.142	E4: 0.116	D4: 0.088	1/8	1/8: 0.519	1/4: 0.259	1/2: 0.082	3/8: 0.031
17	A4	A4: 0.156	E4: 0.116	D4: 0.088	F4: 0.076	1/8	1/8: 0.445	1/4: 0.349	1/2: 0.056	3/8: 0.039
18	F4	F4: 0.144	E4: 0.104	G4: 0.087	C5: 0.079	1/8	1/8: 0.452	1/4: 0.286	1/2: 0.093	3/8: 0.045
19	G4	G4: 0.148	A4: 0.134	E4: 0.103	D4: 0.099	1/8	1/8: 0.489	1/4: 0.329	1/2: 0.065	3/8: 0.034
20	E4	E4: 0.139	A4: 0.120	C5: 0.093	F4: 0.077	1/8	1/8: 0.495	1/4: 0.296	1/2: 0.082	3/8: 0.041

Table 3 presents the ablation experimental results of HITS@k in the autoregressive generation task. For the melody prediction, in HITS@k (k = 1, 3, 5, and 10), the MRBERT achieved the average of 51.70%, 2.77% higher than *w/o cross-attn.*, and 3.65% higher than *w/o separated embed.*, and 7.94% higher than the RNN. For the rhythm prediction, it achieved the average of 81.79%, 0.37% higher than *w/o cross-attn.*, and 0.78% higher than *w/o separated embed.*, and 2.56% higher than the RNN.

Table 3. Ablation experimental results of the autoregressive generation task.

Model	HITS@1 (%)		HITS@3 (%)		HITS@5 (%)		HITS@10 (%)	
	Mel.	Rhy.	Mel.	Rhy.	Mel.	Rhy.	Mel.	Rhy.
MRBERT	15.87	51.53	42.03	83.01	61.53	92.81	87.36	99.81
w/o cross-attn.	14.74	51.44	38.96	82.65	57.45	91.88	84.58	99.80
w/o separate embed.	14.27	51.16	38.14	82.17	55.90	90.91	83.88	99.79
RNN	12.51	48.24	33.60	79.28	50.28	89.67	78.63	99.72

The experimental results revealed that the MRBERT outperformed the models of the ablation experiment in all metrics, especially in the melody prediction. Since *w/o cross-attn.* utilized separate embedding, the performance is slightly higher than that of *w/o separated embed.* Furthermore, pre-training considerably improved the prediction of the melody and rhythm.

4.4. Results of Conditional Generation

In the conditional generation, the melody and rhythm dropped at random positions were used as the evaluation data. The pre-trained MRBERT with the output layers of the conditional generation predicted the missing part of the melody and rhythm based on a given melody and rhythm. Figure 8 displays the predictions of the model and correct answers for the missing parts of the head, middle, and tail of a piece of music. The leadsheet reveals that the missing part in the middle of the bar (or measure) could be easily predicted, but misjudgments occurred at the position at which the bar was switched.

Figure 8. Leadsheets of conditional generated results and reference.

Table 4 presents the details of the predictions in Figure 8. The model presents strong confidence in the rhythm prediction with a high accuracy, whereas the probabilities of the melody candidates did not differ considerably. Although the model predicted *F4* as *G4*, *F4* appeared as the second candidate immediately after. Furthermore, the rhythm *1/8* was accurately predicted at this time but the probability of the first candidate did not have an absolute advantage because, during the bar switching stage, the prediction of the rhythm fluctuates, which is a normal phenomenon.

Table 4. Details of conditional generation.

Masked Pitch Sequence	Probabilities of Pitch	Masked Rhythm Sequence	Probabilities of Rhythm
<BOS>, D4, E-4 [1], F4, G4, …	E-4: 0.276; G4: 0.130; B-4: 0.118; A-4: 0.114; F4: 0.087; Rest: 0.069	<BOS>, 1/6, 1/6, 1/6, 1/2, …	1/6: 0.626; 3/16: 0.098; 1/4: 0.094; 1/2: 0.048
…, C5, B4, A4, G4, F#4, …	A4: 0.229; Rest: 0.164; G4: 0.160; C5: 0.141; B4: 0.096; D5: 0.033	…, 1/8, 1/8, 1/8, 1/8, 1/8, …	1/8: 0.785; 1/4: 0.109; 3/8: 0.040; 1/2: 0.038
…, G4, F4, F4, F4, <EOS>	G4: 0.280; F4 [2]: 0.127; A4: 0.116; E4: 0.105; D4: 0.086; F#4: 0.083	…, 3/8, 1/8, 1/2, 1/2, <EOS>	1/8: 0.280; 1/2: 0.197; 1/4: 0.086; 3/8: 0.080

[1] The underline "__" indicates the covered pitch or rhythm. [2] Model predicted G4, but the correct answer is F4.

Table 5 presents the ablation experimental results of HITS@k in the conditional generation task. For the melody prediction, in HITS@k (k = 1, 3, 5, and 10), the MRBERT achieved the average of 54.86%, 1.49% higher than *w/o cross-attn.*, and 5.22% higher than *w/o separated embed.*, and 9.95% higher than the BiRNN. For the rhythm prediction, it achieved the average of 81.85%, 0.55% higher than *w/o cross-attn.*, and 2.09% higher than *w/o separated embed.*, and 3.16% higher than the BiRNN.

Table 5. Ablation experimental results of the conditional generation task.

Model	HITS@1 (%)		HITS@3 (%)		HITS@5 (%)		HITS@10 (%)	
	Mel.	Rhy.	Mel.	Rhy.	Mel.	Rhy.	Mel.	Rhy.
MRBERT	18.67	51.14	45.86	82.78	65.05	93.69	89.84	99.79
w/o cross-attn.	18.07	50.93	43.94	82.02	63.35	92.55	88.10	99.69
w/o separate embed.	15.69	48.61	40.27	80.11	57.68	90.73	84.91	99.57
BiRNN	13.07	48.11	34.91	78.48	51.95	89.03	79.71	99.12

The experimental results revealed that the MRBERT outperformed the other ablation models, and the accuracy of the rhythm prediction was higher than that of the other models. Compared to the autoregressive generation, since information from two directions was considered in the conditional generation, the accuracy was slightly higher.

4.5. Results of Seq2Seq Generation

In the Seq2Seq generation, the melody with the chords was used as the evaluation data. Figure 9 shows an example of the real chords and predicted chords based on the pre-trained MRBERT with the output layer of the Seq2Seq generation. The predicted chords contained "F," "BbM," and "C7." They were all included in the real chords.

Figure 9. Leadsheets of given melody sequence with generated chords and reference chords.

Table 6 presents the ablation experimental results of HITS@k in the Seq2Seq generation task. The MRBERT achieved the average of 49.56%, 0.61% higher than *w/o cross-attn.*, and 1.83% higher than *w/o separated embed.*, and 5.14% higher than the BiRNN.

Table 6. Ablation experimental results of Seq2Seq generation task.

Model	HITS@1 (%)	HITS@3 (%)	HITS@5 (%)	HITS@10 (%)
MRBERT	22.94	45.90	57.42	71.97
w/o cross-attn.	22.61	45.24	56.75	71.18
w/o separate embed.	22.15	43.46	55.12	70.17
BiRNN	19.70	39.96	51.50	66.51

The experimental results revealed that the MRBERT outperformed the other ablation models in the Seq2Seq generation task. Separate embedding also improved the performance even when predicting the chords rather than the melody and rhythm.

5. Discussion

This paper has conducted ablation experiments for three kinds of tasks, autoregressive generation, conditional generation, and Seq2Seq generation, and has evaluated them at multiple levels by setting different k in HIST@k. The following has been demonstrated by the experimental results: First, pre-trained representation learning can improve the performance of the three kinds of tasks. This is evident in the fact that the performance of the RNN and BiRNN is significantly lower than that of the models using pre-training techniques in all tasks. Second, it is effective to consider the melody and rhythm separately in representation learning. From the ablation results, it can be seen that the model using separate embedding performs better in HITS@k in each task than that not using separate embedding. Third, the assumption that there are weak dependencies between the melody and rhythm is reasonable. The performance of the MRBERT using both separate embedding and semi-cross attention together is slightly higher than that using only separate embedding.

This paper and other music representation learning studies are inspired by language modeling in natural language processing, so this method can only be applied to symbolic format music data. In fact, a large amount of music exists in audio format, such as mp3, wav, etc. This requires the model to be able to handle continuous spectrograms rather than discrete sequences. There have been some studies in computer vision that explore the application of representation learning in image processing [30–32], which is very enlightening for future work.

6. Conclusions

This paper proposed MRBERT, a pre-trained model for multitask music generation. During pre-training, the MRBERT learned representations of the melody and rhythm by dividing the embedding layers and transformer blocks into two groups and implementing information exchanging through semi-cross attention. Compared to the original BERT, the MRBERT simultaneously considered the strong dependencies of the melodies and rhythms on themselves and the weak dependencies between them, which allows it to learn better representations than the original BERT. In the subsequent fine-tuning, the corresponding content was generated according to the tasks. Three music generation tasks, namely autoregressive, conditional, and Seq2Seq generation, were designed to help users compose music, making the composition more convenient. Unlike traditional music generation approaches designed for a single task, these three tasks included multiple functions of melody and rhythm generation, modification, and completion, as well as chord generation. To verify the performance of the MRBERT, ablation experiments were conducted on each generation task. The experimental results revealed that pre-training improves the task performance, and the MRBERT, using separate embedding and semi-cross attention, outperformed the traditional language pre-trained model BERT in the metric of HITS@k.

The proposed method can be utilized in practical music generation applications, including melody and rhythm generation, modification, completion, and chord matching, such as web-based music composers. However, to generate high-quality music, a music corpus composed of leadsheets is used as the training data. These leadsheets must clearly label the melodies, rhythms, and corresponding chords. The problem is that it is difficult to collect this type of data, which limits the expansion of the data volume. In the future, although the application of pre-training techniques in music will continue to be explored, it is equally important to extend the generation tasks to unlabeled music symbolic data and audio data.

Author Contributions: Conceptualization, S.L., and Y.S.; methodology, S.L. and Y.S.; software, S.L. and Y.S.; validation, S.L. and Y.S.; writing—original draft preparation, S.L.; writing—review and editing, Y.S. All authors have read and agreed to the published version of the manuscript.

Funding: This work was supported by the Ministry of Education of the Republic of Korea and the National Research Foundation of Korea (NRF-2021R1F1A1063466).

Institutional Review Board Statement: Not applicable.

Informed Consent Statement: Not applicable.

Data Availability Statement: Restrictions apply to the availability of these data. Data were obtained from https://github.com/00sapo/OpenEWLD and are available accessed on 1 October 2022.

Conflicts of Interest: The authors declare no conflict of interest.

References

1. Zhang, W.; Wu, Q.J.; Yang, Y.; Akilan, T. Multimodel Feature Reinforcement Framework Using Moore–Penrose Inverse for Big Data Analysis. *IEEE Trans. Neural Netw. Learn. Syst.* **2020**, *32*, 5008–5021. [CrossRef] [PubMed]
2. Brown, T.; Mann, B.; Ryder, N.; Subbiah, M.; Kaplan, J.D.; Dhariwal, P.; Neelakantan, A.; Shyam, P.; Sastry, G.; Askell, A.; et al. Language Models are Few-Shot Learners. In Proceedings of the 34th Advances in Neural Information Processing Systems (NeurIPS), Online, 6–12 December 2020; pp. 1877–1901.
3. Dong, H.W.; Hsiao, W.Y.; Yang, L.C.; Yang, Y.H. MuseGan: Multi-Track Sequential Generative Adversarial Networks for Symbolic Music Generation and Accompaniment. In Proceedings of the 32nd AAAI Conference on Artificial Intelligence, New Orleans, LA, USA, 2–7 February 2018; pp. 34–41.
4. Li, S.; Jang, S.; Sung, Y. Automatic Melody Composition Using Enhanced GAN. *Mathematics* **2019**, *7*, 883. [CrossRef]
5. Choi, K.; Fazekas, G.; Sandler, M.; Cho, K. Convolutional Recurrent Neural Networks for Music Classification. In Proceedings of the 2017 IEEE 42nd International Conference on Acoustics, Speech and Signal Processing (ICASSP), New Orleans, LA, USA, 5–9 March 2017; pp. 2392–2396.
6. Qiu, L.; Li, S.; Sung, Y. DBTMPE: Deep Bidirectional Transformers-Based Masked Predictive Encoder Approach for Music Genre Classification. *Mathematics* **2021**, *9*, 530. [CrossRef]
7. Park, H.; Yoo, C.D. Melody Extraction and Detection through LSTM-RNN with Harmonic Sum Loss. In Proceedings of the 2017 IEEE 42nd International Conference on Acoustics, Speech and Signal Processing (ICASSP), New Orleans, LA, USA, 5–9 March 2017; pp. 2766–2770.
8. Li, S.; Jang, S.; Sung, Y. Melody Extraction and Encoding Method for Generating Healthcare Music Automatically. *Electronics* **2019**, *8*, 1250. [CrossRef]
9. McLeod, A.; Steedman, M. Evaluating Automatic Polyphonic Music Transcription. In Proceedings of the 19th International Society for Music Information Retrieval Conference (ISMIR), Paris, France, 23–27 September 2018; pp. 42–49.

10. Jiang, Z.; Li, S.; Sung, Y. Enhanced Evaluation Method of Musical Instrument Digital Interface Data based on Random Masking and Seq2Seq Model. *Mathematics* **2022**, *10*, 2747. [CrossRef]
11. Wu, J.; Hu, C.; Wang, Y.; Hu, X.; Zhu, J. A Hierarchical Recurrent Neural Network for Symbolic Melody Generation. *IEEE Trans. Cybern.* **2019**, *50*, 2749–2757. [CrossRef] [PubMed]
12. Li, S.; Jang, S.; Sung, Y. INCO-GAN: Variable-Length Music Generation Method Based on Inception Model-Based Conditional GAN. *Mathematics* **2021**, *9*, 387. [CrossRef]
13. Makris, D.; Agres, K.R.; Herremans, D. Generating Lead Sheets with Affect: A Novel Conditional Seq2Seq Framework. In Proceedings of the 2021 International Joint Conference on Neural Networks (IJCNN), Shenzhen, China, 18–22 July 2021; pp. 1–8.
14. Devlin, J.; Chang, M.W.; Lee, K.; Toutanova, K. BERT: Pretraining of Deep Bidirectional Transformers for Language Understanding. *arXiv* **2018**, arXiv:1810.04805.
15. Walder, C. Modelling Symbolic Music: Beyond the Piano Roll. In Proceedings of the 8th Asian Conference on Machine Learning (ACML), Hamilton, New Zealand, 16–18 November 2016; pp. 174–189.
16. Hadjeres, G.; Pachet, F.; Nielsen, F. DeepBach: A Steerable Model for Bach Chorales Generation. In Proceedings of the 34th International Conference on Machine Learning, Sydney, Australia, 6–11 August 2017; pp. 1362–1371.
17. Chu, H.; Urtasun, R.; Fidler, S. Song From PI: A Musically Plausible Network for Pop Music Generation. *arXiv* **2016**, arXiv:1611.03477.
18. Mogren, O. C-RNN-GAN: Continuous Recurrent Neural Networks with Adversarial Training. *arXiv* **2016**, arXiv:1611.09904.
19. Noh, S.H. Analysis of Gradient Vanishing of RNNs and Performance Comparison. *Information* **2021**, *12*, 442. [CrossRef]
20. Vaswani, A.; Shazeer, N.; Parmar, N.; Uszkoreit, J.; Jones, L.; Gomez, A.N.; Kaiser, L.; Polosukhin, I. Attention is All You Need. In Proceedings of the 31st Conference on Neural Information Processing Systems (NIPS), Long Beach, CA, USA, 4–9 December 2017.
21. Zeng, M.; Tan, X.; Wang, R.; Ju, Z.; Qin, T.; Liu, T.Y. MusicBERT: Symbolic Music Understanding with Large-Scale Pre-Training. In Proceedings of the Findings of the Associations for Computational Linguistics: ACL-IJCNLP, Online, 1–6 August 2021; pp. 791–800.
22. Chou, Y.H.; Chen, I.; Chang, C.J.; Ching, J.; Yang, Y.H. MidiBERT-Piano: Large-scale Pre-training for Symbolic Music Understanding. *arXiv* **2021**, arXiv:2107.05223.
23. Peters, M.; Neumann, M.; Iyyer, M.; Gardner, M.; Clark, C.; Lee, K.; Zettlemoyer, L. Deep Contextualized Word Representations. In Proceedings of the 2018 Conference of the North American Chapter of the Association for Computational Linguistics: Human Language Technologies, Volume 1 (Long Papers), Association for Computational Linguistics, New Orleans, LA, USA, 1–6 June 2018; pp. 2227–2237.
24. Huang, Y.S.; Yang, Y.H. Pop Music Transformer: Beat-based Modeling and Generation of Expressive Pop Piano Compositions. In Proceedings of the 28th ACM International Conference on Multimedia, Seattle, WA, USA, 12–16 October 2020; pp. 1180–1188.
25. Hsiao, W.Y.; Liu, J.Y.; Yeh, Y.C.; Yang, Y.H. Compound Word Transformer: Learning to Compose Full-Song Music over Dynamic Directed Hypergraphs. In Proceedings of the AAAI Conference on Artificial Intelligence, Virtual, 2–9 February 2021; pp. 178–186.
26. Simonetta, F.; Carnovalini, F.; Orio, N.; Rodà, A. Symbolic Music Similarity through a Graph-Based Representation. In Proceedings of the Audio Mostly on Sound in Immersion and Emotion, North Wales, UK, 12–14 September 2018; pp. 1–7.
27. Liu, Y.; Ott, M.; Goyal, N.; Du, J.; Joshi, M.; Chen, D.; Levy, O.; Lewis, M.; Zettlemoyer, L.; Stoyanov, V. RoBERTa: A Robustly Optimized BERT Pretraining Approach. *arXiv* **2019**, arXiv:1907.11692.
28. Shapiro, I.; Huber, M. Markov Chains for Computer Music Generation. *J. Humanist. Math.* **2021**, *11*, 167–195. [CrossRef]
29. Mittal, G.; Engel, J.; Hawthorne, C.; Simon, I. Symbolic Music Generation with Diffusion Models. *arXiv* **2021**, arXiv:2103.16091.
30. Zhang, W.; Wu, Q.J.; Zhao, W.W.; Deng, H.; Yang, Y. Hierarchical One-Class Model with Subnetwork for Representation Learning and Outlier Detection. *IEEE Trans. Cybern.* **2022**, 1–14. [CrossRef] [PubMed]
31. Zhang, W.; Yang, Y.; Wu, Q.J.; Wang, T.; Zhang, H. Multimodal Moore–Penrose Inverse-Based Recomputation Framework for Big Data Analysis. *IEEE Trans. Neural Netw. Learn. Syst.* **2022**, 1–13. [CrossRef] [PubMed]
32. Zhang, W.; Wu, Q.J.; Yang, Y. Semisupervised Manifold Regularization via a Subnetwork-Based Representation Learning Model. *IEEE Trans. Cybern.* **2022**, 1–14. [CrossRef] [PubMed]

Disclaimer/Publisher's Note: The statements, opinions and data contained in all publications are solely those of the individual author(s) and contributor(s) and not of MDPI and/or the editor(s). MDPI and/or the editor(s) disclaim responsibility for any injury to people or property resulting from any ideas, methods, instructions or products referred to in the content.

Article

Vehicle Routing Optimization with Cross-Docking Based on an Artificial Immune System in Logistics Management

Shih-Che Lo * and Ying-Lin Chuang

Department of Industrial Management, National Taiwan University of Science and Technology, Taipei City 106335, Taiwan
* Correspondence: sclo@mail.ntust.edu.tw; Tel.: +886-2-2737-6351

Abstract: Background: Manufacturing companies optimize logistics network routing to reduce transportation costs and operational costs in order to make profits in an extremely competitive environment. Therefore, the efficiency of logistics management in the supply chain and the quick response to customers' demands are treated as an additional source of profit. One of the warehouse operations for intelligent logistics network design, called cross-docking (CD) operations, is used to reduce inventory levels and improve responsiveness to meet customers' requirements. Accordingly, the optimization of a vehicle dispatch schedule is imperative in order to produce a routing plan with the minimum transport cost while meeting demand allocation. Methods: This paper developed a two-phase algorithm, called sAIS, to solve the vehicle routing problem (VRP) with the CD facilities and systems in the logistics operations. The sAIS algorithm is based on a clustering-first and routing-later approach. The sweep method is used to cluster trucks as the initial solution for the second phase: optimizing routing by the Artificial Immune System. Results: In order to examine the performance of the proposed sAIS approach, we compared the proposed model with the Genetic Algorithm (GA) on the VRP with pickup and delivery benchmark problems, showing average improvements of 7.26%. Conclusions: In this study, we proposed a novel sAIS algorithm for solving VRP with CD problems by simulating human body immune reactions. The experimental results showed that the proposed sAIS algorithm is robustly competitive with the GA on the criterion of average solution quality as measured by the two-sample t-test.

Keywords: logistics management; artificial immune systems; vehicle routing problem; cross-docking

MSC: 68W01; 90B06; 97R40

Citation: Lo, S.-C.; Chuang, Y.-L. Vehicle Routing Optimization with Cross-Docking Based on an Artificial Immune System in Logistics Management. *Mathematics* **2023**, *11*, 811. https://doi.org/10.3390/math11040811

Academic Editor: Tao Zhou

Received: 26 December 2022
Revised: 31 January 2023
Accepted: 3 February 2023
Published: 5 February 2023

Copyright: © 2023 by the authors. Licensee MDPI, Basel, Switzerland. This article is an open access article distributed under the terms and conditions of the Creative Commons Attribution (CC BY) license (https://creativecommons.org/licenses/by/4.0/).

1. Introduction

The concept of a smart city includes a high degree of information technology (IT) integration and communication, which is the same concept as supply chain management today, which relies on the use of various ITs and techniques. One of the important elements of smart cities is smart logistics, aiming to help manufacturers gain performance from reusable transport packaging, such as pallets, racks, and bins, as well as tracking packages. By building Internet of Things (IoT) monitoring technology, smart logistics IT systems can be integrated into virtually any transportation asset to track its location in real-time, optimize inventory planning, and monitor environmental conditions, especially when the world enters the fifth-generation mobile communication technology or even the six-generation mobile communication technology in the future [1–3]. However, even with advanced IT today, logistics costs are still an important part of a global company's worldwide operation management to construct an enterprise's competitive edge over competitors, especially when dealing with post-COVID-19 supply chain disruptions. Intelligent logistics network functions allow companies to quickly respond to customer requirements and create their own competitive advantage over competitors in the design of smart logistics by using IT, such as radio frequency identification, to track shipments in real-time.

Moreover, logistics costs weigh significantly on a company's total costs. The authors of [4] identified the logistics costs from three different aspects of a case company: (1) the share of procurement costs reduced from approximately 0.65 (2013) to 0.45% (2015); (2) the share of production costs increased from approximately 50 (2013) to 65% (2015); and (3) the share of sales costs increased from approximately 7 (2013) to 8.5% (2015). As a result, in order to increase overall profits, lower operational costs, and improve a company's service level, a well-designed and highly cost-efficient logistics mechanism becomes essential. The paper focuses on controlling transport costs by optimizing routes and scheduling of vehicles, which is known as the vehicle routing problem (VRP) [5].

VRPs are a fundamental activity in the fields of transportation systems, distribution channel design, and logistics networks. The study of the VRPs is indeed vital in optimizing the physical flow of goods in the logistics operation in order to reduce transport costs and increase supply chain network performance. Among numerous studies of the VRPs, the problem with optimal routes and scheduling of vehicles, considering both pickup and delivery processes simultaneously, is called the VRP with cross-docking (VRPCD). Kulwiec (2004) pointed out that the cross-docking (CD) facility is an important supply chain strategy. They classified the CD facility into six different types. One of the CD operations is "Truck/Rail Consolidation." [6]. Both suppliers' and retailers' sides of the supply chain have to be considered at the same time in the process of transporting goods. Therefore, CD facilities are an important element in a synchronized supply chain as well as in sustainable logistics management. Generally, there would be no interruption between upstream and downstream operations as long as the physical flow of goods in the pickup process is simultaneously delivered at the CD depot and then delivered to customers after the consolidation process. Therefore, no inventory was stocked, and no delay in customer orders occurred at the facility. As a result, the construction of a CD system in the logistics network makes companies able to: (1) facilitate the efficiency and effectiveness of supply chain management; (2) lower space requirements and reduce transportation costs; and (3) better control the distribution process [7]. Figure 1 shows a simple layout of the CD depot.

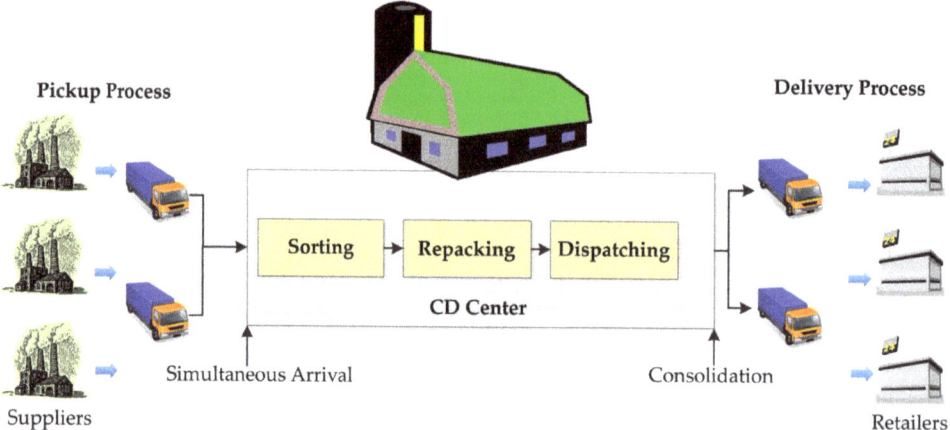

Figure 1. A layout of a typical CD facility.

Studying an efficient heuristics methodology is essential to acquiring an optimal or near-optimal solution within a reasonable amount of computation time because the VRP is a well-known non-deterministic polynomial-time-hard (NP-hard) problem. As the global pandemic of the new coronavirus (COVID-19) has shaken the world since 2020, the study of the human immune system has piqued the interest of many researchers. The Artificial Immune Systems (AIS) is the simulation algorithm of human body defense systems and is applied to solve many research fields, such as clustering/classification, fault detection, combinatorial optimization, and learning problems [8–12].

The AIS has presented numerous studies on solving optimization problems. The results showed that their algorithm was a feasible and effective method for the VRP. For example, the authors of [13] applied clonal selection to tackle the VRP by using clonal selection operators, super mutation operators, and clonal proliferation to improve global convergence speed. The results indicate that their algorithm has a remarkable reliability of global convergence and avoids prematurity when solving the VRP effectively.

This paper aims to propose a two-phase optimization approach based on an artificial immune system combined with the sweep method, called sAIS, to solve the vehicle routing problem with the CD facilities in the logistics network as an important element of smart city infrastructure. The two-phase approach begins with the grouping method to fulfill vehicle capacity constraints and is followed by the optimization engine to find near-optimal solutions for each truck routing sequence while utilizing a minimum number of trucks. The experimental results showed that the proposed sAIS algorithm is robustly competitive with the GA on the criterion of average solution quality.

The remainder of this paper is organized as follows. Section 2 reviews the related literature, and Section 3 defines the VRPCD formulation. Section 4 details the methodology and procedure of our proposed sAIS heuristic algorithm, following a number of experimentation examples presented in Section 5. Section 6 concludes the research with a summary based on the computational results.

2. Related Works

The CD system is a lean supply chain model of transporting raw materials or products from pickup to delivery without ever storing them in the warehouse. It can significantly reduce inventory levels, required space, handling costs, and lead times, as well as customer response times. Packages are unloaded from inbound trucks immediately after arriving at the depot, followed by a sorting, repacking, and dispatching process as shown in Figure 2, then loaded onto outbound trucks for delivery to retailers in a distribution channel [14–18]. The primary objective is to avoid a high inventory level and reduce handling costs so that there will be no inventory being stored in the depot. This is the same concept as the Toyota Production System or lean operations. A well-designed CD operation can provide companies with significant benefits, including decreased inventory levels, low storage space requirements, low transportation costs, a fast response to customer requirements, and better control of the distribution process. Both receiving and shipping processes must be considered simultaneously, to enable the CD facility to be integrated into the logistics network effectively. Lee, Jung, and Lee (2006) first proposed that the most important process for CD operations is the pickup phase, in which all trucks must arrive at the depot at the same time in order to control the start time of warehouse operations [17].

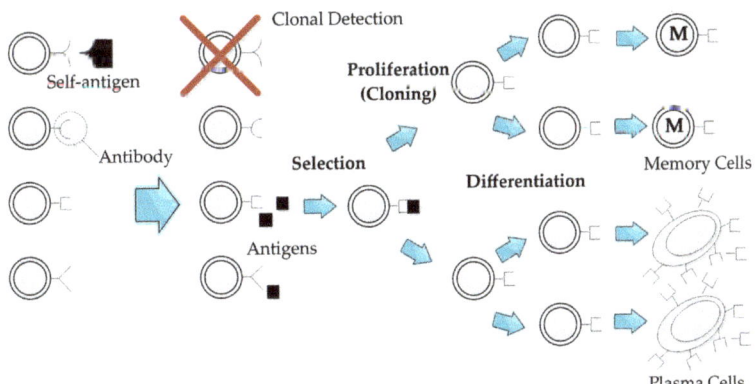

Figure 2. The selection process of antibodies.

Before the CD system served as a mathematical constraint, Dantzig and Ramaser (1959) initially introduced the VRP concept as a solution to the "Truck Dispatching Problem." In their study, a linear programming model was designed to acquire a near-best solution for the truck scheduling problem, which was concerned with the optimum routing of a fleet of delivery trucks supplied by the terminal [19]. Following that, numerous research proposals were made to address the developing VRPs in their study. The VRPs have been studied for many decades. The VRP is a set of customers with known demands who are serviced by a fleet of trucks from one or more depots to a number of geographically dispersed locations and customers based on optimally designed routes [20–24].

There are many solving methods for variants of the VRP proposed in the literature. The authors of [25] dealt with capacitated VRP and distance restrictions by using an integer programming method that used a constraint relaxation approach and sub-tour elimination. The author of [26] proposed tour-partitioning heuristics to solve the pickup and delivery VRPs, whereas the authors of [27] developed a hybrid heuristic method based on the Genetic Algorithm (GA) with neighborhood search to solve the basic VRPs. They showed that the hybrid GA had a significant improvement over the pure GA and was competitive with the simulated annealing approach [28] and the Tabu search approach [29–31] in their experiment results. The authors of [32,33] proposed hybrid ant colony optimizations (ACOs) to solve the VRPs with time windows and found that they were applicable and effective in practical problems. The authors of [34] used an ACO approach for the multiple VRPs with pickup and delivery along with time windows and heterogeneous fleets and applied it to large-scale problems. The authors of [18] developed a matheuristic approach consisting of two phases: adaptive large neighborhood search (ALNS) and setting partitioning to solve VRPCD. The authors of [35] proposed a particle swarm optimization approach to solve VRPCD and carbon emissions reduction. Moreover, sustainable logistics management is a popular research topic nowadays to follow the United Nations' sustainable development goals [36].

Following the same concept to simulate an ant's behavior as ACO, Jerne (1974) proposed the first AIS model to simulate the immune system as a mathematical formulation to solve optimization problems, which had an interaction network of lymphocytes and molecules that had variable regions [37]. Following Jerne's research, Farmer, Packard, and Perelson (1986) proposed the dynamic immune network, which could simulate and solve classification problems, showing the AIS can be extended to solve big data prediction problems nowadays as machine learning pioneers [38]. Kephart (1994) published a paper on the AIS from a biological point of view to auto-distinguish computer viruses [39]. Hunt et al. (1999) devoted themselves to developing clonal selection algorithms and proposing high-frequency variations [40]. Lately, Mrowczynska et al. (2017) used AIS to predict road freight transportation [41]. Mabrouk, Raslan, and Hedar (2022) proposed an immune system programming with local search (ISPLS) algorithm with a tree data structure to be used in the meta-heuristics programming approach to develop new practical machine learning tools [42]. As a result of many years of development, the AIS has become a well-known meta-heuristic that is widely applied to solve combinatorial optimization and abnormal detection problems.

The AIS mainly simulates the relationship between antigens and antibodies, and the core idea of immune reactions includes antibodies' reproduction, clonal expansion, and immune memory properties in the biological immune system. Organisms have two kinds of immunity: the innate immune system and the adaptive immune system. The innate immune system is capable of recognizing molecular patterns in pathogens and signaling other immune cells to start fighting against the pathogens. Adaptive immune systems can maintain a stable memory of known patterns. Living organisms use the immune system to defend their bodies from invasion by outside substances. Lymphocytes are parts of the immune system, which includes T and B cells. Both types of lymphocytes have surface receptors capable of recognizing molecular patterns present on antigens (binding with epitopes). When the receptors bind to epitopes and exceed a threshold, a lymphocyte becomes activated.

Activation triggers a series of reactions that can lead to the elimination of pathogens. During the infection response, the immune system's B cells produced antibodies. Pathogens are bound by antibodies called antigens. Antigens and antibodies can bind together when complementary shapes exist. After binding, the antibody disables the pathogens so that the immune system can easily destroy them. Figure 2 depicts how to select immune system antibodies [43–46].

There are four types of immune mutations running inside the human body: IgM, IgG, IgE, and IgA [47–50]. In this paper, we simulate each mode having a different mathematical function. First, the calculation of affinity is the total correlations between the antigen-antibodies and antibodies-antibodies in our mathematical programming model. If the affinity value of a new string in IgM mode is smaller than that of the old one, a total of four kinds of immune mutations, including IgG mode, IgE mode, and IgA mode, are randomly selected to operate in the next step of mutation in the same generation for optimization purposes.

1. Somatic Hypermutation Simulation Function:
   - IgM mode: Inverse mutation is used in the IgM mode. In the sequence s, randomly selected two positions, i and j. Inverse the sequence of cells between the i and j positions in the neighbor of s. It should be noted if $|i-j| < 2$ it cannot be mutated;
   - IgG mode: Pairwise mutation is used in the IgG mode. In the sequence s, randomly selected two positions, i and j. Swap these two cells in the neighbor of s;
   - IgA mode: Insertion mutation is used in the IgA mode. In the sequence s, randomly selected two positions, i and j. Insert the cell i to the position j in the neighbor of s;
   - IgE mode: Both the swap and insertion mutations are used in the IgE mode. In the sequence s, randomly selected two positions, i and j. A new sequence s' is provided by swapping i and j. Then, in the sequence, s' randomly selected i' and j' to be a cell and a position, respectively. Inserting cell i at position j in the neighbor of s'.

2. Affinity Maturation Simulation Function

   Affinity is a positive or negative correlation between an antigen and an antibody. When the affinity is higher, it can generate a better fit between the interacting surfaces of the antibody and antigen. After somatic hypermutation, some variant antibodies with higher affinities may be produced. Then, in the next response, the cells will have a greater affinity. This phenomenon is called affinity maturation;

3. Elimination Simulation Function

   The human body's bone marrow generates billions of B cells into circulation every day. Those B cells are saved in a catalog, where there is limited storage space for the B cells. The B cells are dead within a certain period if they meet the specific antigen. Hence, the B-cell catalog is not static, and newly produced antibodies are continually tested against antigen infection. Therefore, new antibodies are generated and old ones are deleted.

3. VRPCD Formulation

The VRP is traditionally illustrated as a graph network with vertices denoting terminal points and arcs as vehicle routes, as shown in Figure 3. The basic notations for all VRPs are shown as follows:

$$G = (V, E \cup A),$$

where $V = \{v_0, \ldots, v_n\}$ is a vertex set; v_0 represents the central warehouse from which deliveries are made;

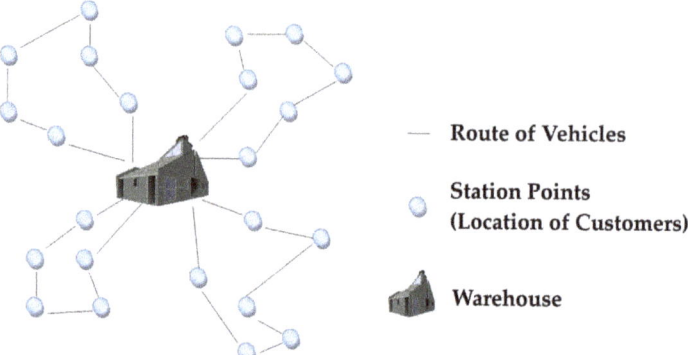

Figure 3. A simple illustration of the VRP routing network.

$A = \{(v_i, v_j): i \neq j, v_i, v_j \in V\}$ represents the directed arc set;
$E = \{(v_i, v_j): i < j, v_i, v_j \in V\}$ is a set of undirected edges.

Lee, Jung, and Lee (2006) addressed the constraints of vehicle routing with the one CD warehouse problem. The CD facility plays a key role in synchronizing the distribution process on both sides of the supply chain [17]. As simulated, the CD facility can be treated as the home depot as in the traditional VRPs, except that the model of CD specifies the simultaneous arrival of each vehicle from the receiving trip. Therefore, several assumptions are made. First, we have n nodes, denoting a total number of suppliers and retailers, who are serviced by m vehicles. Every truck must depart and come back to the depot ($i = 0$), with the simultaneous arrival of trucks from pickup routes. Second, for each customer, only one truck is assigned and associated with a cost amount of C_{ij}. Every customer has a homogeneous demand d, which is related to the capacity limit q_k for truck k. Additionally, a constraint of the planning time horizon T specifies that the total distance traveled by vehicles cannot exceed it. Two types of costs are considered: transportation costs and operational costs. The objective of this research in the mathematical programming model is to find optimized routing solutions by using a minimum number of trucks to service and complete the assignment. The following presents the basic notations of the VRPCD model.

Decision Variables:

X_{ijk}: a binary variable representing the route from i to j is serviced by vehicle k, where

$$X_{ijk} = \begin{cases} 1, & \text{if vehicle } k \text{ is in the tour from } i \text{ to } j; \\ 0, & \text{otherwise.} \end{cases}$$

Notation of Variables:

Y_{ijk}: loaded quantity of vehicle k from pickup trip i to j;
Z_{ijk}: unloaded quantity of vehicle k from delivery trip i to j;
tc_{ijk}: the transportation cost of vehicle k from customer i to j;
et_{ijk}: time for vehicle k to move from i to j;
δ_{ik}: service time required by vehicle k to load/unload the quantity demanded at i;
m: number of vehicles;
n: number of customers;
c_k: fixed cost of vehicle k;
q_k: maximum capacity for each vehicle k;
T: planning horizon;
P: set of unit demand from each pickup stop;
D: set of unit demand from each delivery stop;
DT_{jk}: departure time of vehicle k at node j;
AT_k: arrival time at the depot of vehicle k.

Objective Function:

$$\text{Minimize } Z = \sum_{i=0}^{n}\sum_{j=0}^{n}\sum_{k=1}^{m} tc_{ij}X_{ijk} + \sum_{k=1}^{m}\sum_{j=1}^{n} c_k X_{0jk} \tag{1}$$

Subject to:

$$\sum_{i=0}^{n}\sum_{k=1}^{m} X_{ijk} = 1, \text{ for } j = 1, 2, \ldots, n; \tag{2}$$

$$\sum_{j=0}^{n}\sum_{k=1}^{m} X_{ijk} = 1, \text{ for } i = 1, 2, \ldots, n; \tag{3}$$

$$\sum_{i=1}^{n} X_{ihk} = \sum_{j=1}^{n} X_{hjk}, \text{ for } k = 1, 2, \ldots, m; \, h = 1, 2, \ldots, n; \tag{4}$$

$$\sum_{j=1}^{n} X_{0jk} \leq 1, \text{ for } k = 1, 2, \ldots, m; \tag{5}$$

$$\sum_{i=1}^{n} X_{i0k} \leq 1, \text{ for } k = 1, 2, \ldots, m; \tag{6}$$

$$Y_{ijk} + Z_{ijk} \leq \sum_{i=1}^{n} Q_i \sum_{j=1}^{n} X_{ijk}, \text{ for } k = 1, 2, \ldots, m; \tag{7}$$

$$Y_{jik} - Y_{ijk} = \begin{cases} P_j, & \text{if } j \in P, i = 1, 2, \ldots, n, \\ 0, & \text{if } j \in D, i = 1, 2, \ldots, n, \\ -\sum_{i=1}^{n} P_i, & \text{if } j \in 0, i = 1, 2, \ldots, n; \end{cases} \tag{8}$$

$$Z_{ijk} - Z_{jik} = \begin{cases} 0, & \text{if } j \in P, i = 1, 2, \ldots, n, \\ d_i, & \text{if } j \in D, i = 1, 2, \ldots, n, \\ \sum_{i=1}^{n} d_i, & \text{if } j \in 0, i = 1, 2, \ldots, n; \end{cases} \tag{9}$$

$$\sum_{i=0}^{n}\sum_{j=0}^{n} \delta_{ik} X_{ijk} + \sum_{i=0}^{n}\sum_{j=0}^{n} et_{ijk} X_{ijk} \leq T, \text{ for } k = 1, 2, \ldots, m; \tag{10}$$

$$DT_{jk} = (et_{ij} + DT_{ik} + \delta_j) X_{ijk}, \text{ for } k = 1, 2, \ldots, m; \tag{11}$$

$$AT_k = (et_{i0} + DT_{ik}) X_{i0k}, \text{ for } k = 1, 2, \ldots, m; \tag{12}$$

$$AT_a = AT_b, \text{ for } a \neq b. \tag{13}$$

Equation (1) is the objective function whose goal is to minimize both transportation costs and fixed costs. The constraints of each customer being serviced by only one vehicle are described in Equations (2) and (3), while Equation (4) represents that each vehicle arriving at the node must also leave from the same node. Equations (5) and (6) state the constraints of each vehicle being only permitted to start from and return to the cross-docking depot and being used to serve at most one route, respectively. The loaded and uploaded demand from pickup and delivery processes cannot exceed the vehicle quantity limit detailed by Equation (7), while Equations (8) and (9) each represent the quantity limit for pickup and delivery en route. The total distance visited and time traveled cannot exceed the planning horizon, which is limited by Equation (10). The departure and arrival times are functioned by Equations (11) and (12), respectively. The vehicles' simultaneous arrival at the CD hub is stated by Equation (13).

4. Proposed sAIS Algorithm

4.1. Clustering Method

In order to minimize total cost, each dispatched vehicle must serve the maximum number of customers within its capacity limit while traveling the shortest distance possible. In this research, we simulate this practical strategy to solve the problem of generating vehicle route sequences with one CD operation in the supply chain. Moreover, for faster convergence, we use a two-phase algorithm to solve VRPCD.

In the initial route-generating phase, we use the sweep method as the first phase to provide the initial solution for the second phase of sAIS. Usually, the sweep method is applied to a polar coordinate system, and the center of the coordinate system serves as the depot of the VRP. In this case, for each traveling distance of route O_i ($i = 1, 2, \ldots, n$, where n denotes the number of customers), the ith customer's C_i served as the first customer in the cluster. Next, search for the closest customer from C_{i+1} to C_i by increasing the angle, and add it to the same cluster without exceeding vehicle capacity. When a customer cannot be added to the current cluster due to a vehicle capacity limit, this customer becomes the first customer in the next cluster. After all customers are clustered, we calculate the objective value of this route. After $O_1, O_2, \ldots, O_n$, were calculated, we chose the minimum distance of n routes as the initial solution of the AIS algorithm. Figure 4 illustrates an example of the clustering process for 12 nodes.

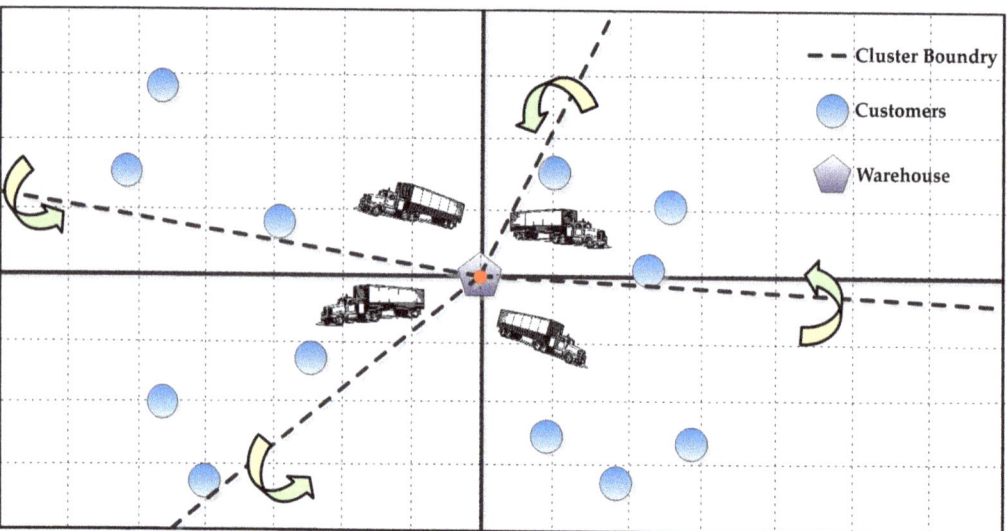

Figure 4. An illustration of clustering by the sweep method.

The total cost is accumulated by the fixed cost of vehicles used (operational cost) and transportation costs as vehicles travel from one customer to another. In some cases, the aggregated service time consumed by each customer is also considered. Overall, the shorter the distance traveled by vehicles, the lower the total cost incurred. Figure 5 exemplifies the hierarchies of the proposed two-phase algorithm for 10 customers with homogeneous demand served by 2 vehicles as well as the chromosome encoding format in this study.

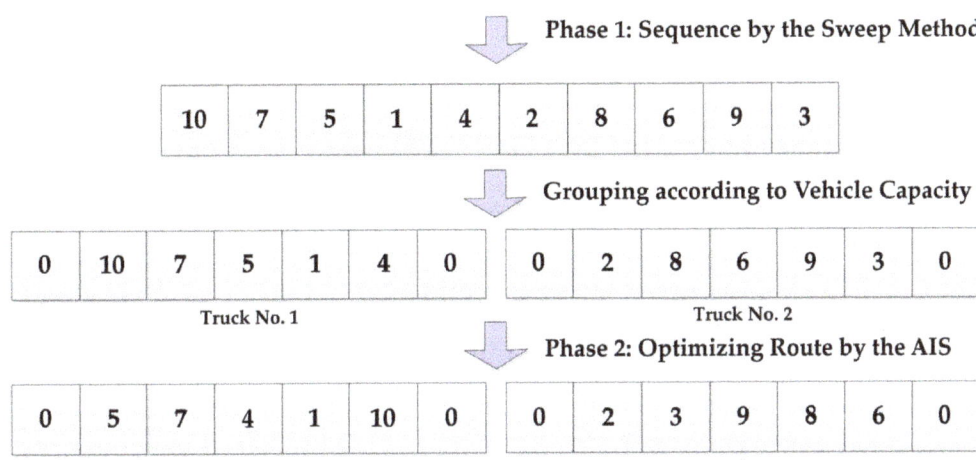

Figure 5. An illustration of 10 nodes with homogeneous demand served by 2 vehicles.

4.2. AIS Procedure

As mentioned previously, the AIS was successfully implemented to solve combinatorial optimization and abnormal detection problems. For data representation, we used chromosomes to denote routing sequences. All suppliers and retailers were assigned a unique number. We made the variation field of each cell, and its dimensions (length of chromosome) equivalent to the suppliers' (for pickup routes) or customers' (for delivery routes) numbers to be served, as shown in Figure 5. Therefore, the cells' chromosomes represent the nodes of the positions to be visited. In the meantime, the suppliers' or customers' sequences also mean the routing of orders. First, somatic hypermutation will be selected to make cells evolve, which can search for any feasible cells in the solution field. Next, we calculate the affinities between the antigen-antibodies and antibodies-antibodies according to the objective function. After iterations, the relationship between antigens and antibodies has a greater affinity. Moreover, elimination is a mechanism that will delete worse cells with each iteration. With affinity maturation and elimination, the cells will mutate toward the better-quality field of solution. In this case, each iteration individually will preserve the best cell, which means a higher affinity value.

In the proposed sAIS optimization algorithm, the principles of each antibody mutation have four parts. The basic components of the sAIS applied in the VRPCD are shown as follows:

- Antigen: the antigen mimics the equations of the VRPCD model, which represent the formulas for the objection function and constraint functions;
- Antibody: The antibody is the candidate solution for the VRPCD model. The strings of solutions refer to the visiting sequence of suppliers or customers. The antibodies are feasible sets of models for the problem;
- Cell: the cell represents the ID of suppliers or customers;
- Population size: the number of antibodies (feasible solutions of the VRPCD model) that are used per iteration;
- Number of clones for each cell: number of times antibodies are reproduced per iteration;
- Stopping criterion: the sAIS optimization procedure will not be terminated until the maximum number of iterations is reached.

The proposed sAIS optimization approach has a mechanism with the inside operation processes:

1. Somatic Recombination

Somatic recombination is one of the gene rearrangement processes that involves cutting out small regions of DNA and then putting the remaining pieces of DNA back together in an error-prone way in the adaptive immune system. For every iteration of our proposed algorithm, we randomly create a new set of antibodies by using the somatic recombination process in order to search for optimized solutions;

2. Somatic Hypermutation

There are five types of immune mutations that we use in our proposed sAIS algorithm. Each type has a different function. If the cost of objection function of antibodies in IgM is larger than the cost of the old ones, we randomly selected one of four kinds of immune mutations to operate in the next step of mutation in the same iteration. In addition to the traditional four types of immune mutations, we proposed a new immune mutation, called IgG_2, to further improve the performance of the sAIS optimizations:

- IgM mode: In the vehicle's route of sequence s, randomly select two suppliers or customers, i and j. Inverse the sequence of suppliers or customers between i and j as shown in Figure 6. It is noted that if $|i - j| < 2$ it is not allowed to be mutated;
- IgG mode: In the vehicle's route of sequence s, randomly select two suppliers or customers, i and j. Swap these two suppliers or customers in the neighbor of s;
- IgA mode: In the vehicle's route of sequence s, randomly select two suppliers or customers, i and j. Insert the suppliers or customers i to the sequence's jth position in the neighbor of s as shown in Figure 7;
- IgG_2 mode: In the vehicle's route of sequence s, let i_1, i_2, j_1, and j_2 be randomly selected as four suppliers or customers in the sequence. Swap i_1 to j_1 and i_2 to j_2 in the neighbor of s as shown in Figure 8;
- IgE mode: Both the IgG mode and the IgA mode are applied in this mutation. In the vehicle's route of sequence s, randomly select two suppliers or customers, i and j. A new sequence s' is provided by swapping i and j. Then, in the sequence s' randomly selected i' and j' will be suppliers and customers, respectively, and have a position in the sequence. Inserting the suppliers or customers i to the sequence position j in the neighbor of s';

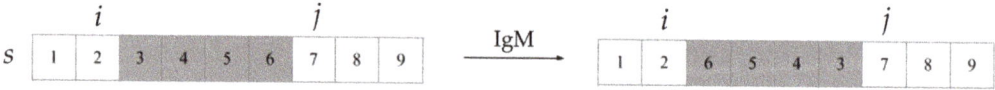

Figure 6. The operation of IgM mode.

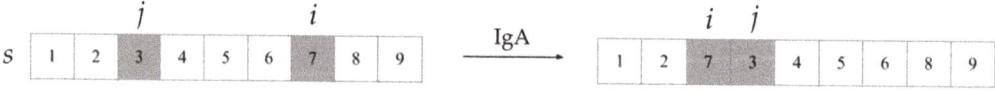

Figure 7. The operation of IgA mode.

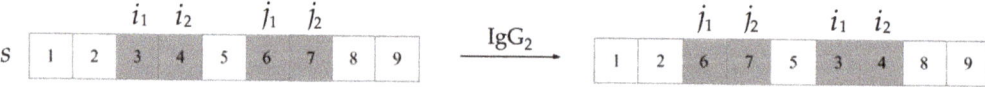

Figure 8. The operation of IgG_2 mode.

3. Affinity Maturation

Affinity means the total cost of the vehicles routed from the objection function of the VRPCD model. Some mutant antibodies with lower costs may be generated after several iterations of somatic hypermutation. Then, from iteration to iteration, the cost of producing antibodies will steadily decrease. This phenomenon is called affinity maturation;

4. Elimination Process

The antibodies will be stored in a limited list per iteration. Except for the best antibody, the antibodies that were produced and mutated per iteration were deleted from previous iterations. As a result, antibodies will search for alternative solution spaces for the VRPCD;

5. Escape Criterion

We designed an escape criterion for searching the antibody in the global optimization to prevent the search from entering the same solution space and remaining in the local optimum.

Figure 9 and Algorithm 1 show the proposed procedure of the sAIS algorithm.

Algorithm 1: The proposed sAIS algorithm.

1. Initialization: Create a population of p antibodies randomly (p is the size of the antibody population)
2. For each iteration do:
3.   For each antibody do:
4.   Somatic recombination
5.   Calculate affinity of the antibody
6.   Somatic hypermutation:
7.   IgM
8.   Decode the new string
9.   If the objective function (new) < the objective function (old):
10.   antibody = new string;
11.   else:
12.   Choose IgG, IgE, IgA or IgG_2
13.   Decode the new string
14.   If the objective function (new) < the objective function (old):
15.   antibody = new string
16.   else:
17.   antibody = antibody
18.   Eliminate antibodies except the best antibody in the population
19.   Reserve the best antibody in the population to affect velocity
20.   If the objective function (new) = the objective function (old):
21.   Count++
22.   If count attain list length:
23.   Generate the new antibodies randomly
24.   End For Loop
25.   If stopping criteria = false:
26.   Continue
27.   else:
28.   Break
29. End For Loop

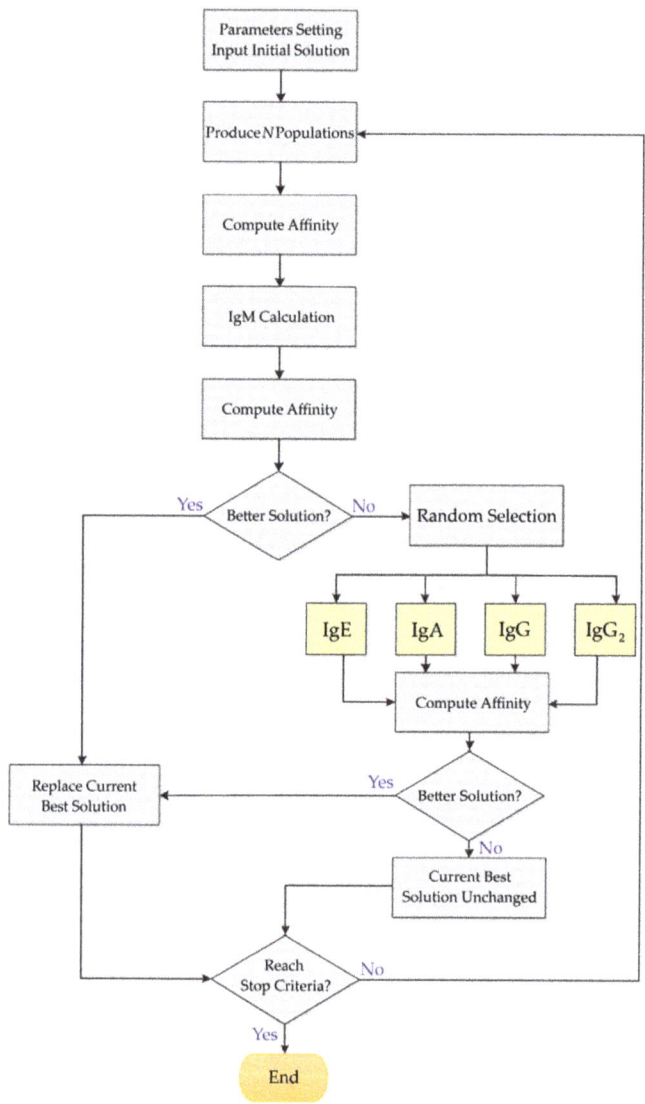

Figure 9. The processes of the proposed sAIS flowchart.

5. Computational Experiments

First, a preliminary investigation of the optimal parameter settings for the proposed algorithm is presented here. Next, 60 VRPPD benchmark problems were retrieved from the VRP Web (http://www.bernabe.dorronsoro.es/vrp/ accessed on 3 February 2023) as the criteria to evaluate the performance of the proposed heuristics. The comparison set is based on the GA algorithm, which is functioned by the customized software Palisade Evolver (https://www.palisade.com/evolver/) industrial edition 5.5.1, the Genetic Algorithm Solver plug-in for Microsoft Excel 2016.

5.1. Preliminary Tests

In the preliminary experiment, the design of experiments (DOE) was conducted to decide the optimal parameter settings for the sAIS optimization. The size of the population and escape list were acquired through the experimentation methodology. One randomly selected instance from the 60 testing problems was used to execute the experiment methodology. The parameter of population size, after an initial trial-and-error process, was located in the interval of [100, 500], and we used the set of {100, 200, 300, 400, and 500} to run the single factor factorial design experiment at 5 levels. Figure 10 shows the mean plot of the population size factor from the results of the experiments. The variable y is the objective function's minimized value (fitness value), as is the y-axis in Figures 10 and 11.

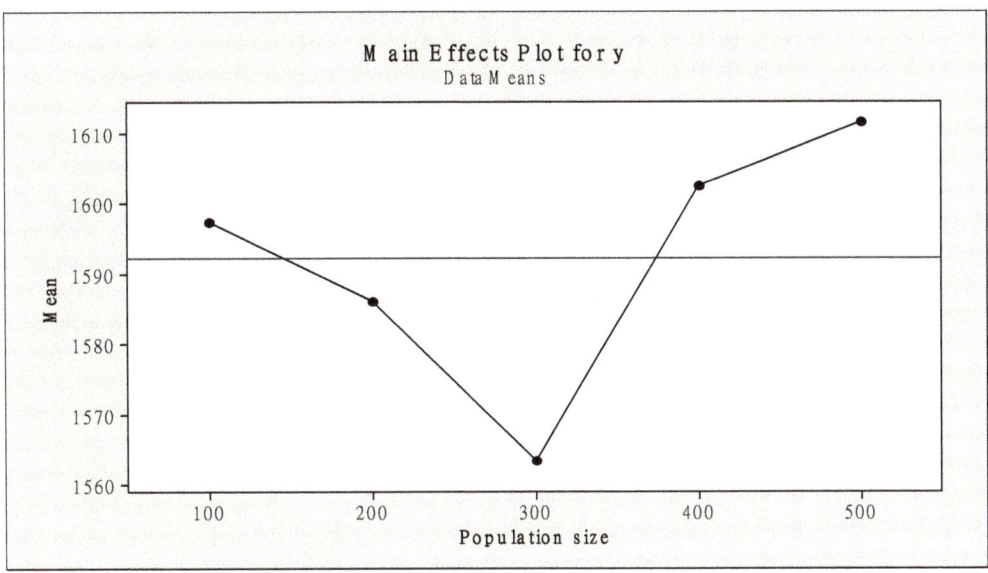

Figure 10. The mean plot of population size for a one-factor factorial design.

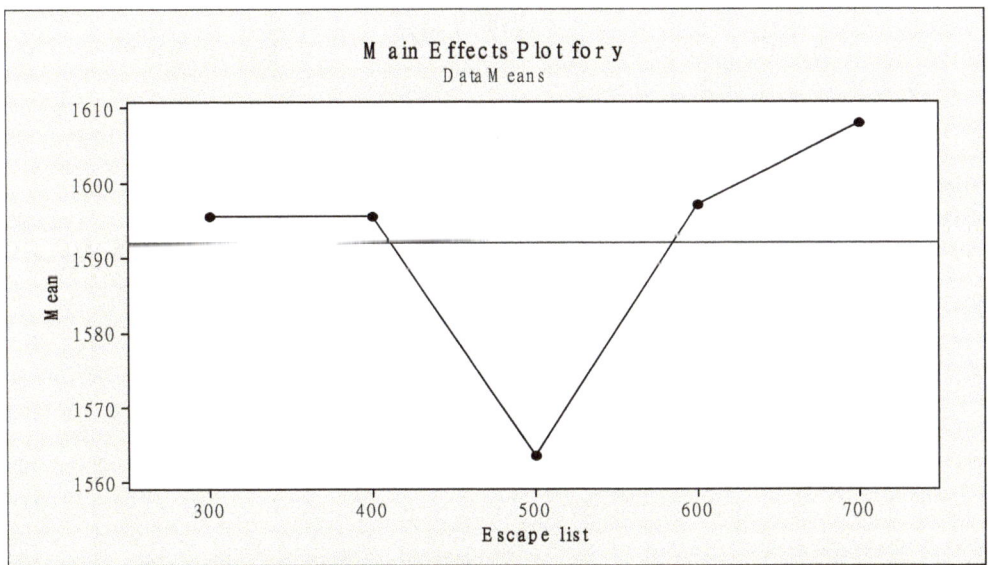

Figure 11. The mean plot of the escape list for a one-factor factorial design.

When the length of the escape list is attained, the AIS algorithm will jump out of the present field. The DOE also determined the length from large numbers in the interval [300, 700], and we chose {300, 400, 500, 600, and 700} as the 5 levels for the single factor factorial design experiment. Figure 8 shows the mean plot of the escape list factor from the results of the experiment.

It is found that the sAIS method can generate a better-quality solution when the population size and escape list factors are assigned to 300 and 500. According to the literature review, the maximum iteration was set at 100,000 trials as the termination criterion in our experiments. These settings were used in the following experiment for the sAIS algorithm. On the other hand, the population size of genes in the GA method was set at 50; the mutation rate is 0.06; and the crossover rate is 0.15. The maximum iteration number was 5000 trials with 30 replications for each instance.

5.2. Experiment Results

A total of 60 benchmark datasets with homogeneous demands were used in our experiment. Each instance is replicated for 30 runs for both the sAIS algorithm and the GA method. The solution from the sweep method, which generates proper clusters for shipment grouping of vehicles, is then picked up as the initial solution for both the sAIS and the GA methods. The comparison of performance between the two methods is computed based on the average improvement rate (AIR), as shown in Equation (14). The experimentation results are given in Table 1.

$$\text{Average Improvement Rate (AIR)} = \frac{|\text{AIS}_{\text{Average Cost}} - \text{GA}_{\text{Average Cost}}|}{\text{GA}_{\text{Average Cost}}} \times 100\%. \quad (14)$$

Table 1. Performance comparisons between sAIS and GA.

No. Instances	GA		sAIS		AIR
	Average Cost	Average Time (s)	Average Cost	Average Time (s)	
1P1	1683.22	604.5	1563.57	120.64	7.11%
2P1	1831.25	624	1671.51	111.38	8.72%
3P1	2075.44	624	1971.64	108.68	5.00%
4P1	1446.27	604.5	1439.02	126.73	0.50%
5P1	1515.79	624	1508.69	116.22	0.47%
6P1	1895.14	624	1819.36	112.09	4.00%
7P1	1790.83	643.5	1580.49	123.12	11.75%
8P1	1826.89	624	1659.31	104.11	9.17%
9P1	2429.49	624	1651.10	111.32	32.04%
10P1	1735.36	624	1488.57	103.91	14.22%
11P1	1859.02	643.5	1651.24	136.64	11.18%
12P1	2244.29	624	2031.68	136.61	9.47%
13P1	1604.56	624	1538.53	138.81	4.12%
14P1	1853.96	643.5	1680.49	140.23	9.36%
15P1	2091.15	663	1971.21	131.98	5.74%
16P1	1393.43	702	1363.70	170.57	2.13%
17P1	1487.11	663	1457.43	143.20	2.00%
18P1	1972.85	624	1799.52	137.73	8.79%
19P1	1120.58	624	1076.95	179.50	3.89%
20P1	1181.41	643.5	1170.37	164.43	0.93%
21P1	1641.65	624	1519.44	135.39	7.44%
22P1	1243.36	624	1132.10	176.54	8.95%
23P1	1246.59	663	1221.70	157.51	2.00%
24P1	1685.82	663	1550.75	137.61	8.01%
25P1	1035.99	643.5	1021.97	172.06	1.35%

Table 1. Cont.

No. Instances	GA Average Cost	GA Average Time (s)	sAIS Average Cost	sAIS Average Time (s)	AIR
26P1	1132.80	663	1116.50	170.57	1.44%
27P1	1721.06	643.5	1460.14	137.45	15.16%
28P1	1242.39	624	1202.44	183.15	3.22%
29P1	1338.65	663	1284.38	163.36	4.05%
30P1	1747.52	643.5	1616.69	138.48	7.49%
31P1	991.99	663	960.42	112.47	3.18%
32P1	1291.67	663	1202.92	113.12	6.87%
33P1	1721.57	663	1626.53	100.73	5.52%
34P1	971.77	663	956.98	117.75	1.52%
35P1	1180.81	624	1140.58	101.94	3.41%
36P1	1746.42	624	1554.76	101.45	10.97%
37P1	1070.18	604.5	944.67	109.23	11.73%
38P1	1274.88	624	1143.66	119.46	10.29%
39P1	1767.73	624	1553.02	115.70	12.15%
40P1	1090.22	643.5	1001.72	123.07	8.12%
41P1	1276.28	624	1212.92	101.59	4.96%
42P1	1679.75	624	1640.76	121.74	2.32%
43P1	1153.37	624	975.59	123.60	15.41%
44P1	1356.32	643.5	1166.58	111.69	13.99%
45P1	1723.25	624	1573.59	104.94	8.68%
46P1	1195.50	624	1083.37	103.39	9.38%
47P1	1373.71	643.5	1233.93	100.70	10.18%
48P1	1697.67	663	1618.59	114.34	4.66%
49P1	1286.97	702	1264.74	113.89	1.73%
50P1	1278.76	663	1264.71	101.67	1.10%
51P1	1741.72	643.5	1662.47	140.89	4.55%
52P1	1314.23	663	1154.11	138.25	12.18%
53P1	1451.27	624	1305.02	132.65	10.08%
54P1	1952.70	624	1742.00	124.55	10.79%
55P1	1308.87	624	1192.67	137.26	8.88%
56P1	1418.42	643.5	1333.62	136.96	5.98%
57P1	1888.41	624	1792.38	132.35	5.09%
58P1	1344.08	624	1153.09	139.39	14.21%
59P1	1371.34	663	1311.74	140.85	4.35%
60P1	1822.68	663	1760.34	136.58	3.42%
Avg. AIR		639.275		129.37	7.26%
Std. of AIR					0.0521
Max. AIR					32.04%
Min. AIR					0.47%

As listed, the 60 benchmark problems were sorted into 20 subgroups with three instances in each, based on the node coordinates assigned. Instances within one group are given identical node coordinates, except for the position where the cross-docking facility is located. Each set of the 60 instances contains 100 nodes, comprising both pickup and delivery customers. Each node is associated with a known demand of 10 units, while each vehicle dispatched is constrained by a capacity limit of 100 units. Examples of optimized routing sequences are shown in the Appendix A.

The computational results showed that the solution quality of the sAIS method is superior to the GA, outperforming each with an average improvement rate and lowest improvement rate of 11.98% and 9.47%, respectively, on the basis of average solution quality. In addition, the sAIS optimization, which has the lowest cost, was able to discover new, better solutions than the GA did in all 60 benchmarks, even though the computation time of the sAIS algorithm method takes longer; however, it is still a reasonable amount of time. Moreover, the maximum rate of improvement on average solution quality is 30.03%, whereas the minimum rate is acquired at 1.28%, indicating that the performance of the sAIS method is robust and competitive with the GA method. Nevertheless, all problems' average improvement rate was better able to discover new solutions than the GA did.

Finally, a one-sided, two-sample t-test was conducted to verify the performance of the two methods. The hypothesis test is:

$$H_0: \mu_{GA} - \mu_{sAIS} = 0$$

$$H_A: \mu_{GA} - \mu_{sAIS} > 0$$

the results showed that the t-value = 2.09 and the p-value = 0.019. Because the p-value is less than the 0.05 significant level, we reject the null hypothesis and conclude that μ_{GA} is significantly greater than μ_{sAIS}. That is, the total cost, including transportation costs and operational costs, generated by the sAIS approach is smaller than the total cost generated by the GA in our experiments.

6. Conclusions and Future Research

In this research, a novel sAIS algorithm is proposed to approach the combinatorial optimal solution of the VRPCD. The primary objectives of this work include the integration of the operation of cross-docking and the optimal vehicle routing schedule into the design of supply chain optimization. A significant development lies in the synchronization between upstream suppliers and downstream retailers, where both sides of the supply chain are simultaneously considered to collaborate on the physical flow of goods in each inbound and outbound process. Manufacturers can reduce logistics costs by building IoT monitoring technology into smart logistics IT systems to track its location in real-time, reduce inventory levels in warehouses, monitor environmental conditions, and optimize the routing sequence for trucks for smart city infrastructure.

The computational results show that the sAIS model is effective for solving the VRPCD. The effectiveness of the method comes from the two-phase mechanism. In the initial route generation phase, the initial solution was generated by the sweep method before being input into the route's optimization phase with the AIS algorithm. The combination of the two-phase approach ensures that the sAIS method yields quality solutions.

A total of 60 benchmark problems were deployed to investigate the applicability of the proposed sAIS method. The experimental results showed that the sAIS method was able to produce significant improvements over the GA, surpassing each testing problem. Additionally, the sAIS method was able to discover better solutions than the GA method for all 60 benchmark problems, and the sAIS's search time is faster than the GA. It found sAIS to be a useful methodology. As artificial intelligence research rapidly increases, more simulations from human body systems could be used to improve the solution quality of the AIS optimization, and the AIS optimization could be applied to other research problems in the operations research field, such as multiple-criteria decision-making problems or supplier selection problems, etc.

Author Contributions: Conceptualization, S.-C.L. and Y.-L.C.; methodology, S.-C.L. and Y.-L.C.; validation, S.-C.L. and Y.-L.C.; formal analysis, S.-C.L. and Y.-L.C.; experimental, S.-C.L. and Y.-L.C.; writing—original draft preparation, S.-C.L. and Y.-L.C.; writing—review and editing, S.-C.L. and Y.-L.C.; visualization, S.-C.L. and Y.-L.C.; supervision, S.-C.L. and Y.-L.C.; funding acquisition, S.-C.L. All authors have read and agreed to the published version of the manuscript.

Funding: This research received no external funding.

Data Availability Statement: Not applicable.

Conflicts of Interest: The authors declare no conflict of interest.

Appendix A

Examples of optimized routing sequences are shown in the appendix.

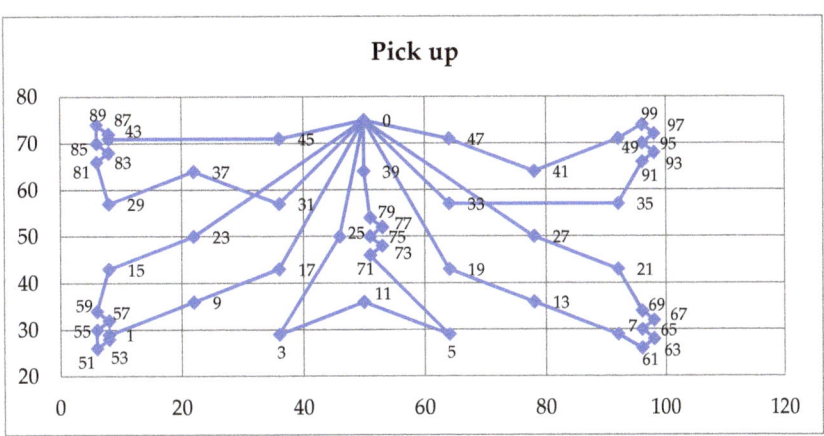

Figure A1. Optimized pickup routes from sAIS for instance 53P1.

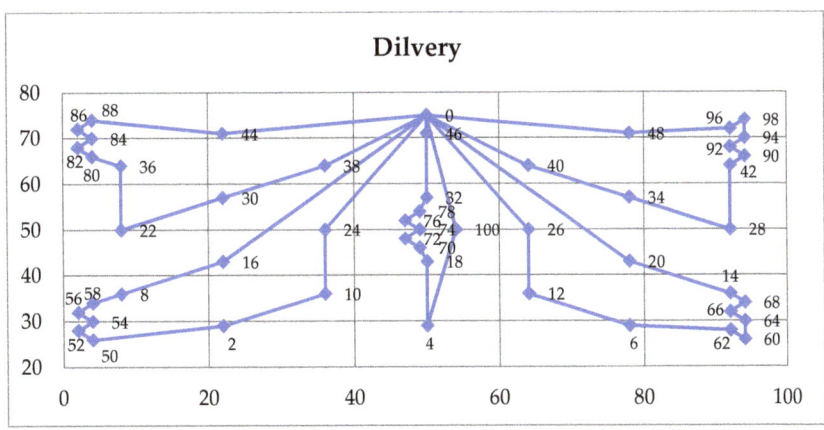

Figure A2. Optimized delivery routes from sAIS for instance 53P1.

Figure A3. Optimized pickup and delivery routes from sAIS for instance 53P1.

References

1. Khanh, Q.V.; Hoai, N.V.; Manh, L.D.; Le, A.N.; Jeon, G. Wireless communication technologies for IoT in 5G: Vision, applications, and challenges. *Wirel. Commun. Mob. Comput.* **2022**, *2022*, 3229294. [CrossRef]
2. Kamruzzaman, M.M. Key technologies, applications and trends of Internet of Things for energy-efficient 6G wireless communication in smart cities. *Energies* **2022**, *15*, 5608. [CrossRef]
3. Qadir, Z.; Le, K.N.; Saeed, N.; Munawar, H.S. Towards 6G Internet of Things: Recent advances, use cases, and open challenges. *ICT Express* **2022**, *In press*. [CrossRef]
4. Kulwiec, R. Crossdocking as a supply chain strategy. Association for Manufacturing Excellence. 2004. Available online: https://www.ame.org/sites/default/files/target_articles/04-20-3-Crossdocking.pdf (accessed on 23 January 2023).
5. Stępień, M.; Łęgowik-Świącik, S.; Skibińska, W.; Turek, I. Identification and measurement of logistics cost parameters in the company. *Transp. Res. Procedia* **2016**, *16*, 490–497. [CrossRef]
6. Laporte, G. Fifty years of vehicle routing. *Transp. Sci.* **2009**, *43*, 408–416. [CrossRef]
7. He, M.; Shen, J.; Wu, X.; Luo, J. Logistics space: A literature review from the sustainability perspective. *Sustainability* **2018**, *10*, 2815. [CrossRef]
8. Astachova, I.F.; Zolotukhin, A.E.; Kurklinskaya, E.Y.; Belyaeva, N.V. The application of artificial immune system to solve recognition problems. *J. Phys. Conf. Ser.* **2019**, *1203*, 012036. [CrossRef]
9. Wang, D.; Liang, Y.; Dong, H.; Tan, C.; Xiao, Z.; Liu, S. Innate immune memory and its application to artificial immune systems. *J. Supercomput.* **2022**, *78*, 11680–11701. [CrossRef]
10. Silva, G.C.; Dasgupta, D. A survey of recent works in artificial immune systems. In *Handbook on Computational Intelligence*; Angelov, P.P., Ed.; World Scientific Publishing Co Pte Ltd.: Singapore, 2016; pp. 547–586. [CrossRef]
11. Park, H.; Choi, J.E.; Kim, D.; Hong, S.J. Artificial immune system for fault detection and classification of semiconductor equipment. *Electronics* **2021**, *10*, 944. [CrossRef]
12. Miralvand, M.; Rasoolzadeh, S.; Majidi, M. Proposing a features preprocessing method based on artificial immune and minimum classification errors methods. *J. Appl. Res. Technol.* **2015**, *13*, 106–112. [CrossRef]
13. Ma, J.; Gao, L.; Shi, G. An Improved Immune Clonal Selection Algorithm and Its Applications for VRP. In Proceedings of the 2009 IEEE International Conference on Automation and Logistics, Shenyang, China, 5–7 August 2009. [CrossRef]
14. Arabani, A.R.B.; Ghomi, S.M.T.F.; Zandieh, M. Meta-heuristics implementation for scheduling of trucks in a cross-docking system with temporary storage. *Expert Syst. Appl.* **2011**, *38*, 1964–1979. [CrossRef]
15. Arabani, A.R.B.; Zandieh, M.; Ghomi, S.M.T.F. Multi-objective genetic-based algorithms for a cross-docking scheduling problem. *Appl. Soft Comput.* **2011**, *11*, 4954–4970. [CrossRef]
16. Arabani, A.R.B.; Zandieh, M.; Ghomi, S.M.T.F. A cross-docking scheduling problem with sub-population multi-objective algorithms. *Int. J. Adv. Manuf. Technol.* **2012**, *58*, 741–761. [CrossRef]
17. Lee, Y.H.; Jung, J.W.; Lee, K.M. Vehicle routing scheduling for cross-docking in the supply chain. *Comput. Ind. Eng.* **2006**, *51*, 247–256. [CrossRef]
18. Gunawan, A.; Widjaja, A.T.; Vansteenwegen, P.; Yu, V.F. A matheuristic algorithm for the vehicle routing problem with cross-docking. *Appl. Soft Comput.* **2021**, *103*, 107163. [CrossRef]
19. Dantzig, G.B.; Ramser, J.H. The truck dispatching problem. *Manage. Sci.* **1959**, *6*, 80–91. [CrossRef]
20. Vidal, T.; Crainic, T.G.; Gendreau, M.; Prins, C. Heuristics for multi-attribute vehicle routing problems: A survey and synthesis. *Eur. J. Oper. Res.* **2013**, *231*, 1–21. [CrossRef]
21. Hertrich, C.; Hungerländer, P.; Truden, C. Sweep algorithms for the capacitated vehicle routing problem with structured time windows. In *Operations Research Proceedings 2018*; Springer: Cham, Switzerland, 2019; pp. 127–133. [CrossRef]
22. Agárdi, A.; Kovács, L.; Bányai, T. Ontology support for vehicle routing problem. *Appl. Sci.* **2022**, *12*, 12299. [CrossRef]
23. Kamruzzaman, M.M. Hybrid modified ant system with sweep algorithm and path relinking for the capacitated vehicle routing problem. *Heliyon* **2021**, *7*, e08029. [CrossRef]
24. Borčinová, Z. Kernel search for the capacitated vehicle routing problem. *Appl. Sci.* **2022**, *12*, 11421. [CrossRef]
25. Laporte, G.; Nobert, Y.; Desrochers, M. Optimal routing under capacity and distance restrictions. *Oper. Res.* **1984**, *43*, 1050–1073. [CrossRef]
26. Mosheiov, G. Vehicle routing with pick-up and delivery: Tour partitioning heuristics. *Comput. Ind. Eng.* **1998**, *34*, 669–684. [CrossRef]
27. Baker, B.M.; Ayechew, M.A. A genetic algorithm for the vehicle routing problem. *Comput. Oper. Res.* **2003**, *30*, 787–800. [CrossRef]
28. Osman, I.H. Metastrategy simulated annealing and tabu search algorithms for the vehicle routing problem. *Ann. Oper. Res.* **1993**, *41*, 421–451. [CrossRef]
29. Taillard, É. Parallel iterative search methods for vehicle routing problems. *Networks* **1993**, *23*, 661–673. [CrossRef]
30. Gendreau, M.; Hertz, A.; Laporte, G. A Tabu search heuristic for the vehicle routing problem. *Manage. Sci.* **1994**, *40*, 1276–1290. [CrossRef]
31. Taillard, É.; Badeau, P.; Gendreau, M.; Guertin, F.; Potvin, J.-Y. A tabu search heuristic for the vehicle routing problem with soft time windows. *Transp. Sci.* **1997**, *31*, 101–195. [CrossRef]
32. Bell, J.E.; McMullen, P.R. Ant colony optimization techniques for the vehicle routing problem. *Adv. Eng. Inform.* **2004**, *18*, 41–48. [CrossRef]

33. Wu, H.; Gao, Y.; Wang, W.; Zhang, Z. A hybrid ant colony algorithm based on multiple strategies for the vehicle routing problem with time windows. *Complex Intell. Syst.* **2021**, 1–18. [CrossRef]
34. Ky Phuc, P.N.; Phuong Thao, N.L. Ant colony optimization for multiple pickup and multiple delivery vehicle routing problem with time window and heterogeneous fleets. *Logistics* **2021**, *5*, 28. [CrossRef]
35. Lo, S.-C. A particle swarm optimization approach to solve the vehicle routing problem with cross-docking and carbon emissions reduction in logistics management. *Logistics* **2022**, *6*, 62. [CrossRef]
36. Lo, S.-C.; Shih, Y.-C. A genetic algorithm with quantum random number generator for solving the pollution-routing problem in sustainable logistics management. *Sustainability* **2021**, *13*, 8381. [CrossRef]
37. Jerne, N.K. Towards a network theory of the immune system. *Ann. Immunol.* **1974**, *125C*, 373–389.
38. Farmer, J.D.; Packard, N.H.; Perelson, A.S. The immune system, adaption, and machine learning. *Physica. D.* **1986**, *22*, 187–204. [CrossRef]
39. Kephart, J.O. A biologically inspired immune system for computers. In *Artificial Life IV: The Fourth International Workshop on the Synthesis and Simulation of Living Systems*; Brooks, R.A., Maes, P., Eds.; The MIT Press: Cambridge, MA, USA, 1994; pp. 130–139. [CrossRef]
40. Hunt, J.; Timmis, J.; Cooke, E.; Neal, M.; King, C. Jisys: The envelopment of an artificial immune system for real world applications. In *Artificial Immune Systems and Their Applications*; Dasgupta, D., Ed.; Springer: Berlin/Heidelberg, Germany, 1999; pp. 157–186. [CrossRef]
41. Mrowczynska, B.; Ciesla, M.; Krol, A.; Sladkowski, A. Application of artificial intelligence in prediction of road freight transportation. *Promet—TrafficTransp.* **2017**, *29*, 363–370. [CrossRef]
42. Mabrouk, E.; Raslan, Y.; Hedar, A.-R. Immune system programming: A machine learning approach based on artificial immune systems enhanced by local search. *Electronics* **2022**, *11*, 982. [CrossRef]
43. Cutello, V.; Nicosia, G. An immunological approach to combinatorial optimization problems. In *Advances in Artificial Intelligence—IBERAMIA 2002*; Garijo, F.J., Riquelme, J.C., Toro, M., Eds.; Lecture Notes in Computer Science book series; Springer: Berlin/Heidelberg, Germany, 2002; Volume 2527, pp. 361–370. [CrossRef]
44. Parham, P. *The Immune System*, 4th ed.; Garland Science Publishing: New York, NY, USA, 2014; ISBN 978-08153443667.
45. Kim, Y.; Lee, H.; Park, K.; Park, S.; Lim, J.-H.; So, M.K.; Woo, H.-M.; Ko, H.; Lee, J.-M.; Lim, S.H.; et al. Selection and characterization of monoclonal antibodies targeting middle east respiratory syndrome coronavirus through a human synthetic fab phage display library panning. *Antibodies* **2019**, *8*, 42. [CrossRef]
46. Yadav, D.; Agarwal, S.; Pancham, P.; Jindal, D.; Agarwal, V.; Dubey, P.K.; Jha, S.K.; Mani, S.; Dey, A.; Jha, N.K.; et al. Probing the immune system dynamics of the COVID-19 disease for vaccine designing and drug repurposing using bioinformatics tools. *Immuno* **2022**, *2*, 344–371. [CrossRef]
47. Engin, O.; Döyen, A. A new approach to solve hybrid flow shop scheduling problems by artificial immune system. *Future Gener. Comput. Syst.* **2004**, *20*, 1083–1095. [CrossRef]
48. Chung, T.-P.; Liao, C.-J. An immunoglobulin-based artificial immune system for solving the hybrid flow shop problem. *Appl. Soft Comput.* **2013**, *13*, 3729–3736. [CrossRef]
49. Pan, S.; Manabe, N.; Yamaguchi, Y. 3D structures of IgA, IgM, and components. *Int. J. Mol. Sci.* **2021**, *22*, 12776. [CrossRef] [PubMed]
50. de Sousa-Pereira, P.; Woof, J.M. IgA: Structure, function, and developability. *Antibodies* **2019**, *8*, 57. [CrossRef] [PubMed]

Disclaimer/Publisher's Note: The statements, opinions and data contained in all publications are solely those of the individual author(s) and contributor(s) and not of MDPI and/or the editor(s). MDPI and/or the editor(s) disclaim responsibility for any injury to people or property resulting from any ideas, methods, instructions or products referred to in the content.

Article

Broad Embedded Logistic Regression Classifier for Prediction of Air Pressure Systems Failure

Adegoke A. Muideen [1,2], Carman Ka Man Lee [1,3,*], Jeffery Chan [1], Brandon Pang [1] and Hafiz Alaka [2]

1 Centre For Advances in Reliability and Safety (CAiRS), Hong Kong, China
2 Big Data Technologies and Innovation Laboratory, University of Hertfordshire, Hatfield AL10 9AB, UK
3 Department of Industrial and Systems Engineering, The Hong Kong Polytechnic University, Hong Kong, China
* Correspondence: ckm.lee@polyu.edu.hk

Abstract: In recent years, the latest maintenance modelling techniques that adopt the data-based method, such as machine learning (ML), have brought about a broad range of useful applications. One of the major challenges in the automotive industry is the early detection of component failure for quick response, proper action, and minimizing maintenance costs. A vital component of an automobile system is an air pressure system (APS). Failure of APS without adequate and quick responses may lead to high maintenance costs, loss of lives, and component damages. This paper addresses classification problem where we detect whether a fault does or does not belong to APS. If a failure occurs in APS, it is classified as positive class; otherwise, it is classified as negative class. Hence, in this paper, we propose broad embedded logistic regression (BELR). The proposed BELR is applied to predict APS failure. It combines a broad learning system (BLS) and logistic regression (LogR) classifier as a fusion model. The proposed approach capitalizes on the strength of BLS and LogR for a better APS failure prediction. Additionally, we employ the BLS's feature-mapped nodes for extracting features from the input data. Additionally, we use the enhancement nodes of the BLS to enhance the features from feature-mapped nodes. Hence, we have features that can assist LogR for better classification performances, even when the data is skewed to the positive class or negative class. Furthermore, to prevent the curse of dimensionality, a common problem with high-dimensional data sets, we utilize principal component analysis (PCA) to reduce the data dimension. We validate the proposed BELR using the APS data set and compare the results with the other robust machine learning classifiers. The commonly used evaluation metrics, namely Recall, Precision, an F1-score, to evaluate the model performance. From the results, we validate that performance of the proposed BELR.

Keywords: artificial intelligence; automotive; condition monitoring; machine learning; predictive maintenance

MSC: 68T07

1. Introduction

Air Processing System (APS) is a critical component in any brake system of heavy-duty vehicles. It plays an essential role in gauging brakes, controlling suspensions, shifting gears, etc. The effects of faulty APS are numerous. For instance, a faulty APS can cause improper functioning of gears, brakes, and suspension. These may lead to unpleasant/undesired situations such as total breakdown of the vehicles, which may lead to high maintenance costs and sometimes, in a critical situation, loss of life. To mitigate this side effect, the proper functioning of APS should be ensured; hence, its monitoring is vital. APS is said to be working properly when the APS supplies compressed air to its major components in an efficient, adequate, and timely manner.

Typically, in an automobile, the main components of APS are control units, circuit protection valves, and air dryers. A circuit-protection valve controls various circuits. Some of the circuits are a service brake circuit, a parking brake circuit, an auxiliary circuit, etc. It simply does this by activating them using different pre-set pressures. Furthermore, the air dryer removes excess moisture from the inlet air generated at the compressor. The control units dictate when to activate the compressor based on the pressure level in the APS. The control units consist of pressure sensors and temperature sensors.

APS failure detection is a key area of research [1,2]. It is a problem to detect whether an APS failure is the cause of a complete system breakdown or not. APS failures can result in huge maintenance costs and sometimes life-threatening situations. In recent years, machine learning-based techniques for APS failure detection are becoming increasingly popular. This is partly due to the large historical data set and the emergence of Industry 4.0 and the Industrial Internet of Things (IIoT). The core problems for APS failure detection/prediction are associated with:

- High volume of missing values in the data.
- Strongly imbalanced distribution of classes.

Figure 1 presents the missing values and imbalanced class distribution for APS failure data sets. From the figures, we notice many missing values in the data set. Hence, to tackle the problem, we cannot use the commonly used deletion method, as the missing value are many and deletion methods will cause large chunks of the data to be deleted. This will leave no or fewer data to be explored or used for the machine learning task. It is obvious from Figure 1 that the number of negative class cases is far higher than the number of positive class cases. Hence, the data set is highly imbalanced.

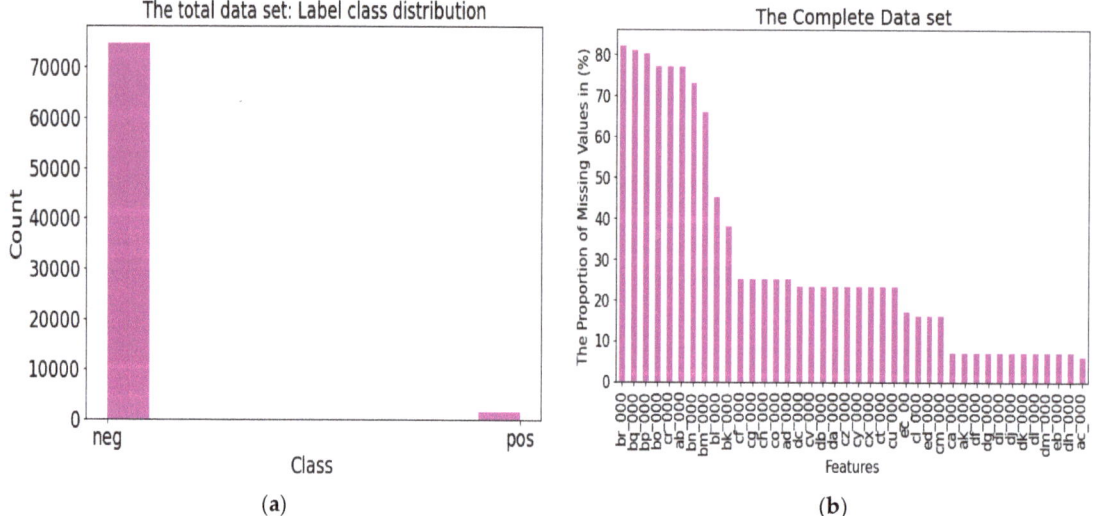

Figure 1. The distribution of the data set: (**a**) shows the class distribution and the imbalance of class distribution for the complete data set; (**b**) shows the percentage of missing values in each feature of the data set.

The two problems, namely class imbalance and missing values, can affect the performance of any machine learning algorithm if proper care is not taken [3,4]. Many researchers have worked on various techniques for handling missing data in APS data sets [1,5]. The existing techniques combined the classical data imputation methods with the traditional machine learning methods. However, the impact of modern data imputation methods is not explored. This could improve the performance of the machine learning method significantly. Additionally, a using modern machine learning method such as flat structure neural networks can enhance performance when the data is skewed to the positive class or negative class.

Additionally, a deep neural network with traditional classifiers can be used for many classification tasks. For instance, in [6], a deep neural network is trained together with a classifier where highly efficient features are extracted from raw data by a deep neural network, and a classifier, logistic regression [7], is used for classification. However, using a deep neural network requires high computation resources, and it takes a long time to train. Instead of using deep structure, some researchers have investigated random vector functional-link neural networks (RVFLNN). Chen and Liu [8] proposed BLS based on the concept of RVFLNN and obtained a promising result in classification accuracy and learning speed. The BLS network [8,9] is different from the deep neural network in many aspects, and its structure can be constructed widely. Additionally, the BLS network adopted incremental learning, which has quick remodelling without needing to re-train the network from scratch, provided that the performance of the initial network is not acceptable. In essence, the BLS network can be trained quickly and has good generalization performance. Additionally, BLS is regarded as a universal approximator with sufficient nodes in the network.

This paper explores the strength of a broad learning system and logistic regression for APS failure prediction. The BLS network is a flat structure neural network. It has a feature-mapped layer and a feature-enhancement layer. In addition, another common issue in a typical real-life big data set is high dimension. The high dimensional data set can affect the machine learning algorithm's performance. Additionally, it will increase the computational cost. To handle this, we explore principal component analysis (PCA) [10]. PCA is the widely used dimensionality reduction algorithm. Hence, to prevent the issue of the curse of dimensionally [11], we use PCA to reduce the dimension of the data set.

Furthermore, to the best of our knowledge, previous studies on APS failure detection have not investigated the performance of a flat structure neural network. A typical flat structure neural network example is a broad learning system. It has a broad layer structure where nodes are connected widely. More details of the network will be given in Section 3.

Generally, many machine learning models have difficulty handling imbalanced class distribution problems. However, the proposed approach can perform well under imbalanced class distribution problems. The proposed BELR does not require an additional or external method for imbalanced class distribution, as the feature-mapped nodes can extract features discriminative enough to enhance a classifier to separate classes from each other. The feature can be further enhanced by feature-enhancement nodes to uniquely classify each of the classes.

In summary, our method performance is reliable under challenging data sets such as the APS data set, which has an imbalance distribution problem. The idea of a missing mechanism is formalized in [12,13] where the study of missing data such as Missing at random (MAR), Missing not at random (MNAR), and Missing completely at random (MCAR) are presented in details. The data we employ in this paper have missing values across the feature set. A total of 169 features have missing values out of 170 features. Figure 2 shows the pattern of missing values in the data set across the features. From the Figure, the purple color represents the missing values, while the white or clear space represents where values exist in the data.

Additionally, the distribution of the data set and missing data is presented in [14]. In addition, Figure 2 shows the pattern of the missing values. From the idea in [12,13] and from the literature, the pattern of the missing values in the APS data set may be missing completely at random (MCAR). In our paper, the focus is not to categorize the pattern of the missing value in the APS data set. However, an appropriate method can be selected based on missing data mechanism in the data set. Thus, to prevent the destruction of the data set that could come from some missing value imputation method, we employ KNN imputer. In other words, we impute the missing value using the KNN technique [15]. Other methods such as imputation based on generative adversarial network (GAN) [14] could be explored. In [16], median imputation is explored for the problem of missing value. In this paper, we explore KNN imputation concept to tackle the problem of missing value. Figure 3 shows the pipeline of the proposed approach.

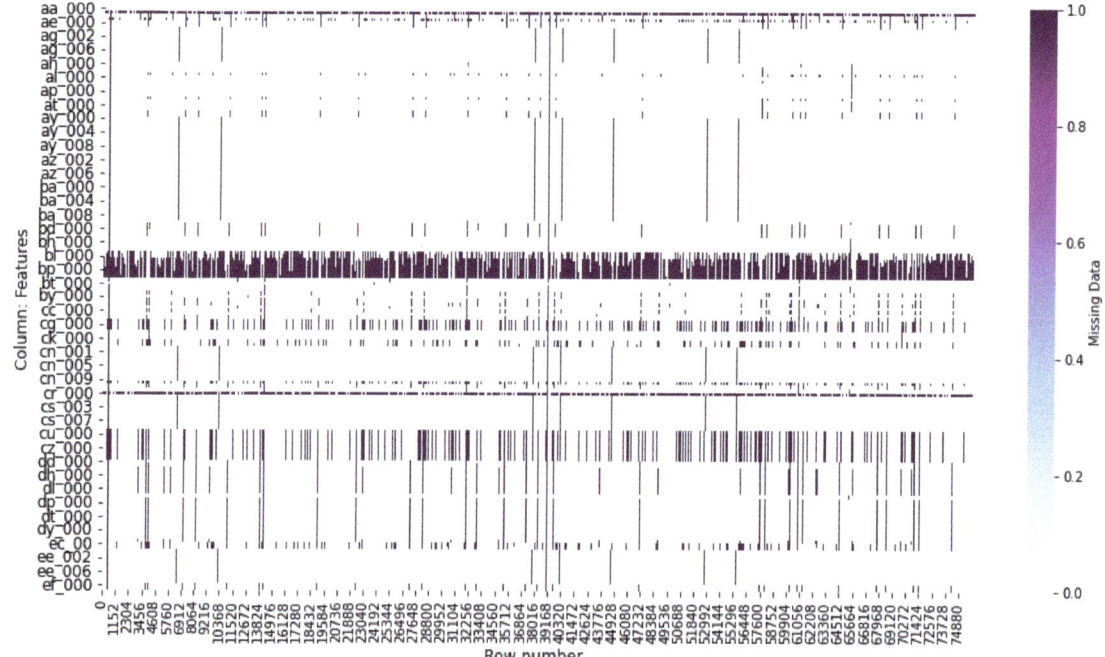

Figure 2. Pattern of the missing values in the data set across the features.

In summary, the contributions of this paper are summarized as follows:

- We propose broad embedded logistic regression (BELR). It is the fusion of broad learning system and logistic regression. We apply the proposed BELR to predict APS's failure.
- We propose a hybrid objective function based on the classical logistic regression objective function.
- We impute the missing value using the KNN algorithm.
- We propose and explore feature-mapped nodes of the BLS to extract discriminative features from the input data and enhancement nodes for further separation of the two classes such that the skewed distribution data set cannot affect the performance of the proposed broad embedded logistic regression (BELR).
- We explore principal component analysis (PCA) for dimensionality reduction and combine BLS and logistic regression classifier for the prediction of air pressure failure detection.

The rest of the paper is presented as follows. Section 2 presents related work on APS failure prediction from the literature. In Section 3, we describe the broad learning system (BLS) and give the mathematical model of the BLS. Additionally, Logistic regression (LogR) is discussed. Section 4 presents the experiment where the APS data set is described, and the numerical results are presented. In addition, in Section 4, the performances of the comparison algorithms and results are discussed. Section 5 gives the conclusion.

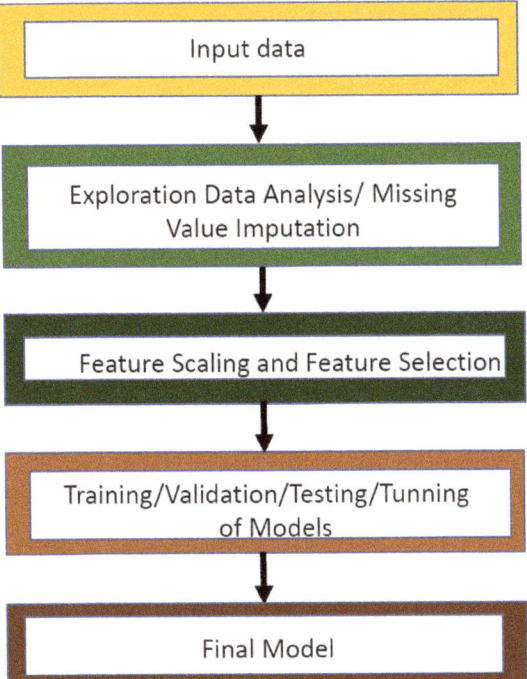

Figure 3. The Flow Chart of the Experimental Process.

2. Related Work

Diagnosis of transportation systems is a common task in the automotive industry. The problem is commonly handled using data analysis and machine learning methods. In this section, we focus on related works to APS failure prediction. Additionally, we present related work on the imbalanced classification problem from the literature.

2.1. APS Failure Prediction

First, standard machine learning approaches for APS failure prediction have been applied to the mentioned task. There are works on APS failure prediction. For instance, in [16,17], the failure of APS of heavy-duty vehicles is studied. In the paper, the weighted loss function is employed to improve the performance of the network architecture used. In addition, in [18], a fuzzy-based machine learning algorithm is utilized for air pressure failure prediction. The fuzzy based algorithm was combined with a relaxed prediction horizon for better air-pressure failure-prediction performance. Furthermore, APS failure prediction was analyzed by [16,19] using various machine learning algorithms, namely Support vector machines (SVM), Multi-Layer Perception (MLP), and Naive Bayes. The author extracts a feature from the raw data set using the feature engineering method namely histogram. In addition, feature ranking was implemented in their feature-selection approach. In the work, the preprocessing method used for the missing value replacement is KNN imputation, where the nearest neighbour in each feature column replaces the missing value. The metric used in terms of cost is based on total misclassification by the algorithm. In the metric, fp is set as a false positive, which predicts the failure wrongly, and fn is set as a false negative, which is missing a failure. In their proposed approach, missing a failure has a cost of 500, while the cost of falsely predicting a failure is given by 10. In their approach, a mean cost of 0.6 was achieved. The mean cost is given by $\frac{1}{Number\ of\ test\ sample}(10 * fp + 500 * fn)$.

Additionally, to consider imbalance class issues, in some works, weighted data classifiers are used for APS failure prediction [14], logistic regression (LogR), and SVM classifiers. In their method, class-specific weights were integrated into the classifier. The value of the weight for each class is chosen such that it is inversely proportional to the number of samples in a class. Other classical machine learning methods have been applied to the APS data set. For instance, the performance of many machine learning techniques on the APS data set was investigated in Refs. [20–22]. The problem is a binary classification task. In their approach, they resolve the class imbalance problem with the aid of SMOTE (Synthetic Minority Oversampling Technique) algorithm to balance the positive class and negative class examples. Additionally, the author performs feature engineering before applying the machine learning algorithm. Besides, a new method for predicting APS failure was proposed in Ref. [23]. The method maximizes Area Under the Curves (max AUC) by utilizing a linear decision boundary. It is specifically designed to handle imbalance class distribution in the data set.

From all the previous studies on APS failure prediction, most authors focus on exploring the classical machine learning algorithms such as SVM, KNN, NB, LogR, etc. In summary, to the best of our knowledge, no work on APS failure prediction has used the neural network or flat structure-based machine learning methods, namely extreme learning machine (ELM) [24–26] and broad learning system (BLS) [8,26–29]. However, ELM and BLS algorithms are popular among researchers, and they are widely used in many applications. This is partly because they are universal approximators; with sufficient hide nodes, they can estimate any functions. Additionally, they are fast and easy to implement. Hence, in this work, we proposed to combine a broad learning system (BLS) and logistic regression (LogR) to predict APS failure. The background details of BLS and LogR are given in the next sections.

2.2. Broad Learning System (BLS) and Logistic Regression (LogR)

2.2.1. Broad Learning System (BLS)

The concept of BLS [8] is a new technique. BLS and other variants [8,30,31] connect hidden nodes of a neural network broadly. As shown in Figure 4, the nodes are put together in a broad flat structure. A BLS network contains two hidden layers, namely the enhancement layer and feature-mapped layer.

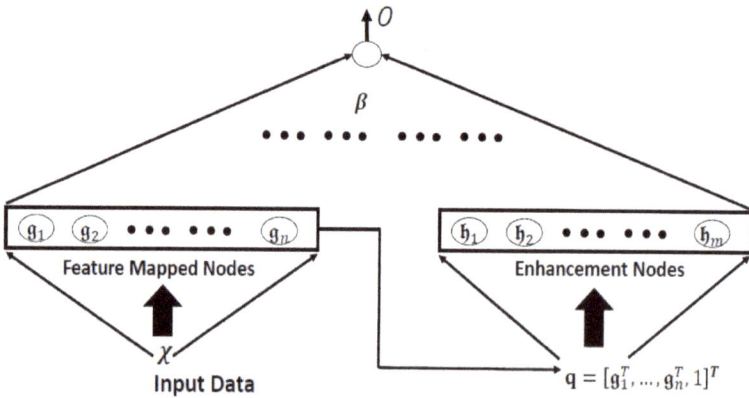

Figure 4. A typical structure of a BLS network.

The concept introduced in the BLS framework is promising. It is an efficient, simple learning algorithm. Due to the efficient feature-extraction capacity of the nodes in the feature-mapped layer and enhancement layer of the BLS, the original BLS and hybrid methods, where feature-mapped layer of BLS and other techniques are combined, have been used in many applications. However, much work has not been completed using neural network-based algorithms to predict APS failure in the case of APS failure. In view of the points and that BLS's feature-mapped nodes and enhancement nodes can extract effective features from the input data, which can enhance the performance of a classifier, we combine BLS and logistic regression (LogR) to study APS failure prediction. Thus, we propose broad embedded logistic regression (BELR) for APS failure prediction.

2.2.2. Operation of BLS Networks

This subsection gives background knowledge on the operation of a BLS network. This paper proposed BLS for solving the air pressure system failure classification problem. In this paper, the classification problem is formulated as nonlinear logistic regression, where the input of a logistic regression algorithm is the feature from the BLS network. The final output is the sign of the predicted value or the probability of the predicted output. In other words, if the sign is positive, then the predicted value belongs to the positive class. Otherwise, the predicted class is negative. Let $\mathbf{x} \in \mathbb{R}^D$ be the input data to the BLS network, where D is the dimension of the input data, and $o \in \mathbb{R}$ be the output of a BLS network. In this section, for smooth and clear presentation, we present the input $\mathbf{x}$ augmented with 1 as $\chi = [\mathbf{x}^T, 1]^T$.

(a) Feature-mapped nodes

The BLS network has two main layers, namely feature-mapped layer and enhancement layer. The feature-mapped layer is to extract features from input data. For the feature-mapped layer, there are n groups of the feature-mapped nodes. These n groups are concatenated together to form one main feature extraction. The output of the main feature-extraction group is passed to the output layer, and another layer is called the enhancement layer. Each group from the n groups is used to extract distinctive features. Each group has it on a specific number of nodes. For instance, in this paper, f_i represents the i-th group of the feature-mapped nodes. Hence, for n groups of features-mapped nodes, the total number of features-mapped nodes is the following:

$$f = \sum_{i=1}^{n} f_i \qquad (1)$$

It should be noted that f_i for $i = 1, \ldots n$ may not be equal. For each group of the feature-mapped node, which is the i-th group of features-mapped nodes, there is an associated learned projection matrix, and the i-th learned projection matrix is given by:

$$\mathbf{\Psi}_i = \begin{pmatrix} \psi_{i,1,1} & \cdots & \psi_{i,1,(D+1)} \\ \vdots & \ddots & \vdots \\ \psi_{i,f_i,1} & \cdots & \psi_{i,f_i,(D+1)} \end{pmatrix} \qquad (2)$$

where $\mathbf{\Psi}_i \in \mathbb{R}^{f_i \times (D+1)}$. It is designed to generate features from the input data. The i-th group of mapped features g_i are obtained by projecting the input data with the matrix $\mathbf{\Psi}_i$. They are given by the following:

$$\begin{aligned} \mathfrak{g}_i &= [g_{i,1}, \cdots, g_{i,f_i}]^T \\ &= \mathbf{\Psi}_i \chi \qquad \forall i = 1, \cdots, n, \end{aligned} \qquad (3)$$

where $g_{i,u}$ is the u-th feature of the u-th group, where $i = 1, \cdots, n$, and $u = 1, \cdots, f_i$.

In the classical BLS, $\mathbf{\Psi}_i$'s is constructed based on sparse optimization steps. There are many ways to achieve these steps. One way is to solve sparse optimization problems based on the alternating direction method of multipliers ADMM [32] algorithm. In Section 2.2.3-(a), we present the construction procedure of $\mathbf{\Psi}_i$'s. In the classical BLS scheme, a linear operation is applied on $\mathfrak{g}_i$s. It should be noted that $\mathfrak{g}_i$s is not χ but features-extracted from χ. Similarly, a nonlinear operation can be applied on $\mathfrak{g}_i$'s as well.

In this paper, we apply a linear operation on $\mathfrak{g}_i$'s, that is, this paper follows the classical BLS framework. The outputs from the n group of the feature-mapped nodes are gathered as

$$\mathbf{g} = [\mathfrak{g}_1^T, \cdots, \mathfrak{g}_n^T]^T \in \mathbb{R}^f \tag{4}$$

Additionally, we let

$$\mathbf{q} = [\mathbf{g}^T, 1]^T \in \mathbb{R}^{f+1} \tag{5}$$

for a smooth mathematical model presentation and as the augmented vector of $\mathbf{g}$.

(b) Enhancement nodes

Like the feature-mapped nodes, the enhancement nodes of the BLS network have m groups of enhancement nodes. In the enhancement layer, the j-th group of enhancement nodes has e_j nodes. The total number of enhancement nodes in the BLS network is given by

$$e = \sum_{j=1}^{m} e_j \tag{6}$$

In addition, the output of j-th group of enhancement nodes is given by

$$\mathfrak{H}_j = \left[\mathfrak{H}_{j,1}, \ldots \mathfrak{H}_{j,e_j}\right]^T = \xi(\mathbf{W}_j \mathbf{q}) \tag{7}$$

where $j = 1, \cdots, m$ and $\mathbf{W}_j$ is the weight that connects the output of feature-mapped nodes to the input of the enhancement nodes together. It should be known that, in the original BLS framework, $\mathbf{W}_j$ is a randomly generated. The elements of $\mathbf{W}_j$ are denoted as

$$\mathbf{W}_j = \begin{pmatrix} w_{j,1,1} & \cdots & w_{j,1,f+1} \\ \vdots & \ddots & \vdots \\ w_{j,e_j,1} & \cdots & w_{j,e_j,f+1} \end{pmatrix}. \tag{8}$$

It should be known that $\xi(\cdot)$ is the activation function for enhancement nodes. Each group of enhancement nodes can have its activation function. In the original BLS algorithm, the hyperbolic tangent is employed as the activation function for all the enhancement nodes. This paper uses hyperbolic tangent as the activation function for all enhancement nodes. We gather all the enhancement node outputs together as

$$\mathbf{\eta} = [\mathfrak{h}_1^T, \cdots, \mathfrak{h}_m^T]^T \in \mathbb{R}^e \tag{9}$$

(c) Network Output

For a given input vector $\mathbf{x}$, the output of the network is

$$o = [\mathbf{g}^T | \mathbf{\eta}^T] \boldsymbol{\beta} \tag{10}$$

where $\boldsymbol{\beta}$ is the output weight vector. The number of elements in $\boldsymbol{\beta}$ is equal to $f + e$. Hence, its components are given by

$$\boldsymbol{\beta} = [\beta_1, \ldots, \beta_{f+e}]^T \tag{11}$$

2.2.3. Construction of Weight Matrices and Vectors

Given N training pairs $\mathbb{D}_{train} = \{(\mathbf{x}_k, y_k) : k = 1, \ldots, N\}\}$, where $\mathbf{x}_k = [x_{k,1}, \cdots, x_{k,D}]^T$ is a D dimensional training input and y_k is the corresponding target output as the training set. Consider that the training data matrix is formed by packing all the input $\mathbf{x}_k$'s together. The augmented data matrix denoted as $\mathbf{X}$ is given by

$$\mathbf{X} = \begin{pmatrix} \mathbf{x}_1^T & | & 1 \\ \vdots & | & \vdots \\ \mathbf{x}_N^T & | & 1 \end{pmatrix} \tag{12}$$

(a) Construction of the Projection Matrix $\mathbf{\Psi}_i$

For each group of features-mapped nodes, one important thing in the framework of BLS is building the projection matrix $\mathbf{\Psi}_i$. An important question then arises as follows: how to build the projection matrix? The approach presented here follows the procedures of [8,33]. In the BLS, a random matrix $\mathcal{P}_i \in \mathbb{R}^{(D+1) \times f_i}$ is generated first for each group of features-mapped nodes. Afterwards, we can obtain a random-projection data matrix $\mathbf{Q}_i$, given by

$$\mathbf{Q}_i = \mathbf{X} \mathcal{P}_i \tag{13}$$

The projection matrix $\mathbf{\Psi}_i$ is the result of the sparse approximation problem given by

$$\min_{\mathbf{\Psi}_i} \left\{ \| \mathbf{Q}_i \mathbf{\Psi}_i - \mathbf{X} \|_F^2 + \rho \| \mathbf{\Psi}_i \|_1 \right\} \tag{14}$$

where in (14), the term $\rho \| \mathbf{\Psi}_i \|_1$ is to enforce the solution of (14) to be a sparse matrix. Additionally, ρ is a regularization parameter for sparse regularization. In addition, F is the popular Frobenius norm and $\| . \|_1$ is norm 1.

(b) Construction of the Weight Matrices of the Enhancement Nodes

To some degree, the construction step of $\mathbf{W}_j$'s is a bit straightforward. For instance, as detailed in [8,33,34], the traditional BLS algorithm and other variants randomly generate the weight matrices for each group of the enhancement nodes. Similarly, this paper follows the same procedure to generate $\mathbf{W}_j$'s.

(c) Construction of Output Weight Vector

This section gives the procedure to construct the output weight vector $\boldsymbol{\beta}$. Given the projection matrix $\mathbf{\Psi}_i$'s $\forall i = 1, \cdots, n$ of the feature-mapped nodes, and the training data matrix $\mathbf{X}$, the i-th training data feature matrix for all training samples is given by

$$\mathbf{Z}_i = \begin{pmatrix} \mathbf{z}_{i,1}^T \\ \vdots \\ \mathbf{z}_{i,N}^T \end{pmatrix} = \mathbf{X} \mathbf{\Psi}_i^T \tag{15}$$

where $\mathbf{z}_{i,k} = [z_{i,k,1}, \cdots, z_{i,k,f_i}]^T$, and

$$z_{i,k,u} = \sum_{\iota=1}^{D} \psi_{i,u,\iota} x_{k,\iota} + \psi_{i,u,D+1} \tag{16}$$

Let $\mathcal{Z}$ be the collection of all training data feature matrices. Hence, we have

$$\mathcal{Z} = [\mathbf{Z}_1, \cdots, \mathbf{Z}_n] \tag{17}$$

In this way, $\mathcal{Z}$ is an $N \times f$ matrix, denoted as

$$\mathcal{Z} = \begin{pmatrix} \mathcal{Z}_{1,1} & \cdots & \mathcal{Z}_{1,f} \\ \vdots & \ddots & \vdots \\ \mathcal{Z}_{N,1} & \cdots & \mathcal{Z}_{N,f} \end{pmatrix} = \begin{pmatrix} \mathcal{Z}_1^T \\ \vdots \\ \mathcal{Z}_N^T \end{pmatrix} \tag{18}$$

where the k-th row vector $\mathcal{Z}_k^T$ of $\mathcal{Z}$ is the inputs of the enhancement nodes (the outputs of the feature-mapped nodes) for the k-th training input vector $\mathbf{x}_k$. To handle input biases, we augment one vector into $\mathcal{Z}$, given by

$$\mathcal{Z}' = \begin{pmatrix} \mathcal{Z}_1^T & 1 \\ \vdots & \vdots \\ \mathcal{Z}_N^T & 1 \end{pmatrix} = \begin{pmatrix} \mathcal{Z}'_1{}^T \\ \vdots \\ \mathcal{Z}'_N{}^T \end{pmatrix} \qquad (19)$$

Furthermore, given $\mathcal{Z}$, the enhancement node outputs of the j-th enhancement group for all training data are given by

$$\mathbf{H}_j = \zeta\left(\mathcal{Z}' \mathbf{W}_j^T\right) = \begin{pmatrix} \mathbf{h}_{j,1}^T \\ \vdots \\ \mathbf{h}_{j,N}^T \end{pmatrix} \qquad (20)$$

for $j = 1, \cdots, m$, where

$$\mathbf{h}_{j,k} = [h_{j,k,1}, \cdots, h_{j,k,e_j}]^T \qquad (21)$$

and

$$h_{j,k,v} = \zeta\left(\sum_{\tau=1}^{f+1} w_{j,v,\tau} \mathcal{Z}'_{k,\tau}\right) \qquad (22)$$

Packing all the enhancement node outputs together, we have

$$\mathcal{H} = [\mathbf{H}_1, \cdots, \mathbf{H}_m] \qquad (23)$$

where $\mathcal{H}$ is a $N \times \left(\sum_{j=1}^m e_j\right) = N \times e$ matrix.

Define $\mathcal{A} = [\mathcal{Z}|\mathcal{H}]$. The output weight vector β can be calculated based on least square techniques:

$$\arg\min_{\beta} \|\mathcal{A}\beta - \mathbf{y}\|_\rho^\rho + \varrho \|\beta\|_\lambda^\lambda \qquad (24)$$

where $\mathbf{y} = [y_1, \cdots, y_N]^T$ is the collection of all training outputs. Equation (24) means that we can have different cost functions by setting different values of ρ, ϱ, λ. It should be noted the value of ρ and λ are not necessarily the same. In this paper, to explore BLS for air pressure failure prediction, we reformulate the objective function (24) like that of logistic regression. In the next subsection, we give background details of logistic regression (LogR).

2.2.4. Logistic Regression

Logistic regression (LogR) is a widely used and popular probabilistic statistical classification technique. It is designed for binary classification problems. Logistic regression is detailed in [35]. The technique aims to maximize the likelihood function given by

$$J_{LogR} = \prod_{k=1}^N t_k^{y_k}\{1 - t_k\}^{1-y_k}; t_k = \sigma\left(\mathbf{w}^T \mathbf{x}_k\right) \qquad (25)$$

where $\sigma(z) = \frac{1}{1+\exp^{-z}}$ and $\mathbf{x}_k$ is the k-th input vector. We can further modify (25) as a minimization problem. With manipulations, we turn (25) to a well-known cross-entropy error function (26). By taking the negative logarithm of the likelihood function (25), we arrive at

$$J(w) = -\log(J_{LogR}) = -\sum_{k=1}^N \{y_k \log(t_k) + (1 - y_k)\log(1 - t_k)\} \qquad (26)$$

The gradient descent can be used to optimize the error function (25) to obtain an optimal output weight $\mathbf{w}$.

3. The Proposed Technique

In the proposed approach, we capitalize on the strength of a broad learning system (BLS) and logistic regression (LogR). Figure 5 shows the structure of the fused BLS network with logistic regression classifier.

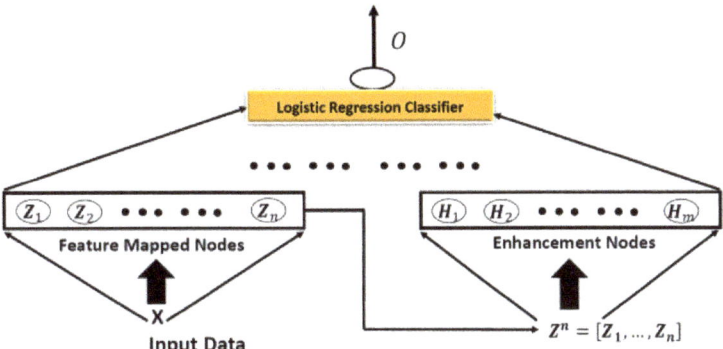

Figure 5. The Flowchart of the proposed network and procedure.

In Figure 5, input **X** is passed to the feature-mapped layer, where the feature Z^n is extracted and obtained. This feature is further enhanced to obtain an enhanced feature H^m. Both features are combined as $\mathcal{A} = [Z^n | H^m]$. The concatenated features are then passed to the logistic regression classifier for making the decision. The fusion of logistic regression and broad learning system, with the effectiveness of the feature-extraction layer and enhancement layer improves the performance of the network. For instance, when the feature nodes extract features from the input X, the enhancement nodes further enhance the features such that the distance between the positive class and negative class is widened. Hence, it able to separate between class even when the two classes are in balance.

In our approach, we incorporate the objective function of BLS (24) into the objective function of LogR (25). In other words, for the proposed broad embedded logistic regression model, we assume a non-linear relationship between the input of the logistic regression classifier and the output of logistic regression classifier. For easy notation and explanation, we let

$$\mathcal{A} = \begin{bmatrix} \mathcal{A}_1, \cdots, \mathcal{A}_{f+e} \end{bmatrix} = \begin{bmatrix} a_{1,1} & \cdots & a_{1,f+e} \\ \vdots & \ddots & \vdots \\ a_{N,1} & \cdots & a_{N,f+e} \end{bmatrix}$$

Additionally, the probability that $y_k = 1$ is given by p_k. In other words, when the model predicts that $y_k = 1$, the prediction probability is given by p_k. Hence, we formulate the relationship between feature $\mathcal{A}$ obtained from the BLS network and the output weight $\beta = [\beta_1, \ldots, \beta_{f+e}]^T$. In addition, we add a bias term β_0 and $\mathcal{A}_0 = [1, 1, 1 \ldots 1]^T$ into the relationship. Hence, for k-th input, we have

$$l_k = a_{k,0} \beta_0 + \sum_{r=1}^{f+e} a_{k,r} \beta_r = \log_b \frac{p_k}{1 - p_k} \quad (27)$$

where l_k is the log-odds for the k-th. Furthermore, it should be noted that b is an additional generalization, it is the base of the model.

For a more compact notation and to take the bias term into consideration, we specify the feature variables $\overline{\mathcal{A}}$ and $\overline{\beta}$ as $(f+e+1)$—dimensional vectors. They are given by

$$\begin{aligned}\overline{\mathcal{A}} &= \begin{bmatrix}\mathcal{A}_0, \mathcal{A}_1, \cdots, \mathcal{A}_{f+e+1}\end{bmatrix} \\ \overline{\beta} &= [\beta_0, \beta_1, \ldots, \beta_{f+e+1}]^T\end{aligned} \quad (28)$$

where $\mathcal{A}_0 = [a_{1,0}, \ldots a_{N,0}]^T$, $\mathcal{A}_1 = [a_{1,1}, \ldots a_{N,1}]^T, \ldots, \mathcal{A}_{f+e+1} = [a_{1,f+e+1}, \ldots a_{N,f+e+1}]^T$. Hence, we rewrite the logit, l_k as

$$l_k = \sum_{r=0}^{f+e} a_{k,r} \beta_r = \log_b \frac{p_k}{1-p_k} \quad (29)$$

Now, solving for the probability p_k that the model predicts $y_k = 1$. yields.

$$p_k = \frac{e^{l_k}}{1+e^{l_k}} = \sigma(l_k) \quad (30)$$

where b is substituted by e and it is exponential function and where $\sigma(.)$ is the sigmoid function. With (30), we can easily compute the probability that $y_k = 1$ for a given observation. The optimum β can be obtained by minimizing the negative log-likelihood of (30). Hence, the log-likelihood may be written as follows:

$$\begin{aligned}J &= \sum_{k=1}^{N} \{-y_k \log(p_k) - (1-y_k)\log(1-p_k)\} + \rho \parallel \beta \parallel_\lambda^\lambda \\ &= \sum_{j=1}^{N} \{-y_k \log(\sigma_k) - (1-y_k)\log(1-\sigma_k)\} + \rho \parallel \beta \parallel_\lambda^\lambda\end{aligned} \quad (31)$$

where

$$\sigma_k = \frac{1}{1+exp^{(l_k)}} = \frac{1}{1+exp^{(\sum_{r=0}^{f+e} a_{k,r}\beta_r)}} \quad (32)$$

We employ gradient descent to optimize the proposed objective function (31). We name our proposed technique broad embedded logistic regression (BELR).

From (26) and (31), it should be noted that the traditional logistic regression can only manage the linear relationship between dependent variables and independent variables effectively. In other words, the classical logistic regression does not consider any possible nonlinear relationship between the dependent variable and independent variables. Unlike the classical logistic regression classifier, where the raw data are used as its input directly, in this paper, from (31), the output of the feature-mapped node and enhancement node of BLS is the input of the logistic regression classifier. In other words, enhanced features serve as the input of the logistic regression classifier. This improves the performance of the algorithm.

In addition, the objective function (31) of the proposed approach contains the regularizer $\rho \parallel \beta \parallel_\lambda^\lambda$, where λ can be chosen or set to different values to have different scenarios and to improve the performance of the network. For instance, for $\lambda = 1$, the output weight of the proposed method will have a sparse solution. This setting can allow the network to automatically select a relevant feature from $\overline{\mathcal{A}}$, which may enhance the network performance. Similarly, if λ is set to 2, the output weight will have dense values and the values will be small. This will prevent the network from overfitting. In this paper, our focus is not to have a sparse solution. Hence, in our experiment, we utilize $\lambda = 2$.

4. Experiment and Settings

In this section, we compare the proposed BELR with other linear and non-linear algorithms, namely the original logistic regression (LogR), Random Forest classifier (RF), Gaussian Naive Bayes (GNB), K-nearest neighbour (KNN), and Support Vector Machine

(SVM). We use four evaluation metrics in our comparison. Table 1 presents the evaluation metrics used to evaluate the performance of the comparison algorithms.

Table 1. The METRICS FOR THE MODELS comparison.

Evaluation Metrics	Equivalent Equation
Precision	$\frac{TP}{(TP+FP)}$
Recall	$\frac{TP}{(TP+FN)}$
F1-Score	$\frac{2*(Precision*Recall)}{(Precision+Recall)}$
Accuracy	The fraction of the predictions the model executed correctly $\frac{TP+TN}{(TP+TN+FP+FN)}$

From the Table, False Positive (FP) is the number of examples which are predicted to be positive by the model but belong to the negative class. False Negative (FN) is the number of examples which are predicted to be negative by the model but belong to the positive class. True Positive (TP) is the number of examples which are predicted to be positive by the model and belong to the positive class.

Furthermore, for a fair comparison, in all the comparison algorithms, we use standard settings for all the parameters suggested in the scikit-learn machine learning package [36]. Additionally, we use APS data set [37,38]. This benchmark data set is commonly used to evaluate machine learning algorithms, specifically for APS failure prediction tasks. There are two problems with the data set. First, the data set contains a high number of missing values. Second, the data set has a high imbalance in class distribution.

In some papers, median imputation has been used to fill missing data. For instance, in [16], the median imputation technique was utilized to handle missing values. However, median imputation can cause destruction to the data. Hence, we employ a robust imputer, namely the KNN imputation method. Thus, we replace the missing values in each column using KNN. The data set used in this paper is quite challenging, as it has the issue of imbalanced class distribution. Our proposed BELR has a comparable good performance. This may be attributed to the ability of feature-mapped layer (nodes) to extract features from the input data and enhancement layer (nodes) for further enhancement of the feature such that the classes are separated from each other. Hence, this improves the performance of BELR under skew data set. This is validated when we compare the original logistic regression classifier and the proposed BELR.

After filling the missing data using KNN imputer, we use cross validation method to fit the comparison models. Furthermore, inside cross-validation, we extract features by using BLS on training set, then fit logistic regression on a feature from the training set, then used the test set to estimate quality metrics.

The total data points are split into 10-fold using stratified method of scikit-learn machine learning package and run each algorithm 10 times. For instance, in the first run we combine nine samples of the divided data as the training set and the remaining one sample for test set. We repeat this process 10 times using different set of data points as the training set and test set. Table 2 summarize the details of the data set used in the first run. In the experiment, we present the average performance of each compared algorithm.

Table 2. Details of the data set and further details of the data set.

Total Number of Data Points	No Rows of Training Data	No Rows of Test Data	
76,000	68,400	7600	
Training Set		Test Set	
Negative Case	Positive Case	Negative Case	Positive Case
67,162	123	7462	137

From the table, the ratio of positive case to negative case in the training set is 0.001831, and for the test set, it is 0.018360. It should be noted that we have used stratified method of scikit-learn, a machine learning package, in our cross-validation methods. It takes into consideration the imbalance class of the data to split the data into 10-fold.

The Comparison of the Performance of the Compared Algorithms

In the subsection, we compare the proposed BELR and the original logistic regression (LogR), Random Forest classifier (RF), Gaussian Naive Bayes (GNB), K-nearest neighbour (KNN), and Support Vector Machine (SVM). The average performance in terms of the metrics listed in Table 1 is presented for the comparison algorithms. First, to prevent the effect of the curse of dimensionality, we use principal component analysis (PCA) to reduce the dimension and select an important feature from the input data. A total of 81 principal components are created after applying the PCA technique with a covariance value of 0.95. The initial dimension of input data is 170; however, after applying PCA, the dimension is reduced to 81, which is almost 50% of the feature variables compared to the initial feature variables. After applying PCA, we then apply comparison algorithms on the feature from PCA. We use 10-fold cross-validation concept. In the experiment, the total number of data point is 76,000. For each fold, there are 7600 data points after applying stratified cross-validation, ensuring that each fold has the same proportion of observations with a given categorical value. In the first run, we take one group (7600 data points) as the test set and the remaining nine groups (9 × 7600 data points) for training of the model. In the second run, we pick another 76,000 data points (a new group) as the test set and the remaining nine groups (9 × 7600 data points) to train the models. The process continues until we reach the 10th run or trial. The training set contains 67,162 negative cases and 123 positive cases. Similarly, the test set contains 7462 negative cases and 137 positive cases. Table 2 shows the details. From the experiment, the results obtained are presented in Table 3.

Table 3. The performance of comparison algorithms under certain metrics.

Score (%)	GNB	LogR	RF	SVM	KNN	BELR
Precision	32.45	77.81	82.6	92.05	80.23	80.91
Sensitivity (Recall)	79.35	57.89	57.67	27.78	55.78	62.25
F1-Score	46.06	66.39	67.92	42.68	65.81	70.39
Accuracy	96.64	98.94	99.01	98.65	98.95	99.05

From Table 3, we notice that GNB has a recall of 79.35, and the performance looks better than the rest of the algorithms. However, GNB has a very poor performance in precision. It has a precision score of 32.45. In addition, it has a very poor performance in F1-score, with a score of 46.06.

For other algorithms, it is notice that SVM has a very good score in precision but a very poor score in recall. This resulted in a poor value of F1-score. However, LogR, RF, KNN, and the proposed BELR have good precision and recall scores from the Table. Their performances in terms of precision are relatively equal. The proposed BELR has the best average score in terms of Sensitivity (Recall). In addition, when we compared the performance of the compared algorithms in terms of average F1-score, the proposed BELR has the best F1-score, as shown in Table 3. Other scores for other evaluation metrics are presented in the Table. We use boxplot to present the average F1-score of all the compared algorithms. Figure 6 presents the average F1 score of the performance of the compared algorithms. It is noticed that the proposed BELR has a better F1 score from the box plot.

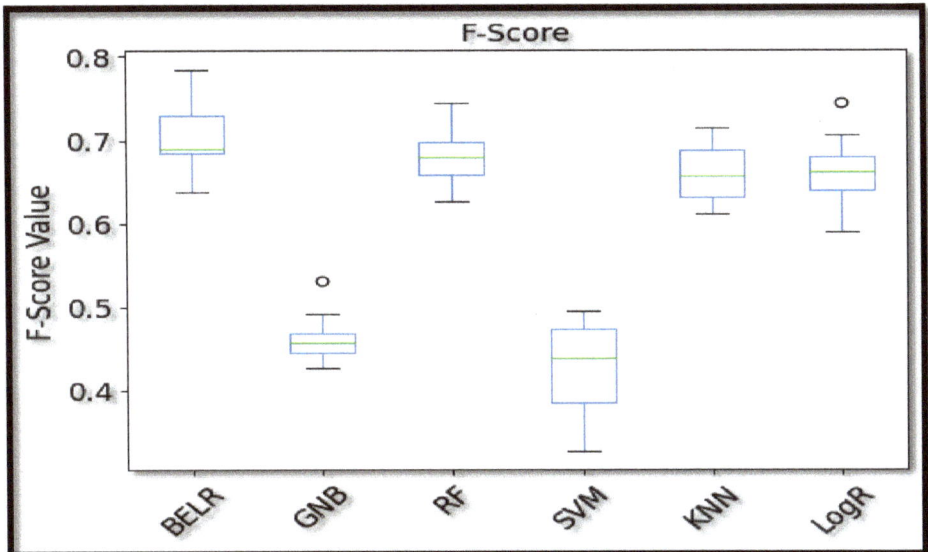

Figure 6. The average F1-score of the compared algorithms.

Overall, we notice that the performance of the proposed BELR is better than the other comparison algorithms under an imbalanced data set.

5. Conclusions

This paper proposes broad embedded logistic regression (BELR) for classification problems, specifically for APS failure prediction. In addition, its performance is studied under an exceedingly difficult data situation and an imbalanced class distribution problem. The feature-mapped nodes and enhancement nodes of the BLS are employed to handle imbalance data set due to the ability of the two types of nodes to generate/extract features that can uniquely separate two classes from each other. Hence, it improves the classification capacity of logistic regression classifier.

Furthermore, the APS data set has a problem of missing data, and in this paper we explore KNN imputation method to solve the problem of missing data using KNN_imputer from Sklearn. Sklearn is a machine learning package commonly used for processing data, building machine learning model. It should be noted that other missing data imputation methods such as generative adversarial network (GAN), etc., could be explored.

The performance of the proposed algorithm is better than other comparison algorithms, namely Gaussian Naive Bayes (GNB), Random Forest, K-nearest neighbor (KNN), Support Vector Machine (SVM), and Logistic Regression (LogR). The performance of the comparison algorithms is evaluated using popular and commonly used metrics in the literature, namely average F1-score, average Recall, average Precision, and average Accuracy. In terms of the F1-score, the performance of the proposed algorithm is the best among the comparison algorithms. The Table and the Figures presented in the experimental section validate that the proposed BELR performances are comparable with other algorithms.

Author Contributions: Validation, B.P.; Writing—original draft, A.A.M.; Writing—review & editing, H.A.; Supervision, C.K.M.L.; Project administration, J.C.; Funding acquisition, C.K.M.L. All authors have read and agreed to the published version of the manuscript.

Funding: ITC-InnoHK Clusters-Innovation and Technology Commission.

Institutional Review Board Statement: Not Applicable.

Informed Consent Statement: Not Applicable.

Data Availability Statement: Available upon request.

Acknowledgments: The work was supported by the Centre for Advances in Reliability and Safety (CAiRS) admitted under AIR@InnoHK Research Cluster.

Conflicts of Interest: The authors declare no conflict of interest.

Abbreviations

ML	Machine learning
APS	Air Pressure System
BELR	Broad Embedded Logistic Regression
BLS	Broad Learning System
LogR	Logistic Regression
PCA	Principal Component Analysis
RVFLNN	Random Vector Functional-link neural networks
IIoT	Industrial Internet of Things
SVM	Support Vector Machine
MLP	Multi-layer Perceptron
SMOTE	Synthetic Minority Oversampling Technique
ELM	Extreme Learning Machine
KNN	K-Nearest Neighbour
ADMM	Alternating Direction Method of Multipliers
RF	Random Forest
GNB	Gaussian Naïve Bayes
ROC	Receiver Operating Characteristics
max AUC	Maximizes Area Under the Curves
MAR	Missing at random
MNR	Missing not at random
MCAR	Missing completely at random
GAN	Generative Adversarial Network
f	Total number of feature-mapped nodes in the BLS network
e	Total number of enhancement nodes in the BLS network

References

1. Yuantao, F.; Nowaczyk, S.; Antonelo, E.A. Predicting air compressor failures with echo state networks. *PHM Soc. Eur. Conf.* **2016**, *3*, 1.
2. Lokesh, Y.; Nikhil, K.S.S.; Kumar, E.V.; Mohan, G.K. Truck APS Failure Detection using Machine Learning. In Proceedings of the 2020 4th International Conference on Intelligent Computing and Control Systems (ICICCS), Madurai, India, 13–15 May 2020; IEEE: Piscataway, NJ, USA, 2020.
3. Qu, W.; Balki, I.; Mendez, M.; Valen, J.; Levman, J.; Tyrrell, P.N. Assessing and mitigating the effects of class imbalance in machine learning with application to X-ray imaging. *Int. J. Comput. Assist. Radiol. Surg.* **2020**, *15*, 2041–2048. [CrossRef] [PubMed]
4. Zolanvari, M.; Teixeira, M.A.; Jain, R. Effect of imbalanced datasets on security of industrial IoT using machine learning. In Proceedings of the IEEE International Conference on Intelligence and Security Informatics (ISI), Miami, FL, USA, 9–11 November 2018; IEEE: Piscataway, NJ, USA, 2018.
5. Akarte, M.M.; Hemachandra, N. *Predictive Maintenance of Air Pressure System Using Boosting Trees: A Machine Learning Approach*; ORSI: Melle, Belgium, 2018.
6. Wang, G.K.; Sim, C. Context-dependent modelling of deep neural network using logistic regression. In Proceedings of the IEEE Workshop on Automatic Speech Recognition and Understanding, Olomouc, Czech Republic, 8–12 December 2013; IEEE: Piscataway, NJ, USA, 2013.
7. Wright, R.E. Logistic regression. In *Reading and Understanding Multivariate Statistics*; Grimm, L.G., Yarnold, P.R., Eds.; American Psychological Association: Washington, DC, USA, 1995; pp. 217–244.
8. Chen, C.P.; Liu, Z. Broad learning system: An effective and efficient incremental learning system without the need for deep architecture. *IEEE Trans. Neural Netw. Learn. Syst.* **2017**, *29*, 10–24. [CrossRef] [PubMed]
9. Adegoke, M.; Leung, C.S.; Sum, J. Fault Tolerant Broad Learning System. In *International Conference on Neural Information Processing*; Springer: Cham, Switzerland, 2019; pp. 95–103.
10. Abdi, H.; Williams, L.J. Principal component analysis. *Wiley Interdiscip. Rev. Comput. Stat.* **2010**, *2*, 433–459. [CrossRef]
11. Köppen, M. The curse of dimensionality. In Proceedings of the 5th Online World Conference on Soft Computing in Industrial Applications (WSC5), Online, 4–18 September 2000; Volume 1.
12. Rubin, D.B. Inference and missing data. *Biometrika* **1976**, *63*, 581–592. [CrossRef]

13. Little, R.J.; Rubin, D.B. *Statistical Analysis with Missing Data*; John Wiley & Sons: Hoboken, NJ, USA, 2019; p. 793.
14. Guo, Z.; Wan, Y.; Ye, H. A data imputation method for multivariate time series based on generative adversarial network. *Neurocomputing* **2019**, *360*, 185–197. [CrossRef]
15. Zhang, S. Nearest neighbor selection for iteratively kNN imputation. *J. Syst. Softw.* **2012**, *85*, 2541–2552. [CrossRef]
16. Gondek, C.; Daniel, H.; Oliver, R.S. Prediction of failures in the air pressure system of scania trucks using a random forest and feature engineering. In *International Symposium on Intelligent Data Analysis*; Springer: Cham, Switzerland, 2016.
17. Rengasamy, D.; Jafari, M.; Rothwell, B.; Chen, X.; Figueredo, G.P. Deep learning with dynamically weighted loss function for sensor-based prognostics and health management. *Sensors* **2020**, *20*, 723. [CrossRef] [PubMed]
18. Nowaczyk, S.; Prytz, R.; Rögnvaldsson, T.; Byttner, S. Towards a machine learning algorithm for predicting truck compressor failures using logged vehicle data. In Proceedings of the 12th Scandinavian Conference on Artificial Intelligence, Aalborg, Denmark, 20–23 November 2013; IOS Press: Washington, DC, USA, 2013; pp. 20–22.
19. Costa, C.F.; Nascimento, M.A. Ida 2016 industrial challenge: Using machine learning for predicting failures. In *International Symposium on Intelligent Data Analysis*; Springer: Cham, Switzerland, 2016.
20. Cerqueira, V.; Pinto, F.; Sá, C.; Soares, C. Combining boosted trees with meta feature engineering for predictive maintenance. In *International Symposium on Intelligent Data Analysis*; Springer: Cham, Switzerland, 2016.
21. Ozan, E.C.; Riabchenko, E.; Kiranyaz, S.; Gabbouj, M. An optimized k-nn approach for classification on imbalanced datasets with missing data. In *International Symposium on Intelligent Data Analysis*; Springer: Cham, Switzerland, 2016.
22. Jose, C.; Gopakumar, G. An Improved Random Forest Algorithm for classification in an imbalanced dataset. In Proceedings of the 2019 URSI Asia-Pacific Radio Science Conference (AP-RASC), New Delhi, India, 9–15 March 2019; IEEE: Piscataway, NJ, USA, 2019.
23. Syed, M.N.; Hassan, R.; Ahmad, I.; Hassan, M.M.; De Albuquerque, V.H.C. A Novel Linear Classifier for Class Imbalance Data Arising in Failure-Prone Air Pressure Systems. *IEEE Access* **2020**, *9*, 4211–4222. [CrossRef]
24. Huang, G.B.; Zhu, Q.Y.; Siew, C.K. Extreme learning machine: Theory and applications. *Neurocomputing* **2006**, *70*, 489–501. [CrossRef]
25. Huang, G.B.; Ding, X.J.; Zhou, H.M. Optimization method based extreme learning machine for classification. *Neurocomputing* **2010**, *74*, 155–163. [CrossRef]
26. Ding, S.; Zhao, H.; Zhang, Y.; Xu, X.; Nie, R. Extreme learning machine: Algorithm, theory and applications. *Artif. Intell. Rev.* **2015**, *44*, 103–115. [CrossRef]
27. Gong, X.; Zhang, T.; Chen, C.L.P.; Liu, Z. Research review for broad learning system: Algorithms, theory, and applications. *IEEE Trans. Cybern.* **2021**, *52*, 8922–8950. [CrossRef] [PubMed]
28. Xu, M.; Han, M.; Chen, C.L.P.; Qiu, T. Recurrent broad learning systems for time series prediction. *IEEE Trans. Cybern.* **2018**, *50*, 1405–1417. [CrossRef] [PubMed]
29. Zhao, H.; Zheng, J.; Xu, J.; Deng, W. Fault diagnosis method based on principal component analysis and broad learning system. *IEEE Access* **2019**, *7*, 99263–99272. [CrossRef]
30. Liu, Z.; Chen, C.P. Broad learning system: Structural extensions on single-layer and multi-layer neural networks. In Proceedings of the 2017 International Conference on Security, Pattern Analysis, and Cybernetics (SPAC), Shenzhen, China, 15–17 December 2017; IEEE: Piscataway, NJ, USA, 2017.
31. Feng, S.; Chen, C.P. Fuzzy broad learning system: A novel neuro-fuzzy model for regression and classification. *IEEE Trans. Cybern.* **2018**, *50*, 414–424. [CrossRef] [PubMed]
32. Boyd, S.; Parikh, N.; Chu, E.; Peleato, B.; Eckstein, J. Distributed optimization and statistical learning via the alternating direction method of multipliers. *Found. Trends Mach. Learn.* **2011**, *3*, 1–122. [CrossRef]
33. Jin, J.; Liu, Z.; Chen, C.L. Discriminative graph regularized broad learning system for image recognition. *Sci. China Inf. Sci.* **2018**, *61*, 112209. [CrossRef]
34. Muideen, A.; Wong, H.T.; Leung, C.S. A fault aware broad learning system for concurrent network failure situations. *IEEE Access* **2021**, *9*, 46129–46142.
35. Bishop, C.M.; Nasrabadi, N.M. *Pattern Recognition and Machine Learning*; Springer: New York, NY, USA, 2006; Volume 4, No. 4.
36. Pedregosa, F.; Varoquaux, G.; Gramfort, A.; Michel, V.; Thirion, B.; Grisel, O.; Blondel, M.; Prettenhofer, P.; Weiss, R.; Dubourg, V.; et al. Scikit-learn: Machine learning in Python. *J. Mach. Learn. Res.* **2011**, *12*, 2825–2830.
37. Asuncion, A.; Newman, D. UCI Machine Learning Repository. 2007. Available online: https://scholar.google.com/scholar?hl=en&as_sdt=0%2C5&q=31.%09Asuncion%2C+A.%3B+Newman%2C+D.+UCI+ma-chine+learning+repository&btnG=#d=gs_cit&t=1676228269803&u=%2Fscholar%3Fq%3Dinfo%3AbqbHDUKR2lMJ%3Ascholar.google.com%2F%26output%3Dcite%26scirp%3D0%26hl%3Den (accessed on 11 November 2022).
38. Available online: https://www.kaggle.com/datasets/uciml/aps-failure-at-scania-trucks-data-set (accessed on 3 October 2022).

Disclaimer/Publisher's Note: The statements, opinions and data contained in all publications are solely those of the individual author(s) and contributor(s) and not of MDPI and/or the editor(s). MDPI and/or the editor(s) disclaim responsibility for any injury to people or property resulting from any ideas, methods, instructions or products referred to in the content.

Article

Alleviating Long-Tailed Image Classification via Dynamical Classwise Splitting

Ye Yuan, Jiaqi Wang, Xin Xu, Ruoshi Li, Yongtong Zhu, Lihong Wan, Qingdu Li and Na Liu *

Institute of Machine Intelligence, University of Shanghai for Science and Technology, Shanghai 200093, China
* Correspondence: liuna@usst.edu.cn

Abstract: With the rapid increase in data scale, real-world datasets tend to exhibit long-tailed class distributions (i.e., a few classes account for most of the data, while most classes contain only a few data points). General solutions typically exploit class rebalancing strategies involving resampling and reweighting based on the sample number for each class. In this work, we explore an orthogonal direction, category splitting, which is motivated by the empirical observation that naive splitting of majority samples could alleviate the heavy imbalance between majority and minority classes. To this end, we propose a novel classwise splitting (CWS) method built upon a dynamic cluster, where classwise prototypes are updated using a moving average technique. CWS generates intra-class pseudo labels for splitting intra-class samples based on the point-to-point distance. Moreover, a group mapping module was developed to recover the ground truth of the training samples. CWS can be plugged into any existing method as a complement. Comprehensive experiments were conducted on artificially induced long-tailed image classification datasets, such as CIFAR-10-LT, CIFAR-100-LT, and OCTMNIST. Our results show that when trained with the proposed class-balanced loss, the network is able to achieve significant performance gains on long-tailed datasets.

Keywords: deep learning; class-imbalance learning; feature clustering; long-tailed classification; classwise splitting

MSC: 68T07

1. Introduction

With the emergence of large-scale and high-quality datasets, such as ImageNet [1] and COCO [2], deep neural networks (DNNs) have achieved resounding success in many visual discriminative tasks, including image recognition, object detection, and semantic segmentation. Most existing datasets are carefully well-designed and maintain a roughly balanced distribution over different categories. However, real-world datasets typically exhibit long-tailed data distributions [3,4], where a few classes occupy plenty of samples but the others are associated with only a few samples. Learning in such a real-world scenario is challenging due to the biased training of high-frequency ones, which undoubtedly hinders the practical applications of DNNs with significant performance degradation [5,6].

To tackle the imbalanced problem, early rebalancing strategies mainly focus on resampling [7,8] and reweighting [9,10] to pay more attention to minority classes. The intuition behind the above methods is to adjust the training data distribution based on importance estimation. Then, logit-based regularization was introduced to calibrate the shifted distribution between the training test data, encouraging the large margins for minority classes. These strategies could improve recognition performance for minority categories; however, the majority categories easily suffer from relatively lower accuracy because of over-emphasizing minority samples. Recently, it was indicated that the mismatch between representative and classifier learning plays a vital role in long-tailed recognition [11–13]. Thus, a two-stage training strategy was developed to decouple feature and classifier learning and has led to significant improvement over joint training. Motivated by this finding, the recent state-of-the-art performance has been attained through either self-supervised pretraining to obtain high-quality representations or employing ensemble experts for fair classifiers, implicitly increasing the training cost [14].

In this work, we argue that better representations and fair classifiers could be jointly obtained by decomposing majority classes into smaller ones. We observe that a naively trained model on decomposed classes with roughly balanced distribution has better recognition performance with respect to the original label space. This motivates our work to incorporate decomposed classes (called the classwise splitting trick) into the end-to-end training mode, while maintaining the original label space for long-tailed recognition. To this end, we exploit three simple techniques to balance both representations and classifiers. We first explore online clustering to split majority classes for balancing representative learning. Then, intra-class clusters are maintained via the moving average approach to reduce computational costs. Finally, a group mapping module is formulated to recover the original label space for balancing classifier learning. Please refer to Figure 1 for an overall framework of our work.

The main contributions can be summarized as follows: (1) We design a novel framework to improve the classification of long-tailed datasets by proposing a classwise splitting (CWS) method. (2) Our framework can achieve significant performance improvement by clustering majority categories into several subclasses, assigning pseudo-labels, and then mapping the predictions to the real labels. (3) Experiments show that our framework can be used as a generic method for visual recognition by outperforming the previous state-of-the-art performances on long-tailed CIFAR-10 and CIFAR-100 datasets [15].

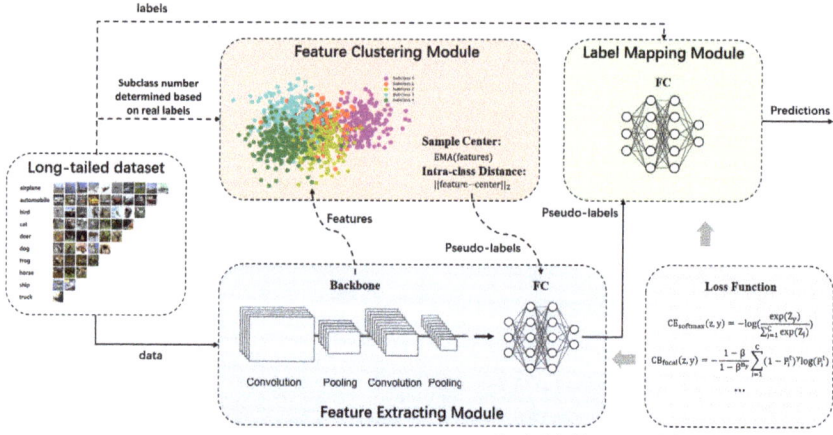

Figure 1. Overall architecture of the classwise splitting (CWS) method. The framework contains three parts: a feature-extracting module, a feature clustering module, and a label-mapping module. During training, the feature-extracting module uses the backbone network to extract the features of input images, and then the feature clustering module assigns pseudo-labels to the features according to their intra-class distances, and finally the feature mapping module maps the pseudo-labels to real labels. During inference, the feature clustering module will be removed.

2. Related Works

Most of the previous efforts on long-tailed datasets could be divided into two regimes: resampling [7,8] and reweighting [9,10].

Resampling. Resampling is a data-level method widely used to address the problem of imbalanced classification. It adjusts the training data distribution by undersampling the majority categories or oversampling the minority categories [16]. However, it is difficult to reconcile the classification performance of the majority and minority categories. Oversampling can easily lead to the overfitting of samples, while undersampling can lead to the loss of some useful information. The more imbalanced the dataset, the more pronounced the shortcomings of the resampling strategy.

Reweighting. Reweighting is a class-level method that is widely used to address the problem of imbalance learning by modulating the weighting factors of categories in the data [17]. The common reweighting methods include focal loss [18], class-balanced (CB) loss [19], and label-distribution-aware margin (LDAM) loss [20]. Among them, focal loss applies a moderation term to cross-entropy loss, focusing on learning the minority categories in the imbalanced dataset. CB loss introduces the effective number to approximate the expected volume of samples of each category instead of the label frequency. LDAM loss addresses the overfitting of the majority categories by regularizing the margins.

Two-stage Training Strategy. The two-stage training strategy was initially used to solve the conflict problem arising from different rebalancing strategies. Due to the overlapping effects between different rebalancing strategies, directly combining two rebalancing strategies for long-tailed data classification tasks will significantly reduce the model's generalization ability [20,21]. Kang et al. [13] applied this strategy to decoupling training, which divides the original joint training method into two stages of training, greatly reducing the degree of coupling between different modules of the model, and allowing the network to search for parameters with stronger generalization ability during the training process. Here, inspired by this strategy, we also adopted a similar approach to [22] to achieve this goal.

Clustering For Classification. Clustering is a typical unsupervised learning method, whose core idea is to divide the whole sample set into multiple disjoint subsets by comparing the distances of samples in a low-dimensional space, so as to complete the classification [23,24]. The imbalance classification task based on clustering has been widely studied in recent years [25,26]. Singh et al. [27] use the distance between a minority class sample and its respective cluster centroid to infer the number of new samples. Swarnalatha et al. [6,28] divide each class into smaller subclasses, and then classify them based on feature metrics to achieve compactness. Indeed, clustering-based methods have proven to be helpful in addressing class imbalance problems in the past. However, they mainly obtain fine subclasses by clustering the samples directly, and the subclass centers are usually invariant in the subsequent training tasks. These static clustering methods may limit the upper optimization of network parameters. Therefore, inspired by previous research, we embed clustering techniques into the training process of deep neural networks, using the extracted features for dynamical clustering to obtain pseudo-labels, which in turn are used to train deep neural networks. Finally, a mapping network is used to establish the correspondence between the pseudo-labels and the real labels.

3. Method

Preliminaries. Given a training set $D = \{(x_i, y_i)\}_{i=1}^{N}$ with N training samples, the x_i represents the i-th training sample and y_i represents the corresponding label. The total number of training samples is $N = \sum_{c=1}^{C} N_c$, where C denotes the total number of categories and N_c denotes the number of training samples of the c-th class. The general assumption of long-tailed distribution is that the classes are sorted in decreasing order of the sample number. Assume that the training sample numbers of the c_1 and c_2 classes are denoted as N_{c_1} and N_{c_2}, respectively, then $N_{c_1} > N_{c_2}$ if $c_1 < c_2$. In this case, the target of the recognition task for long-tailed distributed data is to learn a deep neural network $f(\cdot, \theta)$ with parameter θ, which can achieve good recognition performance on a balanced test set.

Given a training sample x_i, the network predicts its label $y'_i = f(x_i, \theta)$, where the prediction error between y'_i and the ground truth y_i is calculated using a cost function $\mathcal{L}(y'_i, y_i)$, e.g., a cross-entropy (CE) loss. To train the network $f(\cdot, \theta)$, we optimize θ by minimizing $\mathcal{L}(y'_i, y_i)$ over the whole training set D:

$$\theta^* = \arg\min_{\theta} F(\theta; \mathcal{D}) \equiv \sum_{i=1}^{N} \mathcal{L}(f(\mathbf{x}_i; \Theta), y_i) \quad (1)$$

Naively solving Equation (1) produces an imbalanced feature distribution that has biased decision boundaries toward common classes. Therefore, we are motivated to learn a balanced feature extractor by splitting majority classes into sub-classes. Such artificially balanced label distributions can also balance the weights of the classifier for sub-classes, then we can transform this pseudo label space into the original one via a mapping module. The proposed framework is shown in Figure 1.

Our proposed method mainly contains three modules: a feature-extracting module, a feature clustering module, and a label-mapping module. In order to realize the collaborative training of multiple modules, we combine unsupervised learning (clustering techniques) with supervised learning to propose a two-stage classification algorithm. In the first stage, the feature-extracting module uses a backbone network to extract features from input images, and the feature clustering module uses clustering technique to assign pseudo-labels to these features, which are used in the training of the feature-extracting module. We use the pseudo-labels as input to the label-mapping module and then use ground truth labels to train this module.

3.1. Feature Clustering Module

The role of the feature clustering module is to cluster the features into a specified number of subclasses and assign unique pseudo-labels to them. Specifically, during training, a CNN backbone is used to extract the embeddings of training samples. Then features belonging to the same category are divided into several subclasses according to their distance away from the sample center, which is achieved by a dynamic clustering strategy. Finally, each subclass would be given a pseudo-label for calculating loss. The dynamic clustering can be described as follows:

$$d_t = \frac{\max|S_i - SC_t|}{SN} \quad (2)$$

$$\text{if } |S_i - SC_t| \in (nd_t, (n+1)d_t], n \in [0, 1, \ldots, SN-1] \\ \Rightarrow S_i \leftarrow P_n \quad (3)$$

where SC_t denotes the sample center of a certain category in the t-th batch. S_i denotes the i-th sample of this category. SN denotes the subclass number of this category. The maximum distance between the samples and sample center is equally divided into SN intervals and the length of each interval is d_t.

During training, samples are fed into the framework in batches. In each batch, the following operation is repeated for each category of samples: the sample center is first calculated based on the features of all the samples, then the maximum distance between the sample and the sample center is computed; subsequently, the maximum distance is divided into several intervals. Eventually, the distance between each sample and the sample center is counted to decide which interval it belongs to so that a unique pseudo-label is assigned to that sample accordingly. Notably, the subclass number is taken as a hyperparameter whose value is related to the total sample number of the category. The sample center and subclass number are determined as follows:

Sample Center. The mini-batch training strategy is widely used for vision tasks, which leads to an expensive cost for the cluster center calculation. To efficiently calculate the sample center, an exponential moving average method is utilized, which makes the sample center of each category in each batch closer to the overall situation of the corresponding category in the dataset. The sample center is calculated as follows:

$$SC_t = \begin{cases} y_1 & t = 1 \\ \alpha y_t + (1-\alpha)SC_{t-1} & t > 1 \end{cases} \quad (4)$$

where α ($0 < \alpha < 1$) indicates the attenuation degree of the weight. y_t denotes the average value of the features of a certain category in the t-th batch. SC_t denotes the exponential moving average value of the features of a certain category in the t-th batch, i.e., sample center.

Subclass number. The determination of the subclass number depends on the degree of data imbalance and the intra-class distance. On the one hand, our method aims to generate more subclasses for majority categories, especially for heavily imbalanced data. On the other hand, we experimentally analyzed the effect of the subclass number and obtained the following conclusions: the larger the subclass number, the smaller the intra-class distance of the samples, which will reduce the classification accuracy. Therefore, when determining the subclass number, we will perform a cluster analysis on this category. The subclass number should be as large as possible without the intra-class distance being too small. The ablation experiments of this parameter are detailed in Section 4.

3.2. Label-Mapping Module

To map the pseudo-label space to the real label space, we formulate a label-mapping module following the feature-extracting module, which a three-layer perceptron is employed. In the training process, because the feature clustering module will cluster each category of samples into several subclasses, the total number of pseudo-labels will be greater than the number of real labels. Therefore, in order to map all pseudo-labels of samples of the same category to its real label, the input dimension of the three-layer perceptron should be equal to the number of pseudo-labels, and the output dimension should be equal to the total number of real labels.

3.3. Two-Stage Training Strategy

Given that the feature-extracting module and the label-mapping module are relatively independent networks, a two-stage training approach is implemented to update the weight parameters of the entire framework. The two stages involve separate training processes, each focusing on updating the weight parameters of a specific module.

In the first stage, the pseudo-labels generated by the feature clustering module are utilized as the ground truth for the backbone network. The loss is calculated based on the comparison between the predicted pseudo-labels and the generated pseudo-labels, allowing for the update of the weight parameters in the feature-extracting module. This stage aims to optimize the feature extraction process to ensure accurate and discriminative feature representation. Similarly, in the second stage, the real labels are employed as the ground truth for the three-layer perceptron in the label-mapping module. The loss is computed by comparing the predicted labels with the true labels, facilitating the update of weight parameters in the label-mapping module. This stage focuses on fine-tuning the label-mapping process to ensure effective alignment between the pseudo-labels and the true labels.

The first and second stages are performed alternately, allowing for iterative refinement of the framework. Notably, the loss function remains consistent across both stages of training, ensuring that the overall objective remains unchanged. By adopting this two-stage training method, we can effectively optimize the feature extraction and label-mapping processes within the framework, improving the overall performance and accuracy of the model.

4. Experiments and Discussions

4.1. Datasets and Experimental Settings

Long-tailed CIFAR-10 and CIFAR-100. CIFAR-10 and CIFAR-100 are commonly used datasets in long-tailed classification problems; these datasets consist of 60,000 images, with the training dataset containing 50,000 samples and the test dataset containing 10,000 samples [29]. To obtain the long-tailed version of the CIFAR dataset and ensure fairness, we follow [30] to split the existing dataset. Specially, we use the imbalance ratio factor $\beta = \frac{N_{min}}{N_{max}}$ to control the imbalance degree of the dataset, where N_{max} and N_{min} represent the most and the least frequent class numbers from the training samples, respectively. In our experiments, the imbalance factors are set to 0.05, 0.02, 0.01, and 0.1, respectively. Our framework was verified on the long-tailed versions of CIFAR-10 and CIFAR-100 datasets with different imbalance factors. Notably, the test set remains unchanged. The distribution of the long-tailed CIFAR-10 dataset is shown in Figure 2.

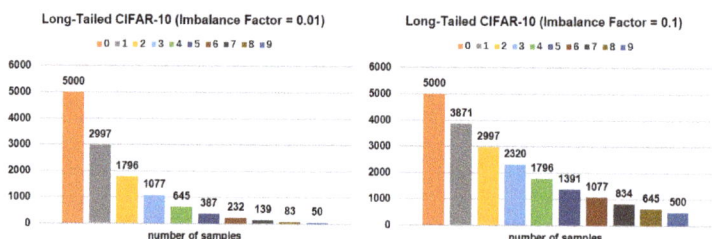

Figure 2. The distribution of the long-tailed CIFAR-10 dataset with imbalance factors of 0.01 and 0.1.

OCTMNIST. OCTMNIST [31] is a new medical dataset built from the previous retinal OCT image classification dataset, which contains 109,309 images. For a fair comparison, we selected four types of data for training and testing. The training dataset is naturally imbalanced, while the test dataset exhibits a balanced distribution in terms of the number of samples. OCTMNIST is an application-oriented dataset from the real world, which can better demonstrate the effectiveness of our method.

Baselines. We compare our method with previous state-of-the-art techniques and their combinations: (1) Cross-entropy (CE) loss [32], which does not change the loss of samples; (2) focal loss [18], which increases the loss for hard samples and down-weights well-classified samples; (3) LDAM loss [20], which regularizes the minority categories to have larger margins; (4) resampling [33], which resamples the samples according to the inverse of the effective number of samples in each category; (5) reweighting [34], which reweights the samples according to the inverse of the effective number of samples in each category; (6) DRW [20], which makes the model learn the initial feature representation and then performs reweighting or resampling. The above three loss functions (i.e., CE loss, focal loss, and LDAM loss) were employed in the experiments, each of which was combined with three training methods (i.e., reweighting, resampling, and DRW). The parameter settings of reweighting and resampling methods were consistent with [19].

Implementation Details. We used PyTorch [35] to implement and train all the models in the work, and we used ResNet [36] architecture for all datasets. For the long-tailed CIFAR-10 and CIFAR-100 datasets, random initialization was used for our model, which adopts ResNet-32 as the backbone network. The networks were trained for 200 epochs with stochastic gradient descent (SGD) (momentum = 0.9). Following the training strategy in [19], the initial learning rate was set to 0.1 and then decayed by 0.01 at 160 epochs and again at 180 epochs. Furthermore, we used a linear warm-up of the learning rate in the first five epochs. We trained the models for the long-tailed CIFAR-10 and CIFAR-100 datasets on a single NVIDIA RTX 3090 with a batch size of 128.

4.2. Classification Experiment Results

Tables 1 and 2 show the test accuracy of our framework on the long-tailed CIFAR-10 and CIFAR-100 datasets under different combinations of loss functions and training methods. The loss curves along with training are shown in Figure 3.

Clearly, without incorporating loss functions and training methods that can mitigate the data imbalance, our framework can achieve comparable performance to the previous state-of-the-art techniques. For example, on the long-tailed CIFAR-10 dataset with the imbalance factor set to 0.1, our framework has a classification accuracy of 87.91%, which almost exceeds the classification accuracy of all other methods and their combinations on this dataset. Compared to the long-tailed CIFAR-10 dataset with the imbalance factor being set to 0.1, our framework improves the baseline performance more significantly on the dataset, with the imbalance factor set to 0.01. For example, on the dataset (imbalance factor = 0.01), the performance improvement of the baseline (CE loss plus none) is up to about 4%, while the performance improvement of this baseline is only 1.5% on the dataset (imbalance factor = 0.1). This means that the more imbalanced the data distribution, the more significant the effect of our framework. The experiments show that our framework can significantly improve the performance of most combinations of loss functions and training methods in the baseline.

Table 1. The test accuracy on the long-tailed CIFAR-10 datasets between our method and the baseline.

Dataset		\multicolumn{8}{c}{Imbalanced CIFAR-10}							
Imbalance Factor		0.05		0.02		0.01		0.1	
Loss	Rule	Baseline	CWS	Baseline	CWS	Baseline	CWS	Baseline	CWS
CE	None	83.27	**85.12**	78.22	**79.44**	71.07	**75.2**	86.39	**87.91**
CE	Resampling	83.16	**84.93**	76.90	**78.89**	71.31	**75.33**	86.79	**87.99**
CE	Reweighting	83.48	**84.88**	78.20	**79.17**	72.2	**75.85**	86.44	**87.41**
CE	DRW	85.14	**85.94**	80.33	**81.24**	74.64	**76.79**	86.43	**88.14**
Focal	None	82.67	**84.07**	76.71	**78.69**	71.07	**73.52**	86.66	**87.83**
Focal	Resampling	85.55	85.09	76.70	**78.24**	70.48	**73.93**	86.16	**87.36**
Focal	Reweighting	83.15	**83.83**	79.27	**80.15**	70.61	**75.65**	87.1	87.6
Focal	DRW	85.75	84.86	80.25	**80.85**	75.3	**76.89**	87.45	**87.98**
LDAM	None	84.00	**84.84**	78.83	**79.31**	73.93	**75.96**	86.96	**87.17**
LDAM	Resampling	83.34	83.24	78.40	78.38	73.1	**75.86**	86.29	**86.98**
LDAM	Reweighting	82.77	**83.96**	78.68	**78.81**	73.74	**73.98**	86.07	**86.57**
LDAM	DRW	85.43	85.33	81.92	80.94	77.68	77.33	88.16	87.24

Baseline: the model without our method; CWS: the model with our method; loss: the loss function of the model; rule: the training method of the model. There are several baselines due to the variety of loss functions and the training method. For each baseline, our method can be combined with it. The values in bold indicate that, under the identical conditions, the accuracy of the model with our method is higher than the model without our method.

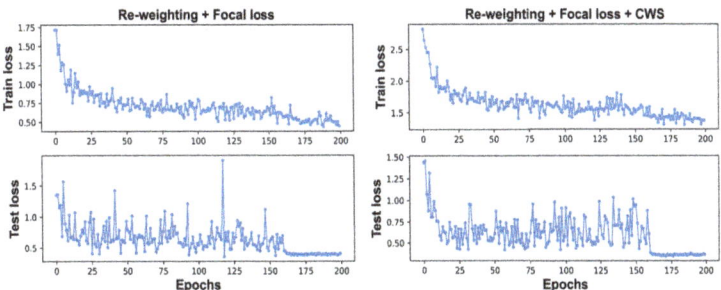

Figure 3. The loss curves of baseline (reweighting plus focal loss) trained on long-tailed CIFAR-10 (imbalance factor = 0.1) with or without the CWS method.

Notably, when there is a large number of categories, it is difficult to determine the subclass number. An inappropriate subclass number can easily lead to non-convergence of the model. For example, our framework combining LDAM loss and the resampling method does not work well on the long-tailed CIFAR-100 dataset. This is because for datasets with a large number of categories, resampling and clustering may result in the absence of samples in some subclasses.

Table 2. The test accuracy on the long-tailed CIFAR-100 datasets between our method and the baseline.

Dataset		Imbalanced CIFAR-100							
Imbalance Factor		0.05		0.02		0.01		0.1	
Loss	Rule	Baseline	CWS	Baseline	CWS	Baseline	CWS	Baseline	CWS
CE	None	50.79	**52.29**	43.71	**46.35**	38.32	**40.28**	55.7	**57.98**
CE	Resampling	51.48	48.86	43.13	39.75	33.44	34.6	55.06	54.71
CE	Reweighting	48.28	**53.28**	45.32	44.92	33.99	**37.93**	57.12	**58.61**
CE	DRW	53.05	52.84	46.84	**47.59**	41.85	**41.88**	57.54	**58.51**
Focal	None	51.08	**52.42**	44.32	44.28	38.71	**40.67**	55.62	**57.91**
Focal	Resampling	50.06	49.43	43.07	39.31	37.88	33.69	56.03	55.43
Focal	Reweighting	47.49	**53.05**	35.65	**44.96**	36.02	**38.69**	57.99	57.87
Focal	DRW	52.43	**53.36**	45.19	**45.62**	38.65	**41.87**	57.64	**58.29**
LDAM	None	51.65	**54.05**	44.32	**46.12**	39.6	**42.64**	56.91	**58.1**
LDAM	Resampling	51.06	-	43.43	-	39.43	-	56.4	-
LDAM	Reweighting	48.20	**50.04**	36.69	**40.92**	29.13	**34.24**	53.69	**56.23**
LDAM	DRW	53.52	**54.21**	47.89	46.80	42.04	**43.28**	58.71	**58.75**

The meanings of baseline, CWS, loss, and rule are the same as in Table 1. '-' in the CWS column indicates that the model does not converge. The values in bold indicate that, under the identical conditions, the accuracy of the model with our method is higher than the model without our method.

To validate the effectiveness of our proposed algorithm in real applications, we report the experimental results of the algorithm on the medical dataset OCTMNIST. Figure 4 shows the classification results of our proposed method on the OCTMNIST dataset after combining it with different backbone networks. It can be seen that our method has achieved optimal ACC and considerably good AUC. Compared with ResNet-50, the accuracy of our proposed method has obtained a nearly 7.5% improvement, while our method only adds two MLP parameters based on ResNet-32. Therefore, this can effectively demonstrate the effectiveness of our proposed method.

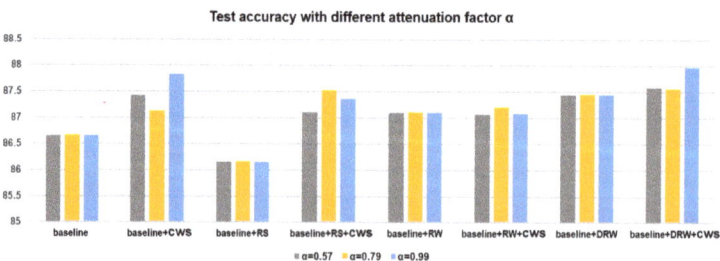

Figure 4. The test accuracy of baselines (focal loss plus different training method) or combinations of baselines and the CWS method on the long-tailed CIFAR-10 (imbalance factor = 0.1) with different attenuation factors α. (RS: resampling, RW: reweighting).

4.3. Ablation Experiment Results

To choose an appropriate subclass number, we performed a series of ablation experiments on the long-tailed CIFAR-10 and CIFAR-100 datasets, and some of the experimental results are shown in Tables 3 and 4. It can be seen that the performance of our framework is not proportional to the subclass number. When the subclass number increases, the classification accuracies of some combinations of baselines and the CWS method increase (e.g., CE plus none, focal plus reweighting), while those of some combinations slightly decrease (e.g., CE plus resampling, LDAM plus resampling). This is because a large subclass number leads to too little discriminability between subclasses. When the subclass number increases to a certain extent, the combinations (e.g., LDAM plus resampling) cannot converge because some subclasses have no samples after clustering. Thus, considering the stability and performance of the framework, the subclass numbers for the long-tailed CIFAR-10 are set to [5, 3, 2, 2, 1, 1, 1, 1, 1, 1]. That is, the samples in the largest category were clustered into five subclasses, and those in the smallest category remained as one category. We repeated each element in [5, 3, 2, 2, 1, 1, 1, 1, 1, 1, 1] ten times as the subclass number for each category in the long-tailed CIFAR-100 dataset, i.e., [5, 5, ..., 5, 3, 3, ..., 3, 2, 2, ..., 2, 1, 1, ..., 1].

We also performed a series of ablation experiments for the attenuation factor α of the exponential moving average in Equation (4), and the experimental results are shown in Figure 4. It can be seen that when the attenuation factor is set to 0.99, our framework combined with other loss functions or training methods can achieve the highest performance. Thus, the attenuation factor α is set to 0.99 in our classification experiments.

Table 3. The test accuracy on the long-tailed CIFAR-10 (imbalance factor = 0.01) with different subclass numbers.

Method		Subclass Number			
		[5,3,2,2,1,1,1,1,1,1]	[10,8,6,5,3,2,2,1,1,1]	[30,24,18,15,3,3,2,2,1,1]	[50,40,30,25,9,9,1,1,1,1]
	CE plus CWS	75.20	76.10	77.48	78.28
	CE plus Resampling plus CWS	75.33	74.68	77.14	77.55
	CE plus Reweighting plus CWS	75.85	76.87	78.49	-
	CE plus DRW plus CWS	76.79	77.82	78.09	-
	Focal plus CWS	73.52	74.12	76.58	77.54
	Focal plus Resampling plus CWS	73.93	75.26	77.15	78.19
	Focal plus Reweighting plus CWS	75.65	76.27	77.44	-
	Focal plus DRW plus CWS	76.89	76.90	77.35	-
	LDAM plus CWS	75.96	75.69	76.27	-
	LDAM plus Resampling plus CWS	75.86	72.73	-	-
	LDAM plus Reweighting plus CWS	73.98	73.54	76.21	-
	LDAM plus DRW plus CWS	77.33	77.08	77.05	-

The meanings of baseline, CWS, loss, and rule are the same as in Table 1. '-' indicates that the model does not converge.

Table 4. The test accuracy on the OCTMNIST dataset. We compared a large number of baseline networks with larger parameter quantities than our proposed method.

Method	AUC	ACC
ResNet-50 (28)	93.9	74.5
ResNet-50 (224)	95.1	75.0
auto-sklearn	88.3	59.5
AutoKeras	95.6	73.6
Google AutoML Vision	96.5	73.2
Ours (ResNet-32 plus CWS)	94.7	**82.5**

The values in bold indicate that, under the identical conditions, the accuracy of our method is higher than other methods.

5. Discussion and Conclusions

In this paper, we propose a novel method to enhance the classification performance of long-tailed datasets by introducing a classwise splitting (CWS) strategy. The core concept revolves around clustering the sample features into multiple subclasses based on their intra-class distance. The method consists of three main modules: the feature extraction module, the feature clustering module, and the label-mapping module. The feature extraction module is responsible for extracting informative features from input images. These extracted features are then fed into the feature clustering module, which performs clustering to group them into distinct subclasses. Additionally, the feature clustering module assigns pseudo-labels to the samples within each subclass. Finally, the label-mapping module is employed to map the pseudo-labels to the corresponding ground truth labels. Experimental results conducted on the CIFAR-10-LT, CIFAR-100-LT, and OCTMNIST datasets validate the effectiveness of our proposed method in tackling long-tailed image classification tasks. The results demonstrate that our approach significantly improves the classification accuracy of long-tailed datasets. By introducing the classwise splitting strategy and leveraging the three modular components, our method demonstrates promising potential in addressing the challenges posed by long-tailed datasets and achieving enhanced classification performance.

The method we proposed, based on the idea of dynamic reclustering, is a general visual framework designed for long-tailed distribution data. The experimental results have demonstrated that our framework can be effectively combined with existing rebalancing strategies, such as resampling, reweighting, focal loss, and LDAM, indicating its strong generality. This means that our framework can be applied to other similar long-tailed distribution tasks.

Moreover, our method introduces a learnable label-mapping network that can efficiently fit a mapping function from pseudo-labels to ground truth labels with a small training cost. This idea holds heuristic significance for other unsupervised and semi-supervised learning tasks, as it provides inspiration for achieving an efficient label-mapping in these scenarios.

However, it is worth noting that the proposed framework's learnable label-mapping network may not perform well in joint learning scenarios. The experimental results have revealed that the upper limit of this method is dependent on the initial subdivision of subclasses. The improper subdivision of subclasses can significantly impact the performance of the final model. Therefore, using our framework requires a two-stage training strategy to ensure the stability of feature extraction and the feasibility of subsequent downstream task training. Extensive experimentation is necessary to identify the most suitable subclass number for each class.

In the future, we will explore ways to automatically determine the optimal number of subclasses and investigate approaches for joint training to further reduce training costs. By addressing these challenges, we aim to enhance the efficiency and effectiveness of the framework.

Author Contributions: Y.Y.: software, formal analysis, and writing—original draft; J.W.: writing—reviewing and editing; X.X.: formal analysis; R.L.: data curation; Y.Z.: data curation; L.W.: formal analysis; Q.L.: writing—reviewing and editing; N.L.: supervision and funding acquisition. All authors have read and agreed to the published version of the manuscript.

Funding: This study is supported by the Young Scientists Fund of the National Natural Science Foundation of China (grant no. 62206175), the Pujiang Talents Plan of Shanghai (grant no. 2019PJD035), and the Artificial Intelligence Innovation and Development Special Fund of Shanghai (grant no. 2019RGZN01041).

Institutional Review Board Statement: Not applicable.

Informed Consent Statement: Not applicable.

Data Availability Statement: The data that support the findings of this study are available from the corresponding author upon reasonable request.

Conflicts of Interest: The authors declare no conflict of interest.

References

1. Deng, J.; Dong, W.; Socher, R.; Li, L.J.; Li, K.; Li, F.F. Imagenet: A large-scale hierarchical image database. In Proceedings of the 2009 IEEE Conference on Computer Vision and Pattern Recognition, Miami, FL, USA, 20–25 June 2009; IEEE: Piscataway, NJ, USA, 2009; pp. 248–255.
2. Lin, T.Y.; Maire, M.; Belongie, S.; Hays, J.; Perona, P.; Ramanan, D.; Dollár, P.; Zitnick, C.L. Microsoft coco: Common objects in context. In Proceedings of the Computer Vision–ECCV 2014: 13th European Conference, Zurich, Switzerland, 6–12 September 2014; Proceedings, Part V 13; Springer: Berlin/Heidelberg, Germany, 2014; pp. 740–755.
3. Liu, Z.; Miao, Z.; Zhan, X.; Wang, J.; Gong, B.; Yu, S.X. Large-scale long-tailed recognition in an open world. In Proceedings of the IEEE/CVF Conference on Computer Vision and Pattern Recognition, Long Beach, CA, USA, 15–20 June 2019; pp. 2537–2546.

4. Yang, L.; Jiang, H.; Song, Q.; Guo, J. A survey on long-tailed visual recognition. *Int. J. Comput. Vis.* **2022**, *130*, 1837–1872. [CrossRef]
5. Buda, M.; Maki, A.; Mazurowski, M.A. A systematic study of the class imbalance problem in convolutional neural networks. *Neural Netw.* **2018**, *106*, 249–259. [CrossRef] [PubMed]
6. Swarnalatha, K.; Guru, D.; Anami, B.S.; Suhil, M. Classwise clustering for classification of imbalanced text data. In Proceedings of the Emerging Research in Electronics, Computer Science and Technology: Proceedings of International Conference, ICERECT 2018, NY, USA, 22–24 August 2018; Springer: Berlin/Heidelberg, Germany, 2019; pp. 83–94.
7. Li, Y.; Vasconcelos, N. Repair: Removing representation bias by dataset resampling. In Proceedings of the IEEE/CVF Conference on Computer Vision and Pattern Recognition, Long Beach, CA, USA, 15–20 June 2019; pp. 9572–9581.
8. Shi, H.; Zhang, Y.; Chen, Y.; Ji, S.; Dong, Y. Resampling algorithms based on sample concatenation for imbalance learning. *Knowl. Based Syst.* **2022**, *245*, 108592. [CrossRef]
9. Peng, H.; Pian, W.; Sun, M.; Li, P. Dynamic Re-Weighting for Long-Tailed Semi-Supervised Learning. In Proceedings of the IEEE/CVF Winter Conference on Applications of Computer Vision, Waikoloa, HI, USA, 2–7 January 2023; pp. 6464–6474.
10. Wang, C.; Men, M.; Zhong, P. Re-weighting regression and sparsity regularization for multi-view classification. *Appl. Intell.* **2022**, *52*, 7442–7458. [CrossRef]
11. Alshammari, S.; Wang, Y.X.; Ramanan, D.; Kong, S. Long-tailed recognition via weight balancing. In Proceedings of the IEEE/CVF Conference on Computer Vision and Pattern Recognition, New Orleans, LA, USA, 18–24 June 2022; pp. 6897–6907.
12. Fu, Y.; Xiang, L.; Zahid, Y.; Ding, G.; Mei, T.; Shen, Q.; Han, J. Long-tailed visual recognition with deep models: A methodological survey and evaluation. *Neurocomputing* **2022**, *509*, 290–309. [CrossRef]
13. Kang, B.; Xie, S.; Rohrbach, M.; Yan, Z.; Gordo, A.; Feng, J.; Kalantidis, Y. Decoupling representation and classifier for long-tailed recognition. *arXiv* **2020**, arXiv:1910.09217.
14. Zhang, Y.; Hooi, B.; Hong, L.; Feng, J. Self-supervised aggregation of diverse experts for test-agnostic long-tailed recognition. *Adv. Neural Inf. Process. Syst.* **2022**, *35*, 34077–34090.
15. Zhu, J.; Wang, Z.; Chen, J.; Chen, Y.P.P.; Jiang, Y.G. Balanced contrastive learning for long-tailed visual recognition. In Proceedings of the IEEE/CVF Conference on Computer Vision and Pattern Recognition, New Orleans, LA, USA, 18–24 June 2022; pp. 6908–6917.
16. Mullick, S.S.; Datta, S.; Das, S. Generative adversarial minority oversampling. In Proceedings of the IEEE/CVF International Conference on Computer Vision, Seoul, Republic of Korea, 27 October–2 November 2019; pp. 1695–1704.
17. Ye, H.J.; Chen, H.Y.; Zhan, D.C.; Chao, W.L. Identifying and compensating for feature deviation in imbalanced deep learning. *arXiv* **2020**, arXiv:2001.01385.
18. Lin, T.Y.; Goyal, P.; Girshick, R.; He, K.; Dollár, P. Focal loss for dense object detection. In Proceedings of the IEEE International Conference on Computer Vision, Venice, Italy, 22–29 October 2017; pp. 2980–2988.
19. Cui, Y.; Jia, M.; Lin, T.Y.; Song, Y.; Belongie, S. Class-balanced loss based on effective number of samples. In Proceedings of the IEEE/CVF Conference on Computer Vision and Pattern Recognition, Long Beach, CA, USA, 15–20 June 2019; pp. 9268–9277.
20. Cao, K.; Wei, C.; Gaidon, A.; Arechiga, N.; Ma, T. Learning imbalanced datasets with label-distribution-aware margin loss. *Adv. Neural Inf. Process. Syst.* **2019**, *32*, 1567–1578.
21. Zhou, B.; Cui, Q.; Wei, X.S.; Chen, Z.M. Bbn: Bilateral-branch network with cumulative learning for long-tailed visual recognition. In Proceedings of the CVPR, Seattle, WA, USA, 13–19 June 2020.
22. Zhong, Z.; Cui, J.; Lo, E.; Li, Z.; Sun, J.; Jia, J. Rebalanced Siamese Contrastive Mining for Long-Tailed Recognition. *arXiv* **2022**, arXiv:2203.11506.
23. Hartigan, J.A.; Wong, M.A. Algorithm AS 136: A k-means clustering algorithm. *J. R. Stat. Soc. Ser. C (Appl. Stat.)* **1979**, *28*, 100–108. [CrossRef]
24. Abdullah, D.; Susilo, S.; Ahmar, A.S.; Rusli, R.; Hidayat, R. The application of K-means clustering for province clustering in Indonesia of the risk of the COVID-19 pandemic based on COVID-19 data. *Qual. Quant.* **2022**, *56*, 1283–1291. [CrossRef] [PubMed]
25. Zhang, Y.; Shuai, L.; Ren, Y.; Chen, H. Image classification with category centers in class imbalance situation. In Proceedings of the 2018 33rd Youth Academic Annual Conference of Chinese Association of Automation (YAC), Nanjing, China, 18–20 May 2018; IEEE: Piscataway, NJ, USA, 2018; pp. 359–363.
26. Johnson, J.M.; Khoshgoftaar, T.M. Survey on deep learning with class imbalance. *J. Big Data* **2019**, *6*, 1–54. [CrossRef]
27. Singh, N.D.; Dhall, A. Clustering and learning from imbalanced data. *arXiv* **2018**, arXiv:1811.00972.
28. Guru, D.; Swarnalatha, K.; Kumar, N.V.; Anami, B.S. Effective technique to reduce the dimension of text data. *Int. J. Comput. Vis. Image Process.* **2020**, *10*, 67–85. [CrossRef]
29. Cui, J.; Liu, S.; Tian, Z.; Zhong, Z.; Jia, J. Reslt: Residual learning for long-tailed recognition. *IEEE Trans. Pattern Anal. Mach. Intell.* **2022**, *45*, 3695–3706. [CrossRef] [PubMed]
30. Shu, J.; Xie, Q.; Yi, L.; Zhao, Q.; Zhou, S.; Xu, Z.; Meng, D. Meta-weight-net: Learning an explicit mapping for sample weighting. *arXiv* **2019**, arXiv:1902.07379.
31. Yang, J.; Shi, R.; Ni, B. Medmnist classification decathlon: A lightweight automl benchmark for medical image analysis. In Proceedings of the 2021 IEEE 18th International Symposium on Biomedical Imaging (ISBI), Nice, France, 13–16 April 2021; IEEE: Piscataway, NJ, 2021; pp. 191–195.

32. Zhang, Y.; Kang, B.; Hooi, B.; Yan, S.; Feng, J. Deep long-tailed learning: A survey. *IEEE Trans. Pattern Anal. Mach. Intell.* 2023, early access.
33. Park, S.; Lim, J.; Jeon, Y.; Choi, J.Y. Influence-Balanced Loss for Imbalanced Visual Classification. In Proceedings of the IEEE/CVF International Conference on Computer Vision, Montreal, QC, Canada, 10–17 October 2021; pp. 735–744.
34. Wang, Y.; Ramanan, D.; Hebert, M.H. *Learning to Model the Tail*; Curran Associates Inc.: Red Hook, NY, USA, 2017.
35. Paszke, A.; Gross, S.; Chintala, S.; Chanan, G.; Yang, E.; DeVito, Z.; Lin, Z.; Desmaison, A.; Antiga, L.; Lerer, A. Automatic Differentiation in Pytorch. 2017. Available online: https://openreview.net/forum?id=BJJsrmfCZ (accessed on 2 July 2023).
36. He, K.; Zhang, X.; Ren, S.; Sun, J. Deep residual learning for image recognition. In Proceedings of the IEEE Conference on Computer Vision and Pattern Recognition, Las Vegas, NV, USA, 27–30 June 2016; pp. 770–778.

Disclaimer/Publisher's Note: The statements, opinions and data contained in all publications are solely those of the individual author(s) and contributor(s) and not of MDPI and/or the editor(s). MDPI and/or the editor(s) disclaim responsibility for any injury to people or property resulting from any ideas, methods, instructions or products referred to in the content.

Article

Deep Learning Architecture for Detecting SQL Injection Attacks Based on RNN Autoencoder Model

Maha Alghawazi *, Daniyal Alghazzawi and Suaad Alarifi

Information Systems Department, Faculty of Computing and Information Technology, King Abdulaziz University, Jeddah 80200, Saudi Arabia; dghazzawi@kau.edu.sa (D.A.); salarifi@kau.edu.sa (S.A.)
* Correspondence: mmohammadalqhtani@stu.kau.edu.sa

Abstract: SQL injection attacks are one of the most common types of attacks on Web applications. These attacks exploit vulnerabilities in an application's database access mechanisms, allowing attackers to execute unauthorized SQL queries. In this study, we propose an architecture for detecting SQL injection attacks using a recurrent neural network autoencoder. The proposed architecture was trained on a publicly available dataset of SQL injection attacks. Then, it was compared with several other machine learning models, including ANN, CNN, decision tree, naive Bayes, SVM, random forest, and logistic regression models. The experimental results showed that the proposed approach achieved an accuracy of 94% and an F1-score of 92%, which demonstrate its effectiveness in detecting QL injection attacks with high accuracy in comparison to the other models covered in the study.

Keywords: SQL injection attacks; recurrent neural network (RNN) autoencoder; ANN; CNN; decision tree; naive Bayes; SVM; random forest; logistic regression

MSC: 68T99

1. Introduction

Structured query language (SQL) is a programming language used to manage, organize, and manipulate relational databases. It also allows the user or an application program to interact with a database by inserting new data, deleting old data, and changing previously stored data. Structured query language injection attacks (SQLIAs) pose a severe security threat to Web applications [1]. These attacks involve the malicious execution of SQL queries on a server, enabling unauthorized access to and retrieval of restricted data stored within databases [2]. Figure 1 illustrates the basic process of an SQLIA.

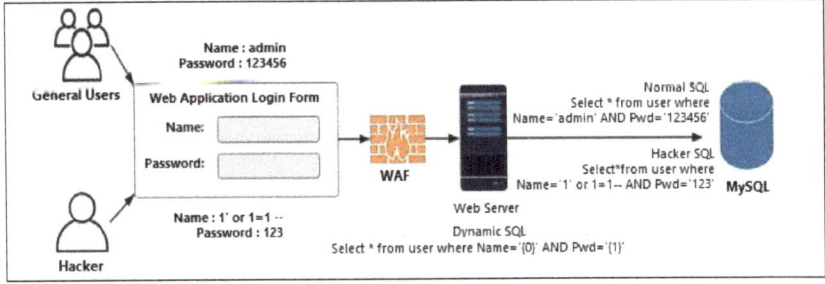

Figure 1. SQL injection attack process adopted from [3].

Attackers can exploit Web applications by injecting SQL statements or sending special symbols through user input to target the database tier and gain unauthorized access to valuable assets [3]. Due to the absence of proper validation in some Web applications, which

is usually the programmer's fault, attackers can bypass authentication mechanisms and gain access to databases, enabling them to retrieve or manipulate data without appropriate authorization [2].

In recent years, researchers have proposed many detection methods, including machine learning algorithms and deep neural network models. Deep neural networks, also known as deep learning, are a rapidly evolving research area within the field of machine learning. They were developed to bring machine learning closer to its original goal of achieving artificial intelligence. Deep learning involves training complex models that can learn the underlying patterns and representations of large datasets. This has proven to be a powerful technique for interpreting various forms of data, including text, images, and sounds. Deep learning has also been successfully applied to Web security detection, highlighting its potential impact on a broad range of applications [4]. However, one of the major drawbacks of using neural networks is their tendency to make overconfident predictions. This means that they have a high degree of certainty in their predictions, even when they are incorrect [5,6]. Even though the models perform well on test data from the same distribution as the training data, they do not know the limits of their knowledge and make erroneous guesses outside that domain. This pitfall arises because neural networks learn highly nonlinear functions that do not output calibrated probability estimates for unfamiliar data [7]. To address this issue, researchers have developed various techniques for estimating predictive uncertainty in neural networks. Lakshminarayanan et al. [7] introduced deep ensembles, where multiple models are independently trained on the same data and their predictions are averaged to capture model uncertainty. Mishra et al. [5] evaluated Bayesian neural networks (BNNs) as a technique that can provide accurate predictions along with reliably quantified uncertainties. Amodei et al. [6] suggested using model rollouts/lookahead during training to avoid reward hacking, improve safety, and reduce overconfidence. In summary, while neural networks have shown great promise in many applications, it is important to be aware of their tendency to make overconfident predictions and the potential pitfalls of overfitting. Estimating predictive uncertainty using techniques such as deep ensembles can help mitigate these issues and improve the reliability of neural network predictions.

Detection of SQL injection attacks is crucial to ensure the security and integrity of Web applications and their associated data. To address this issue, a deep learning architecture based on the recurrent neural network (RNN) autoencoder model is proposed for detecting SQL injection attacks. The RNN autoencoder is a special case of the RNN-based encoder–decoder (RNN-ED) model. The autoencoder consists of an encoder RNN that encodes the input sequence into a hidden state and a decoder RNN that decodes the hidden state back into the original input sequence. The encoder and decoder RNNs are trained jointly using backpropagation to minimize the reconstruction error between the input and output sequences [8].

The aim of this study was to develop an architecture based on a recurrent neural network (RNN) autoencoder to detect SQL injection attacks. Moreover, the proposed approach that addresses this attack is discussed and compared with other approaches. The research questions were:

Q1: Is the proposed RNN autoencoder-based architecture effective for detecting SQL injection attacks?

Q2: How can the RNN autoencoder be optimized to improve its performance in detecting SQL injection attacks?

Q3: Can an RNN autoencoder outperform other SQL injection attack machine learning detection models?

The main contributions of this paper are as follows:

- Proposing an SQLIA detection architecture based on a recurrent neural network (RNN) autoencoder algorithm;
- Comparing the proposed architecture and different machine learning techniques used for detecting and preventing SQLIAs.

The paper is structured as follows: Section 2 reviews the related research in this area. The methodology is discussed in Section 3. Experiment results and the discussion are shown in Section 4. The last section provides the conclusion and discusses future work.

2. Literature Review

This section explores a variety of ML and DL techniques found in the literature for the detection of SQL injection attacks.

Ketema [1] used a deep learning convolutional neural network (CNN) to build a model to prevent an SQLI using a public benchmark dataset. The model was trained using deep learning with different hyperparameter values and five different scenarios. The model achieved an accuracy of 97%. Roy et al. [9] presented a method for detecting SQL injection attacks using machine learning classifiers. The authors used five ML classifiers (logistic regression, AdaBoost, naive Bayes, XGBoost, and random forest) to classify SQL queries as either legitimate or malicious. The proposed model was trained and evaluated using a publicly available dataset of SQL injection attacks on Kaggle. The results of the study showed that the best performance was achieved by the naive Bayes classifier, with an accuracy of 98.33%. Finally, the authors performed a comparison with previous work. Overall, the study demonstrated the potential of machine learning classifiers in improving the accuracy and efficiency of SQL injection attack detection.

S.S. Anandha Krishnan et al. [10] proposed a machine learning-based approach for detecting SQL injection attacks. The authors argued that traditional signature-based approaches are ineffective against advanced attacks, and machine learning can help address this issue. The authors first described the various types of SQL injection attacks and their impact on Web applications. They then outlined the proposed framework, which consisted of preprocessing the data, feature extraction, model training, and evaluation. The results showed that the CNN classifier model performed better than the other classifiers in terms of accuracy, precision, recall, and F1-score. Rahul et al. [11] proposed a novel method of protecting against SQL injection and cross-site scripting (XSS) attacks by augmenting the Web application firewall (WAF) with a honeypot. The WAF filters incoming traffic using established patterns, while the honeypot is designed to attract attackers and capture information about their attack methods, which is then used to improve the WAF's ability to detect and prevent future attacks. The proposed method was evaluated through experiments, and the results suggested that the combination of a honeypot and WAF can effectively protect Web applications from these types of attacks.

Zhang et al. [4] proposed a method for detecting SQL injection attacks using a deep neural network. The authors stated that traditional methods of SQL injection attack detection have limitations, prompting the development of their new approach. The authors gathered a dataset of clean and malicious queries and used it to train a deep neural network classifier with several layers. They then compared the result of the proposed method with the traditional machine learning algorithms, including KNN, DT, and LSTM algorithms. Liu et al. [12] proposed a new approach called DeepSQLi for the automated detection of SQL injection vulnerabilities in Web applications using deep semantic learning techniques. DeepSQLi uses a deep neural network to learn the semantic meanings of SQL queries and identify potential injection vulnerabilities. The model is trained using a dataset of benign and malicious SQL queries and leverages multiple layers of convolutional and recurrent neural networks. The experimental results showed that DeepSQLi outperformed SQLmap, and more SQLi attacks could be identified faster while using a lower number of test cases. Chen et al. [3] presented a novel approach for detecting and preventing SQL injection attacks on Web applications using deep learning algorithms. The authors trained and evaluated the performance of a convolutional neural network (CNN) and a multilayer perceptron (MLP) and compared them in terms of accuracy, precision, recall, and F1-score metrics. The experimental results showed that the CNN and MLP models both performed well for SQL injection attack detection.

In summary, deep learning-based approaches have shown great promise in detecting SQL injection attacks. These approaches can learn the underlying patterns in the input data and detect any anomalies, making them more effective in detecting disguised attacks. In this research, our goal was to explore the effectiveness of the proposed RNN autoencoder in detecting SQL injections.

3. Materials and Methods

The proposed architecture is depicted in Figure 2.

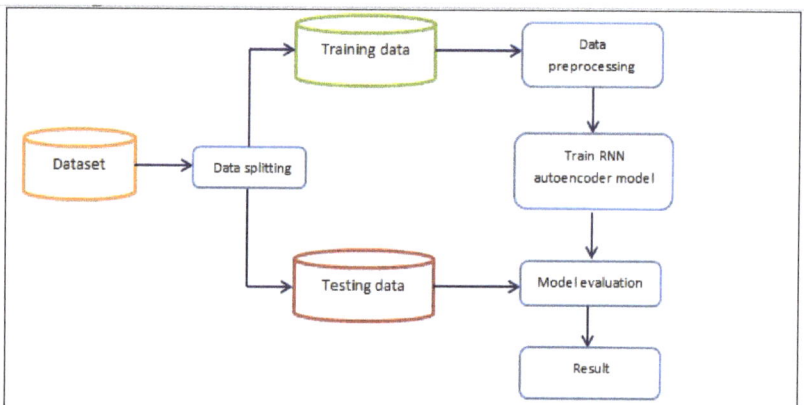

Figure 2. Steps of the proposed architecture.

The architecture consists of the following steps:
- Loading and preprocessing the dataset;
- Splitting the dataset into training and testing sets;
- Building the autoencoder model, which consists of an input layer, an encoder layer, and a decoder layer. The encoder layer reduces the dimensionality of the input data, while the decoder layer reconstructs the original input from the encoded representation;
- Training the autoencoder model on the preprocessed training data;
- Extracting the encoded data from the trained autoencoder model for use in the RNN model;
- Building the RNN model, which consists of an LSTM layer and a dense output layer;
- Training the RNN model on the encoded data;
- Evaluating the model using a set of evaluation techniques.

3.1. Data Preprocessing

The Kaggle dataset [13] was utilized in this research to train, evaluate, and compare the performance of the RNN autoencoder with several classifiers. The dataset was prepared by collecting different SQL injection queries from multiple websites. The dataset contained 30,919 SQL query statements of the form "SELECT FROM" and related variations. Each statement had a binary label, with 1 indicating malicious and 0 benign.

In order to enhance the accuracy of our trained models, we performed data cleaning on the selected dataset. This involved removing any null values and eliminating duplicate records. The removal of missing or null values is crucial, as it prevents the model from learning incorrect relationships or making predictions based on incomplete data. After completing the cleaning process, the dataset consisted of a total of 30,907 records, with 19,529 normal statements and 11,378 malicious statements. The statistics for the dataset are depicted in Figure 3. Each record contained two main features: "Query", which represented the statement itself, and "Label", which indicated whether the statement was normal (0) or malicious (1).

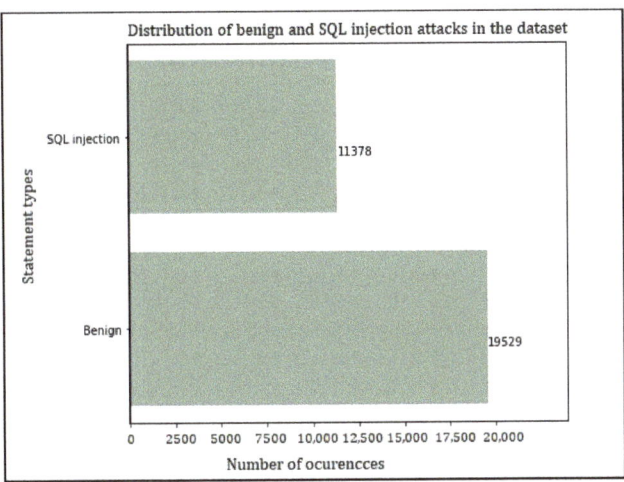

Figure 3. Distribution of benign and SQL injection attacks in the dataset.

Stratified sampling was applied, which ensured that the training and testing sets had similar proportions of each class. This is important for imbalanced datasets like the SQL injection dataset, where the number of malicious queries is much lower than the number of benign queries [14].

3.2. Data Splitting

The dataset was divided into two parts: 80% for training and 20% for testing. This division allowed us to train the proposed approach with the majority of the data and assess its performance with unseen samples.

3.3. Building and Training RNN Autoencoder Model

We developed an architecture for an RNN autoencoder that combines an autoencoder and a recurrent neural network (RNN) for SQL injection attack detection. Figure 4 illustrates the architecture of the proposed model.

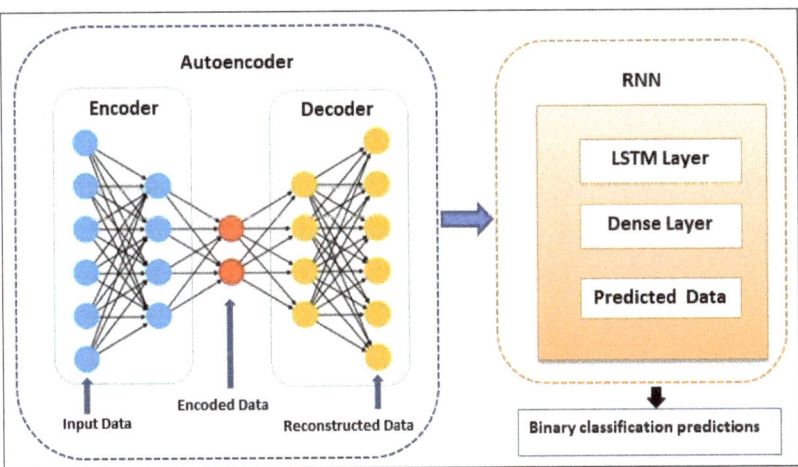

Figure 4. The RNN autoencoder architecture for SQL injection attack detection.

As shown in Figure 4, the proposed architecture consists of two main parts: the autoencoder and the RNN. The autoencoder contains an input layer, an encoder, and a decoder. The encoder takes the input data and compresses it into a lower-dimensional latent space, which is then fed to the decoder. The decoder then reconstructs the input data from the encoded representation. The size of the latent space can affect the performance of the autoencoder and RNN model, as a smaller latent space may lead to loss of information, while a larger latent space may lead to overfitting. The dimensionality of the latent space in an autoencoder is a crucial hyperparameter that should be carefully tuned [15]. In this research, we experimented with different values for the latent space using a grid search technique to find a value that resulted in a good balance between representation power and computational efficiency. The result of the hyperparameter tuning process showed that 64 was the optimal value for the latent space hyperparameter, which meant that the encoder layer compressed the input data into a 64-dimensional latent space. The RNN was designed to take the compressed representation of the input data learned by the autoencoder and use it to make binary classification predictions [16]. The RNN consisted of an LSTM layer and a dense layer, which takes the encoded data from the autoencoder as input and processes it through an LSTM layer, from where it is then fed to a dense layer to make a prediction with the output.

3.4. Model Evaluation

After training the RNN autoencoder model on the training set, we applied it to the testing set and calculated various performance metrics, such as the ROC curve, accuracy, precision, recall, and F1-score, to measure the effectiveness of the RNN autoencoder in detecting SQLIAs. The mathematical representation of these metrics was as follows.

The accuracy metric measures the percentage of correctly classified samples [17], and it is calculated as follows:

$$Accuracy = \frac{TP + TN}{TP + TN + FN + FP} \quad (1)$$

Precision, another important metric, represents the probability that a sample will be correctly classified [17]. It is calculated as follows:

$$Precision = \frac{TP}{TP + FP} \quad (2)$$

Recall, also known as sensitivity or the true-positive rate, indicates the proportion of positive samples that are correctly classified [17]. The recall score is calculated as follows:

$$Recall = \frac{(TP)}{(TP + FN)} \quad (3)$$

The F1-score is a combined metric that considers both precision and recall, providing a balanced measure of model performance [18]. It is calculated as follows:

$$F1Score = 2 * \frac{Precision * Recall}{Precision + Recall} \quad (4)$$

TN is the true-negative rate. It indicates the number of correctly predicted normal requests. TP is the true-positive rate. It indicates the number of correctly predicted malicious requests. FN is the false-negative rate. It indicates the number of incorrectly predicted normal requests. FP is the false-positive rate. It indicates the number of incorrectly predicted malicious requests.

4. Results and Discussion

This section provides a description of the experimental results. The Python environment was used to implement the system. Table 1 summarizes the performance of the RNN autoencoder in terms of the evaluation metrics.

Table 1. Performance metrics for the proposed model.

Performance Metrics	Result
Accuracy	94%
Precision	95%
Recall	90%
F1-Score	92%

The results from Table 1 show that the RNN autoencoder performed better in terms of prediction accuracy. The RNN autoencoder achieved an accuracy of 94% and an F1-score of 92%. Further, we used the receiver operating characteristic (ROC) curve to check the performance of the proposed approach. The ROC curve is a graph that shows the relationship between the true-positive rate (TPR) and false-positive rate (FPR) for different classification thresholds [19].

The AUC curve for the RNN autoencoder model is shown in Figure 5. We obtained the value of 0.94, which indicated that our model could successfully separate 94% of positive and negative rates.

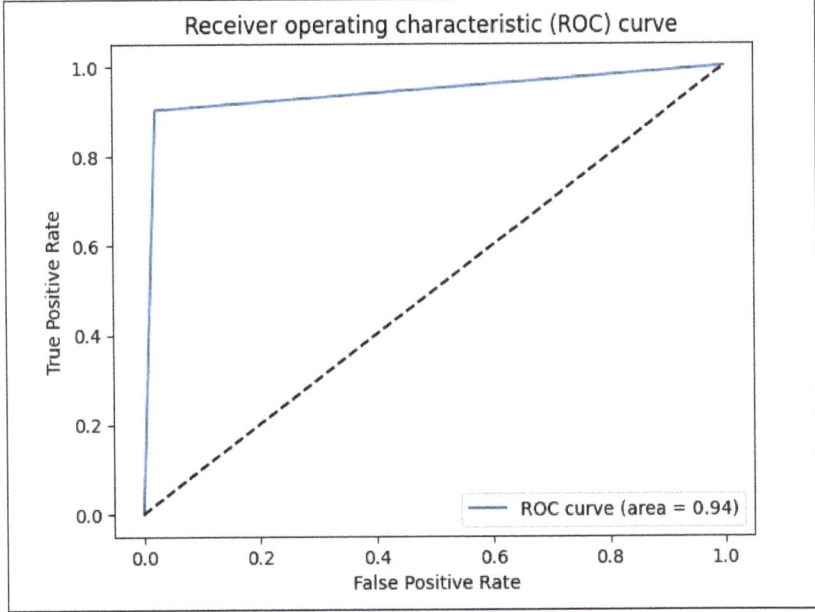

Figure 5. Receiver operating curve (ROC) for our proposed approach.

Regarding RQ1, based on the results provided, it appears that the proposed RNN autoencoder model performed well in correctly identifying instances of SQL injection attacks in the dataset and can be effective for the detection of SQL injection attacks.

Regarding RQ2, one of the most used methods to optimize RNN autoencoders to improve their performance in detecting SQL injection attacks is to adjust the hyperparameters of the model, such as epochs [19]. To find the optimal number of epochs to train the model, we experimented with various numbers of epochs and checked how they affected the accuracy. In the first iteration, we used 10 epochs.

With 10 epochs, we obtained an accuracy of 88%. From Figure 6, we can infer that the validation error decreased. Next, we set the number of epochs to 50.

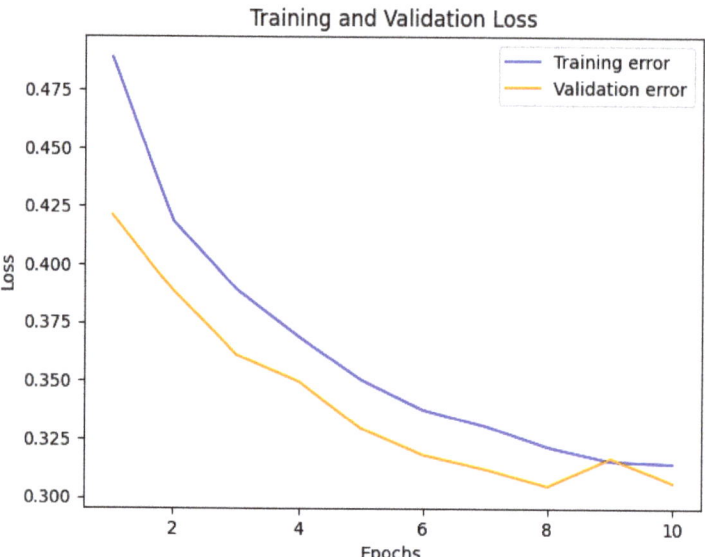

Figure 6. Loss in SQL injection dataset using 10 epochs.

As shown in Figure 7, the accuracy of the model increased to 94% with 50 epochs. Next, we tried to increase the number of epochs to 100.

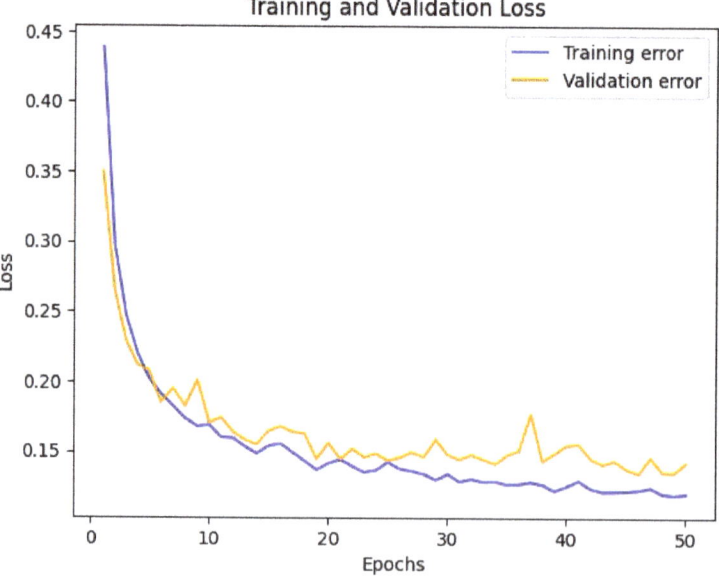

Figure 7. Loss in SQL injection dataset using 50 epochs.

As shown in Figure 8, with 100 epochs, the accuracy increased to 95% but the validation error also increased. This may cause overfitting. Using a small number of epochs, the model cannot capture the underlying patterns in the data, and this may cause underfitting. Furthermore, training the model using many epochs may lead to overfitting, where the model even learns noise or unwanted parts of the data [20]. Therefore, from the this experiment, we deduced that we could stop the training process early at around 50 epochs to obtain better performance from the model without underfitting or overfitting. Then, a grid search technique was used to find the optimal combination of hyperparameters, such as the activation function. Table 2 summarizes the choices for the different hyperparameters after using the grid search.

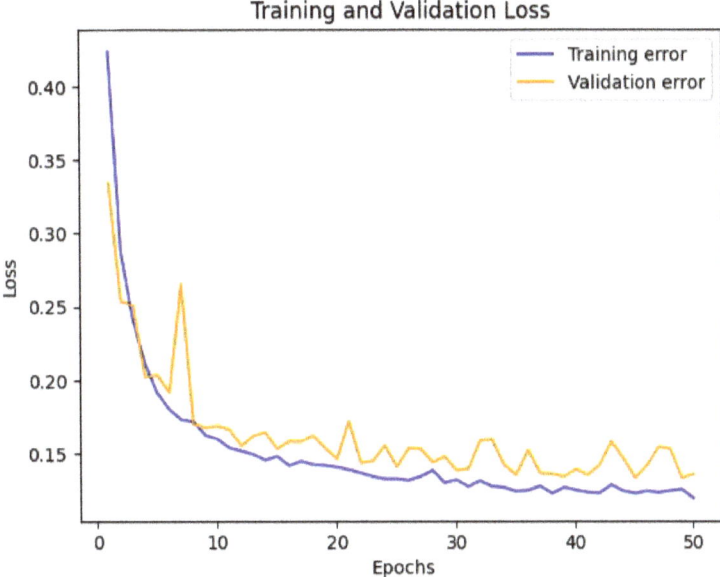

Figure 8. Loss in SQL injection dataset using 100 epochs.

Table 2. Values for several hyperparameters.

Hyperparameters	Value
Number of hidden layers	3
Hidden layer size (neurons)	64 units
Optimizer	Adam
Loss function	Binary cross-entropy
Activation function	ReLU and sigmoid
Number of epochs	50
Batch size	128

The proposed model achieved the best performance when trained for 50 epochs using the Adam optimizer, a batch size of 128, the ReLU activation function for the encoder layer, and the sigmoid activation function for the decoder layer in the autoencoder and output layer in the RNN.

We compared the performance of the proposed approach with the performance of several classifiers, including the ANN, CNN, decision tree, naive Bayes, SVM, random forest, and logistic regression classifiers. The results are presented in Figure 9.

The results in Figure 9 show that the RNN autoencoder and the ANN were effective in detecting SQL injection attacks, achieving a high accuracy of 94% and F1-score of 92%. The RF, LR, and DT models also performed well, achieving accuracy scores of 92%, 93%, and 90%, respectively, and F1-scores of 89%, 90%, and 87%. The CNN model had the highest accuracy of 96% and an F1-score of 49%, indicating its potential for detecting SQL injection attacks. However, the naive Bayes and SVM models had lower accuracy and F1-scores, achieving accuracy scores of 82% and 75%, respectively, and F1-scores of 80% and 49%.

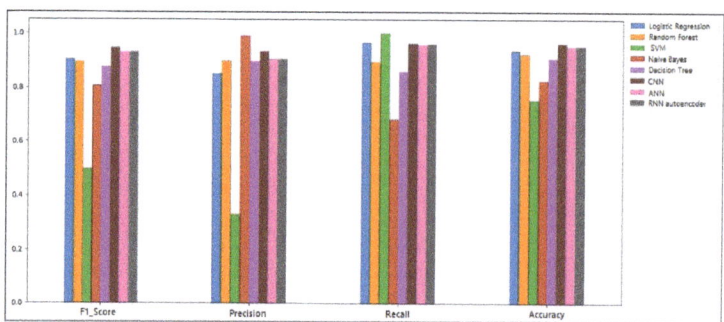

Figure 9. The comparison of evaluation metrics for different ML algorithms.

Regarding RQ3, the results indicated that the RNN autoencoder approach outperformed some of the other algorithms, including the logistic regression, decision tree, random forest, SVM, and naive Bayes algorithms, in terms of accuracy, precision, recall, and F1-score. The RNN autoencoder approach also performed comparably to some of the other algorithms, including the CNN and ANN models, in many NLP tasks, but each architecture has its strengths and weaknesses. According to a study by Yin et al. [21], CNNs perform better at tasks that require local feature extraction, such as sentiment analysis, while RNNs perform better at tasks that require an understanding of longer-term dependencies, such as question answering. They found that both CNNs and RNNs are sensitive when hyperparameter values are varied depending on the task. Banerjee et al. [22] developed CNN and RNN models with similar architectures for classifying radiology reports and found that RNNs were the more powerful model to encode sequential information. However, the study noted that CNNs required less hyperparameter tuning to prevent overfitting and were more stable, while RNNs needed more careful regularization.

In this research, since the SQL queries could contain longer-term dependencies, it made sense that the RNN autoencoder model achieved comparable accuracy to the CNN model. The added memory and sequencing modeling of the RNN likely helped it perform well with the longer query texts, but it may require additional tuning to match the performance of CNNs in some cases. This may explain why the CNN model slightly outperformed the RNN model.

In summary, our results are consistent with previous findings that indicate that RNNs are well suited for longer textual sequences but may require additional tuning to maximize performance compared to CNN models. The strong accuracy of 94% demonstrates the promise of the RNN autoencoder architecture for detecting SQL injection attacks. The key advantage of the RNN autoencoder is that it can learn a compressed representation of the input data, allowing it to capture the underlying patterns and relationships in the data more effectively than traditional methods.

5. Conclusions and Outlooks

A deep learning architecture model based on an RNN autoencoder was proposed for detecting SQL injection attacks. The autoencoder was trained to learn a compressed representation of the input data, while the RNN used this compressed representation to make binary classification predictions. In this study, the RNN autoencoder was trained with different optimization techniques on a public SQL injection dataset. The performance of the model was evaluated using standard evaluation metrics, such as accuracy, precision, recall, and F1-score. Additionally, an ROC curve was calculated to evaluate the model's performance. The experimental results showed that the proposed approach achieved an accuracy of 94% and an F1-score of 92%, indicating that the RNN autoencoder is a promising method for detecting SQL injection attacks. As part of future research, we plan to explore the use of a more complex architecture for the RNN autoencoder to detect SQL injection attacks. Additionally, we acknowledge that the dataset used in this study was relatively small, and we recommend expanding the dataset and implementing the models in real-world scenarios in future investigations.

Author Contributions: Conceptualization, M.A. and D.A.; methodology, M.A.; software, M.A.; validation, M.A., D.A. and S.A.; investigation, M.A.; resources, M.A.; data curation, M.A.; writing—original draft preparation, M.A.; writing—review and editing, S.A.; visualization, M.A.; supervision, D.A. All authors have read and agreed to the published version of the manuscript.

Funding: This research was funded by the Deanship of Scientific Research (DSR) at King Abdulaziz University, Jeddah, under grant no. IFPDP-284-22. The authors, therefore, acknowledge with thanks the DSR's technical and financial support.

Institutional Review Board Statement: Not applicable.

Informed Consent Statement: Not applicable.

Data Availability Statement: Not applicable.

Conflicts of Interest: The authors declare no conflict of interest.

Abbreviations

The following abbreviations are used in this manuscript:

SQL	structured query language
SQLIA	SQL injection attack
RNN-ED	RNN-based encoder–decoder
IDSs	intrusion detection systems
ML	machine learning
DL	deep learning
NB	naive Bayes classifier
DT	decision tree
LR	logistic regression
RF	random forest
SVM	support vector machine
CNN	convolutional neural network
ANN	artificial neural network
MLP	multilayer perceptron
RNN	recurrent neural network
LSTM	long short-term memory

References

1. Ketema, A. Developing Sql Injection Prevention Model Using Deep Learning Technique. Ph.D. Thesis, St. Mary's University, London, UK, 2022.
2. H.R., Y.W.; Kottegoda, H.; Andaraweera, D.; Palihena, P. A Comprehensive Review of Methods for SQL Injection Attack Detection and Prevention. 2022. Available online: https://www.researchgate.net/publication/364935556_A_comprehensive_review_of_methods_for_SQL_injection_attack_detection_and_prevention (accessed on 27 April 2023).
3. Chen, D.; Yan, Q.; Wu, C.; Zhao, J. SQL Injection Attack Detection and Prevention Techniques Using Deep Learning. *J. Phys. Conf. Ser.* **2021**, *1757*, 012055. [CrossRef]
4. Zhang, W.; Li, Y.; Li, X.; Shao, M.; Mi, Y.; Zhang, H.; Zhi, G. Deep Neural Network-Based SQL Injection Detection Method. *Secur. Commun. Netw.* **2022**, *2022*, 4836289. [CrossRef]
5. Mishra, A.A.; Edelen, A.; Hanuka, A.; Mayes, C. Uncertainty quantification for deep learning in particle accelerator applications. *Phys. Rev. Accel. Beams* **2021**, *24*, 114601. [CrossRef]
6. Amodei, D.; Olah, C.; Steinhardt, J.; Christiano, P.; Schulman, J.; Mané, D. Concrete problems in AI safety. *arXiv* **2016**, arXiv:1606.06565.
7. Lakshminarayanan, B.; Pritzel, A.; Blundell, C. Simple and scalable predictive uncertainty estimation using deep ensembles. *Adv. Neural Inf. Process. Syst.* **2017**, *30*, 6405–6416.
8. Yu, W.; Kim, I.Y.; Mechefske, C. Analysis of different RNN autoencoder variants for time series classification and machine prognostics. *Mech. Syst. Signal Process.* **2021**, *149*, 107322. [CrossRef]
9. Roy, P.; Kumar, R.; Rani, P. SQL Injection Attack Detection by Machine Learning Classifier. In Proceedings of the 2022 International Conference on Applied Artificial Intelligence and Computing (ICAAIC), Salem, India, 9–11 May 2022; pp. 394–400.

10. Krishnan, S.A.; Sabu, A.N.; Sajan, P.P.; Sreedeep, A. SQL Injection Detection Using Machine Learning. *Rev. Geintec-Gest. Inov. Tecnol.* **2021**, *11*, 300–310.
11. Rahul, S.; Vajrala, C.; Thangaraju, B. A Novel Method of Honeypot Inclusive WAF to Protect from SQL Injection and XSS. In Proceedings of the 2021 International Conference on Disruptive Technologies for Multi-Disciplinary Research and Applications (CENTCON), Bengaluru, India, 19–21 November 2021; Volume 1, pp. 135–140.
12. Liu, M.; Li, K.; Chen, T. DeepSQLi: Deep semantic learning for testing SQL injection. In Proceedings of the 29th ACM SIGSOFT International Symposium on Software Testing and Analysis, Virtual, 18–22 July 2020; pp. 286–297.
13. Sajid576. SQL Injection Dataset. 2021. Available online: https://www.kaggle.com/datasets/sajid576/sql-injection-dataset (accessed on 27 April 2023).
14. Chindove, H.; Brown, D. Adaptive Machine Learning Based Network Intrusion Detection. In Proceedings of the International Conference on Artificial Intelligence and its Applications, Virtual, 9–10 December 2021; pp. 1–6.
15. Gillette, A.; Chang, T. *ALGORITHMS: Assessing Latent Space Dimension by Delaunay Loss*; Technical Report; Lawrence Livermore National Lab. (LLNL): Livermore, CA, USA, 2020.
16. Do, J.S.; Kareem, A.B.; Hur, J.W. LSTM-Autoencoder for Vibration Anomaly Detection in Vertical Carousel Storage and Retrieval System (VCSRS). *Sensors* **2023**, *23*, 1009. [CrossRef] [PubMed]
17. Mwaruwa, M.C. Long Short Term Memory Based Detection Of Web Based Sql Injection Attacks. Ph.D. Thesis, University of Newcastle, Callaghan, Australia, 2019.
18. Ahmad, M.S.; Shah, S.M. Supervised machine learning approaches for attack detection in the IoT network. In *Internet of Things and Its Applications*; Springer: Berlin/Heidelberg, Germany, 2022; pp. 247–260.
19. Said Elsayed, M.; Le-Khac, N.A.; Dev, S.; Jurcut, A.D. Network anomaly detection using LSTM based autoencoder. In Proceedings of the 16th ACM Symposium on QoS and Security for Wireless and Mobile Networks, Alicante, Spain, 16–20 November 2020; pp. 37–45.
20. Afaq, S.; Rao, S. Significance of epochs on training a neural network. *Int. J. Sci. Technol. Res* **2020**, *9*, 485–488.
21. Yin, W.; Kann, K.; Yu, M.; Schütze, H. Comparative study of CNN and RNN for natural language processing. *arXiv* **2017**, arXiv:1702.01923.
22. Banerjee, I.; Ling, Y.; Chen, M.C.; Hasan, S.A.; Langlotz, C.P.; Moradzadeh, N.; Chapman, B.; Amrhein, T.; Mong, D.; Rubin, D.L.; et al. Comparative effectiveness of convolutional neural network (CNN) and recurrent neural network (RNN) architectures for radiology text report classification. *Artif. Intell. Med.* **2019**, *97*, 79–88. [CrossRef] [PubMed]

Disclaimer/Publisher's Note: The statements, opinions and data contained in all publications are solely those of the individual author(s) and contributor(s) and not of MDPI and/or the editor(s). MDPI and/or the editor(s) disclaim responsibility for any injury to people or property resulting from any ideas, methods, instructions or products referred to in the content.

MDPI
St. Alban-Anlage 66
4052 Basel
Switzerland
www.mdpi.com

Mathematics Editorial Office
E-mail: mathematics@mdpi.com
www.mdpi.com/journal/mathematics

Disclaimer/Publisher's Note: The statements, opinions and data contained in all publications are solely those of the individual author(s) and contributor(s) and not of MDPI and/or the editor(s). MDPI and/or the editor(s) disclaim responsibility for any injury to people or property resulting from any ideas, methods, instructions or products referred to in the content.